MONEY SHOCK

MONEY SHOCK

Ten Ways the Financial Marketplace is Transforming Our Lives

James A. Jorgensen

AMERICAN MANAGEMENT ASSOCIATION

This book is available at a special
discount when ordered in bulk quantities.
For information, contact Special Sales Department,
AMACOM, a division of American Management Association,
135 West 50th Street, New York, NY 10020.

Library of Congress Cataloging-in-Publication Data

Jorgensen, James A.
    Money shock.

    Bibliography: p.
    Includes index.
    1. Financial institutions—United States.
I. Title.
HG181.J595   1986   332.1'0973   86-47596
ISBN 0-8144-5846-7

Printing number

10 9 8 7 6 5 4 3 2 1

To my
favorite companion of 32 years,
Pat Jorgensen

Acknowledgments

Books are rarely written alone.

I would like to thank all those from inside the banking, thrift, brokerage, and mutual fund industries for their help, insight, and ideas. A great deal of material has also come from the research from my previous book on retirement and financial planning, from the experts I've had on my radio and television shows, and from the pages of the *Jorgensen Report*.

I am grateful to my literary agent, Mel Berger, who never lost faith in my ability as a writer. I would especially like to thank Marie Stephens, who has been an important part of every book I have written, for reading and editing my manuscripts and for trying, desperately at times, to keep the subject within the grasp of every reader. And my wife, Pat. Without her support, this book could not have been written.

And last of all, this book is dedicated to everyone who has written to me, called me on the air, and broadened my outlook: You have helped me to better understand not only money and how to accumulate it, but also how thousands of you feel about it.

Introduction

The pageantry of the early 1980s rivaled that of 15th century Florence and its wealthy ruler, Lorenzo de Medici. Tuscan-like standard bearers—in twentieth century garb—hurled their banners high in the air. The archbishop of the Federal Reserve Board gave his blessing as Star Wars music burst into the hall. Bankers, their bellies full after a new kind of banquet, settled back and waited for what financial deregulation would bring.

The feast had several courses. Banks and savings and loans were free at last to compete on equal terms with brokers and mutual funds. State lines would no longer be a barrier to invading the other guy's turf. To the bankers, fireworks had exploded in the night sky. They were now rid of the security blanket of federal regulations. With the Depository Institutions Deregulation Act of 1980, they were free at last to compete.

Then, as if Lorenzo de Medici himself had staged the final encore, Sears, Roebuck and Co. bought a bank. The bankers had quickly been swept into a marketing era that would offer consumers one-stop financial supermarkets, and the transformation from huge brick-and-mortar money places to the counters of Sears, K mart, and J. C. Penney had begun.

Bankers laughed when Sears began offering installment credit back in 1911. They chose to ignore the upstart when the big retailer started selling insurance in 1931. But they took notice when Sears began operating its own statewide savings and loan in California. When Sears bought Coldwell Banker real estate and Dean Witter Reynolds for investment services in 1981, shocked bankers began to wonder if they had missed some angles that would bolster their own deposits. And in 1985 bankers stopped laughing when Sears bought the Greenwood Trust Company in Delaware and announced plans to add a "family bank" in South Dakota. In fact, bankers are downright skittish about

Sears' new credit card, Discover, which is set to compete with the banks' own Visa and MasterCard.

The second money shock of this decade is that passbook savings accounts are dead. Once the bread-and-butter account of banks and savings and loans, passbooks thrived when smokestack America thrived—when the airline, the telephone, and, most of all, the banking industry were highly regulated. But that was back when "made in Japan" was synonymous with "shoddy," when computers filled rooms the size of buildings, and when an apple was something that fell from a tree. Today, halfway through the decade, an era of innovation and high technology has emerged to provide financial products and services undreamed of just five years ago.

And that's not all. In the financial area, deregulation has allowed some of the nation's largest corporations, like General Electric and General Motors, to move outside their corporate cocoons of once-tight regulation and utilize their huge wealth and skills for the marketing of money. These corporations, and dozens more, are already in the process of taking charge of banks, brokers, real estate companies, and insurance companies, and they will set the agenda for the future.

You have to think hard to come up with a metaphor that describes the profound effect of deregulation on the airline, telephone, and financial industries. Nothing like it has ever shaken the bedrock of public confidence and expectations in so short a time. First, long-established airlines began crashing from the sky, while headlines trumpeted the creation of low-fare start-up carriers. Then, before we knew what hit us, zing went the strings of our telephones with the breakup of AT&T. In a single year the number of competing long distance telephone companies soared from 3 or 4 to more than 200. We found we had entered the era of low-cost, discount long distance and "disposable" phones. Deregulation had given birth to a new phenomenon: 50 percent off on our long distance phone bills, and telephones whose life expectancies failed to stretch beyond the 90-day warranty.

Change Is Accelerating

Moving from regulation to deregulation created change. And change, once unleashed, can accelerate and breed even greater change. Take telephone deregulation. A hundred years ago Ma Bell, the high-tech pioneer of its day, gave us long distance telephone calls. Miles of telephone lines boosted the cost, of course, but before air travel and the air mail stamp, it seemed like a bargain.

By the 1980s, America was becoming a new society. Massive shifts were occurring and for the first time in our history more of us worked in information-related service jobs than in the production of goods. Almost overnight the restructuring of the phone business to meet the needs of an information-starved society made long distance phone calls obsolete. Communications technology had collapsed the information "float"—the amount of time information spends between sender and receiver. Increasingly sophisticated computers and satellites had revolutionized the process of making a phone call. Once it became possible to bounce a telecommunications signal off a satellite, every city in the country became, for all practical purposes, the same distance from every other city. Phone companies already want to say goodbye to long distance rates; some are charging just 26 cents a minute to call from anywhere to anywhere.

When AT&T lost its once vise-like grip on its industry, a bewildering number of new players entered the game. Companies like Sprint, MCI, and SBS Skyline jumped on board the train. Changes in the ways we communicate with people, with businesses, and with computers will occur at an ever-increasing pace because of the new freedom to use high technology in a deregulated society. In our lifetime the space shuttles will launch increasing numbers of satellites and dramatically change the way we transmit information. What we think as the stuff of science fiction today will be reality tomorrow. The net effect will be a faster flow of information that will further collapse the information float worldwide and blur the identities of companies that provide information services.

The Bigs Get Bigger

The deregulation of money stands in sharp contrast to the deregulation of telephones. With thousands of players in the money game, no AT&T of money holds most of the cards, yet some giant merchandisers of money are rapidly emerging as the dominant forces in affecting the way we save and invest. Only when we understand the larger patterns, the restructuring of how money is merchandised, will the individual events begin to make sense.

J. C. Penney, aiming for middle America's pocketbook, now offers savings and banking services, insurance, real estate, and stocks and bonds in a financial supermarket that's open seven days a week. The largest order for automatic teller machines was placed by 7-Eleven convenience stores. K mart, with its 2,000 stores visited by up to 15 million people a week, could easily emerge as one of the major nationwide financial firms of the 1980s.

Clearly the future belongs to those who can package and sell financial services. For most banks and savings and loans in the country, their worst fears will become self-fulfilling prophecies. Many will die in the whirlwind of rapid change. Industrial giants like Mobil Oil and General Motors will emerge to provide consumer financial services at bargain rates. Soon you may mortgage a house, borrow money, buy stocks or carry a credit card from mighty General Motors. And GM is no slouch at lending money; they already have $57 billion out on loans.

To stay alive when the financial marketing environment changes this rapidly, a company must reconceptualize its position in the marketplace and learn how to remain competitive with every major giant— in or out of the financial area. Small financial firms, those that don't understand the fast-moving, no-holds-barred world of deregulation, will disappear. Over two-thirds of all the financial firms—banks, S&Ls, brokers, and financial planners—in business today may either merge or go out of business by the end of this decade. The great business lesson of the 1980s will be how to recognize obsolescence before the day-to-day cash runs out.

It's a New Money Game

The key point is this: The old roads to individual wealth and security won't get you there any more. "Proven" strategies of the past can now lead to financial ruin. Both the wealthy and the not-so-wealthy saver and investor must be able to adapt to the rapidly changing conditions or their worst fears about money will become self-fulfilling prophecies.

We have now reached the point where new savings and investments are rushing onto the market so fast that they overwhelm our ability to digest them. And wider variations open new opportunities. Every financial deal that is theoretically doable will be done. In fact, we may no longer learn from experience in precisely the ways we have learned in the past. We must now learn from the present how to anticipate the future.

The purpose of *MoneyShock* is to help you discover the many ways our financial world is being restructured, to understand how the pieces fit together, and to try to see what the new financial products and services will look like. The problem is that deregulation of the financial industry has overtaken everything in its path: Congress, the regulators, financial firms, and investors alike. More changes have occurred in the past five years than in the previous 50. And more changes will occur this year than in the past five. Our thinking, our attitudes, and consequently our decision making about money have not caught up with reality. Changes have been so swift, so fundamental, that in our confusion we fail to see them, or in our uncertainty about what to do we ignore them. Our entire product-driven financial system is moving at the speed of a runaway locomotive; left unchecked, it could jump the rails entirely. Two decades from now, people will look back on the 1980s as the decade of profound change.

MoneyShock is a book about the major shifts occurring in the world of money. Money is being used, saved, invested, and advertised in new ways. Taxation of money is changing, and that will also affect savings and investment plans in new ways. Most of all, *MoneyShock* is a book about money and people. For the average individual the options used to be pretty clear: Either put your money in an insured passbook savings account or play the stock market. Conventional wisdom still says the same old rules should apply—after all, there is more money in passbook savings accounts today than in all the money market and short-term super savings accounts. But conventional wisdom is wrong.

New Options Are Available

All the comforting myths about how we handle money seem to have been shattered. In today's fast-moving financial world we no longer need passbook savings accounts. The irresistible attraction for new investors will be the FSLIC-insured certificates of deposit (CDs) invested in real estate. I call these heads-you-win, tails-you-can't-lose investments. By investing in real estate, earnings-based CDs pay more than three times the interest rate of an insured passbook savings account and carry the same government insurance guarantees. For most Americans, its fast becoming evident that it's time to learn what's happening to money—and learn it well.

There are two consequences when we march to the beat of a new drummer: widespread confusion for many, and remarkable opportunities for those few who clearly understand what is happening. We have entered into a financial environment so different from the past that the old lessons we learned about investing and saving may well be major obstacles to success in the present era. From my (local and national) radio and television shows and from talking with people about how money is changing, the most universal comment I receive goes something like this: "What you are telling me is so different from anything

I've ever known about saving or investing money that I not only don't understand what you're saying, I question if my 'passbook mentality' will even grasp what I'm hearing."

For example, if you want a short-term tax deferral, why not open a high-yield six- or nine-month CD that matures next January? That way you'll escape taxes this year and have until April 15th of the year after next to pay taxes on the earned interest.

Or, if you're afraid that once you retire you'll run out of money before you run out of breath, why not open an individual retirement account, or IRA, and contribute $5,000 or $10,000 or more this year?

Maybe you'd like to buy stocks but you're only interested in dividends not in capital gains. You can buy "Prime" stock at a lower cost and let investors interested in capital gains buy the other half of the common stock, the "score."

Or maybe you've heard of a company where employees fill their fringe benefits plates from a "cafeteria plan" and then pay their bills and save their money with tax-free dollars that never show up on their W-2 forms.

There's No Turning Back

It's too late to recapture a regulated market. There are no passengers on the trip we are about to take into the world of financial supermarkets; we are all members of the crew and we all share the risks.

When I was growing up, with memories and reminders of the Depression all around me, a bank failure often meant the end of the world for people and for a town. When simple interest rates hovered between 2 and 3 percent, the possibility of a passbook savings account building wealth—or even replacing what was lost—was remote indeed. In 1985, with the safety net of federal deposit insurance protecting most savers, hundreds of privately insured financial institutions in 27 states again staged spectacular failures. Deregulation not only brought greater opportunities to save and invest, it also brought with it the opportunity, once again, for financial firms to fail. First there were isolated cases in five states of growth-obsessed, fast-buck money changers, already on a shaky course, going under and leaving depositors unprotected. Those customers found out too late that they were investors, not depositors. After this, the mere perception of weakness was enough to set off a run by depositors at privately insured thrifts, and the governor of Ohio was forced to declare a bank holiday—one of the few in the United States since the Great Depression. Shortly thereafter, the governor of Maryland, to avoid near panic at 102 of the state's privately insured savings and loans, limited the amount of withdrawals each month to $1,000. For many people across the country, deregulation had brought back the bank failures of the Great Depression with a vengeance.

MoneyShock tells us we'll need financial lifeboats in case the new electronic money system crashes into the icebergs of confusion and change. A capitalist society lives and dies with its capital, *and individual Americans own most of the capital.*

When I talk with people—the old and the young, the rich and the poor—about how money is changing, they all seem to be looking for someone they can trust. They sense that money is fast becoming just another product to be merchandised, like detergent or white bread. Supermarkets, department stores, discount brokers, and, yes, banks and S&Ls, all lust after our cash and bury us under a blizzard of ads that leaves us lost in a maze of conflicting claims. In spite of the unprecedented number of financial products to choose from, most people are simply looking for savings and investments that will help them hold onto what they already have.

The problem is, we hear a lot of noise but not much good advice. *MoneyShock* will give you an insider's edge by providing the fundamentals of how saving and investing—how we handle our money—will change, and how your life and your financial security will be affected. We will get a firm grip on these changes and a clear vision of what they mean to your financial planning so you can thrive in the deregulated world of money that lies ahead. You'll learn which direction the financial system will be moving, and you will be able to decide where your comfort zone lies. The decisions are up to you. You may decide you can't fight the system, or take the risks others will grab, but you'll find it helpful to know which way the financial markets are moving.

It's my belief that you'll earn back the price of this book almost every day, and, most important of all, you'll be striking a blow against the fears that keep you awake at night.

At a time when we are drowning in confusion but starved for knowledge, the most reliable way to anticipate change is to learn how the financial industry is changing, to grasp the forces that are at work transforming our money system, and to put ourselves in a position to take advantage of the unprecedented opportunities that lie ahead. That's the premise of this book.

Contents

1

From Regulation to Deregulation

How the Glue Is Coming Unstuck in the Financial Marketplace

The restructuring of America—from an agricultural society to a manufacturing society and now to an information society—has brought about profound shifts in money. For the first time in our history, financial regulations are decreasing instead of increasing. The deregulation train has already left the station, and in this chapter we'll trace its route and explain why it's about to slip into overdrive and hit the main line. Financial power is clearly shifting away from banks, giving new energy to non-bank giants that will shortly become more important personal financial centers than banks. By the end of this decade, we'll all be riding a financial bullet train. The choices—the savings and investment plans, the best deals for our money—will flash by as we speed toward an unknown future in finance where, as in the airlines and telephone companies of the 1980s, free enterprise, unshackled by government regulation, reigns supreme.

Of course, it was not always that way. In fact, from its beginning

1

banking has sought protection from the state. In Renaissance times, bankers demanded from their princes quasi-monopolies to hold and lend money; for providing that state protection, princes extorted hefty sums from those who wanted to start banks. The princes, who generally lacked any savvy about money, did understand the importance of banks: They were simply the place to go when the state needed money. And bankers such as the Medicis and the Fuggers, with their state-licensed money machines, grew wealthy.

So it has been from the time of the oldest bank in the world—the Monte Dei Paschi Di Siena, founded in Italy in 1472—to the mid-1980s. Most people accumulated money in a regulated bank, in some form of passbook savings account. The passbook savings account was easy to understand. You could add to your savings or make withdrawals when the need arose. A bank was, after all, believed to be safe and more important, until a few years ago, your money usually held its value. When you got it back, it would buy just as much as it did when you put it in.

But in the affairs of both men and geology, stresses occur over time in seemingly rock-solid systems. These stresses, evident first as shiverings and then as shakings, increase in frequency and amplitude until they find release in a cataclysm that upsets the system, then restores it to stable well-being. Modern-day financial stresses began in the 1860s, when states' rights allowed banks to issue their own notes backed by the assets of the issuing bank. While bank notes from various banks might have equal face value, all issuing banks were not equal. Some bank notes were taken by investors and traders at par, others got a frigid reception and a hefty discount. Negotiating transactions from one part of the country to another in those days could be the trickiest part of staying in business.

Banks in America Are Regulated

To sidestep the early signs of the banking system's shivering and shaking, Salmon P. Chase, secretary of the Treasury under President Lincoln, pushed through Congress the National Bank Act of 1863, under which he chartered national banks. The national bank notes were now to be backed by U.S. government obligations, which the national banks bought. The system quickly provided an assured market for government bonds as well as a means to stabilize the currency.

However, the 1863 Act only flirted with stability. The banking system continued on its shaky course, with states opposing national banking legislation and defeating every effort to make further nation-wide banking reforms. As a result of this dual system of federal and state bank regulation, no one regulatory body was in effective control of either bankers or bank credit. A merchant in New Jersey trying to arrange a line of credit in Kansas might have to pass through several banks operating under different state laws. Transacting business could be difficult because the value of currency could vary from one state to another.

Finally, the Federal Reserve Act of 1913 gave new powers to the national banks while at the same time making them involuntary members of the Federal Reserve system (also known as the "Fed"). State banks could join the Federal Reserve, but their participation was voluntary. The states, however, were offering a better deal. By clinging to their state charters (each state granted or withheld the right of state-chartered banks to open branches within their borders), state banks could at least think about expanding. Since the National Bank Act of 1863 did not foresee the need for branch banking, it neither forbade nor permitted national banks to have branches. But by the 1920s the urbanization of America had made branch banking a big issue. Without the same rights to branch banks, the national banks were at a disadvantage in competing with state banks in states that allowed branching. As a result, many national banks defected from the national bank system and thus from the Federal Reserve system. In the three years ending in June 1926, for instance, 253 national banks withdrew from the national bank system and grabbed state charters. As more and more national banks gave up their charters and became state banks, the Federal Reserve system found itself scrambling to hang on to what banks it could.

To quell the hubbub and get the national banking system back on track, the Fed sought to make national bank charters at least as attractive as state charters. But from 1913 until the present time, the stumbling block has always been the controversy over branch banking.

State Banks Are Fenced In

In 1923, in the absence of any existing laws, the U.S. Attorney General ruled that national banks could open branch offices in the city or place mentioned in their charters. Immediately Congress began to hear howls of protest from virtually every small-town banker. Thousands of banks hoisted a red warning flag about the rapidly spreading banking giants, asking Congress to put the skids on nationwide banking.

Louis T. McFadden, chairman of the House Banking and Currency Committee, took up the battle and in 1927 Congress enacted the McFadden amendment (known as the McFadden Act) to the National Banking Act. McFadden got his first job as an office boy for the First National Bank of Canton, Pennsylvania. At the age of only 22 he was elected cashier. He later became president of the one-branch bank. Sensing the direction of the political wind in 1926, McFadden played to the emotional issue of local brick-and-mortar branch banking as big-city banks with fancy buildings were flirting with nationwide banking. For McFadden, the passage of the McFadden Act was a victory for small-town bankers who feared that big-city banks could invade their turf and steal their customers.

The McFadden Act made it easier for state banks to merge with national banks, gave national banks the right to deal in investment securities and to hold real estate, and extended indefinitely the charter of the Federal Reserve system. The part of the Act we remember today is the section forbidding banks to open offices outside their home states and denying nationally-chartered banks the right to open branches within a state unless the state-chartered banks have equal rights. The net effect of the McFadden Act, then and now, has been to put the skids on branch banking that jumps state lines.

At its roots, the opposition to interstate branch banking sprang from an instinct genuinely American: the tradition of each bank standing on its own feet, in its own hometown—an American tradition since pioneer days. The tradition dies hard and the stress of state laws that block nationwide banking continues to build. As we'll see, the 60-year-old McFadden Act remains out of touch with the reality of today's deregulated, electronic, high-tech world.

The protective fence so carefully built in the 1920s by Louis McFadden now yields results exactly opposite to those intended by the Act. Banks are locked up behind the regulatory wall while other financial institutions, in growing numbers, are leaping over it. While the major banks grow testy, some savings and loans, mutual funds, insurance companies, and brokers carry on nationwide banking activities. Major retailers such as Sears, K mart, and J. C. Penney are getting into the banking and financial services business. Even nonfinancial, non-retailing firms are stalking the consumer banking business. Mighty General Motors wants to give you its credit card, let you bank with it, and dangle Wall Street under your nose.

This financial free-for-all was unthinkable back when McFadden wrote his amendment. A merchant was a merchant and a banker was a banker. Even so, by the late 1920s, 48 varieties of state banking laws had placed the nation's banking system on the edge of an earthquake fault. Then the earthquake of the Great Depression turned banks into rubble. The nation faced a monumental crisis of failing banks and dying public trust.

In the four years following the 1929 stock market crash, the rate of bank failures rose sharply, with 9,000 banks closing their doors, leaving customers with no protection and no cash. Clearly, there was going to be a scramble for the money in the banks that remained open.

Where Are the Guarantees?

To quell the panic and rescue the nation's banking system, President Franklin Roosevelt was finally forced to close the nation's banks in March 1933 for a historic four-day "bank holiday." At the same time, he called the 73rd Congress into special session to consider H.R. 1491, "An Act to provide relief in the existing national emergency in banking." So hastily had the bill been pulled together that no printed copies of it were available. As the members sat on the hard benches of the House chamber, their knowledge of the bill came from the clerk's reading of the only text then available. That version bore last-minute corrections scribbled in by the bill's sponsor, Alabama's Henry Steagall, a small-town lawyer and chairman of the House Banking and Currency Committee. Steagall told the House that only by voting for the bill could the banks reopen the next day. While the details of the bill to save the nation's banks may have been obscure, the members knew that the country faced financial disaster. Precisely 38 minutes after it had taken up H.R. 1491, the House passed it with a unanimous roar.

Less than half an hour later, as House members crowded the Senate chambers to learn more about what they had already passed, H.R. 1491 came up in the Senate, where Virginia's Senator Carter Glass, the bill's coauthor, was ready to continue his struggle to reform the banking system. Glass knew Roosevelt's New Deal would save its heaviest guns for regulating finance, to save a financial system that was near death. Even so, when his bill to reform banking had first hit the Senate floor the month before, cries of astonishment and alarm had filled the chamber. Private bankers warned that the Glass bill would rivet banks to a monstrous system of guaranteeing bank deposits. Whenever that had been tried, they said, it had been a disastrous failure. At 75, getting old and tired, "Pluck" Glass was still not one to run from a fight— despite those on Capitol Hill betting that the bill was too astonishing and alarming to pass that session. Most people agreed with Senator

Huey Long's assessment: "The bill has no more chance of becoming law this session than I have to become Pope of Rome—and I'm a Baptist. . . . It's [as] dead as a hammer."

But now, the banking bill had been passed unanimously by the House. The Senators were told that without this bill nervous depositors could plunge the country into a financial crisis that would make the Depression seem like a picnic. The Senate, in the end, passed H.R. 1491 by a vote of 73 to 7, with no amendments. Just eight hours after it opened its special session, Congress passed the Glass-Steagall Act of 1933, which gave President Roosevelt the most sweeping power over the American pocketbook ever granted a president in peacetime. A national magazine at the time wrote, "One of the most depressing things about a depression is that to many minds it justifies measures which at some other time would readily be recognized as unwise or dangerous."[1]

"This bill has more lives than a cat," said a grinning President to Carter Glass. "Its been declared dead almost 14 times in the last few months and finally came through." In 1933, America was on its way back from the depths of the Great Depression. Banks would be made safe. A new deal for money would spur the economy.

Like the McFadden Act, the Glass-Steagall Act has become part of the glue that holds our financial system together. The most controversial part of the 1933 law was the bank deposit guarantee scheme, of which most big-city bankers said: "It will placate some depositors, but the plain truth is, it simply won't work." It was an "evil-smelling" trick to force big-city banks into paying a levy to guarantee the deposits of every small-town banker, and it outraged Manhattan bankers.

The government was to launch this revolutionary enterprise by means of a new insurance company called the Federal Deposit Insurance Corporation (FDIC), which was to be financed by $150 million from the U.S. Treasury, about $150 million from the Federal Reserve banks, and another $150 million from the newly insured banks at the rate of .5 percent of their deposits. But what made bankers in the great banking houses of Manhattan wild-eyed with alarm was the requirement, neatly woven into the Glass-Steagall Act, that when the federal guarantee fund sank below about $75 million, the banks would be required to again contribute another .25 percent of their deposits. If the federal guarantee fund continued to sink, they'd have to bolster its assets as long as their banks remained solvent. And that might not be for long according to the *Econostat*, a statistical weekly, which calculated that if the deposit guarantee scheme had been in force from 1928 to 1932, 62 percent of the net profits of solvent banks would have been required just to pay the losses of closed banks.

The American Bankers Association held the Act's provisions for federal deposit insurance to be "unsound, unscientific, unjust, and dangerous." In the past 25 years, it pointed out, eight Western states had tried deposit insurance with disastrous results. Fifty New Hampshire savings banks flatly refused to join on the grounds that the immediate requirements for insurance would cost them more than they'd lost in the last 100 years.

In his book, *Money: Whence It Came From, Where It Went*, John Kenneth Galbraith writes, "The dangers of the proposed [federal deposit insurance] were evident to all. The best banks would now have to accept responsibility for the recklessness of the worst. The worst, knowing that someone else would have to pay, would have a license for reckless behavior that the supervision authorized by the legislation could not hope to restrain. . . . perhaps it [the FDIC] would mean a return to the wildest days of wildcat banking."

On New Year's Day, 1934, federal deposit insurance for banks (FDIC) became a fact. (The Federal Savings & Loan Insurance Corporation, or FSLIC, which insures deposits in savings and loans, was established later in the same year.) The FDIC was soon to insure 100 percent of deposits up to $10,000, 75 percent between that sum and $50,000, and 50 percent on sums over $50,000. The Comptroller of the Currency claimed that the new deposit insurance would insure in full 94 percent of the bank depositors in the country.

In retrospect, it is clear that the federal guarantee on deposits put the brakes on the panicky flight of depositors, many of whom had stuffed their hard-earned cash under their mattresses. The nation's financial system, near death in the 1930s, has scarcely had a sick day since.

New Tasks, New Measures:
The Banks and Wall Street Are Separated

The Glass-Steagall Act had one other major provision: Banks were required to give up either their banking or their securities business. With the 1929 stock market collapse fresh in their minds, millions of Americans wanted the banks barred from the stock market to keep them from using their money to jeopardize the rebuilding of the financial community. Until 1933, banks had been participating in nearly two-thirds of all the new stock and bond issues, and money-center giants such as National City Bank of New York (the forerunner of Citibank) and Chase National (today's Chase Manhattan Bank) were accused of lending money on a cut-rate basis to their own investment affiliates. It was even charged that some banks' own securities departments had tried to prop up the sagging stock prices of parent banks.

Ironically, Wall Street, which has become the villain as the 1929 crash has grown to mythical proportions in the American mind, was dealt with less harshly at first. The Securities Act of 1933, the first federal securities legislation, merely required companies that sold securities to the public to make full disclosure in the offering. The regulatory crunch did not hit Wall Street until early in 1934, when Congress completed its investigation into the causes of the crash and enacted the Securities Exchange Act. Unlike its predecessor, this law had real teeth. It put the exchanges under federal oversight, limited margin buying, and created the Securities and Exchange Commission (SEC) to police Wall Street.

To head the SEC, President Roosevelt picked Joseph P. Kennedy, father of John F. Kennedy. The Boston Irishman had made millions speculating in the stock market during the 1920s, and presumably knew all the tricks of the trade he was being ask to oversee. The SEC's main function was to give investors confidence that the financial markets would never again be manipulated as they had been before the crash.

Insecurity Is Replaced with Guarantees

During the 1930s our traditional faith in ourselves and our financial institutions was badly shaken. We wanted the government to guarantee that our money would be safe in the bank. What we got was a "new" insured passbook savings account and a more regulated stock market. Granted, these ideas were not terribly original, but the laws that made them a reality were as astonishing as is the unravelling of these same laws in the wake of financial deregulation today. Financial security packaged for us in the 1930s won't survive in the fast-changing, deregulated world of the 1980s.

The New Outlook Magazine of April 1933 may have summed up best the public's expectations of bankers—both in the 1930s and in the 1980s—when it said:

> With the storm blown over and survivors coming out of the cellars to cart away the debris and build anew, there is one fundamental to which each banker would do well to return. That foundation of good banking is a realization of the true meaning of the word that is constantly on a banker's lips, the word credit. It is derived from the

Latin *credere*. It means to trust, to believe, to have faith in. It implies a source of honor. That is what a judicious banker looks for in a borrower. That is what a depositor has a right to demand in the character of his banker.

Banks and Thrifts
Revert to Renaissance Times

For the next 30 years, federal regulations gave banks a protected money machine. Recipients of national bank charters were protected from competition, since no neighboring start-up bank would be approved without first demonstrating "economic need" for a nearby bank. "Only a fool could lose money," a banker said. "For years the federal government told us how to operate. They gave us our instruments and priced them for us, then told us to go out and make a lot of executive decisions on how many pots and pans we were going to give away."

With a monopoly, financial institutions had no reason and developed no talent for redesigning their services to attract customers. Wringing their hands, they told us they were paying the "highest interest rate allowed by law," and their profits soared. They gave away their services and their toasters, and waited for consumers to pour through the front doors of their money palaces. Bank stockholders, benefitting for generations from one of the last officially sanctioned monopolies in America, grew rich.

Computers Set Banks Free—and We Pay a Price

The first stage of the technological revolution was internal. Computers, which cut the costs of doing business, were first introduced in ways that did not threaten people. They were thought of merely as tools to manage complexity. Since financial institutions are nothing more than giant countinghouses, it was easy to run the entire customer list past the computer each day. Interest, which had been posted once a month or once a quarter, could now be posted every night. Splashy ads proclaimed, "interest from date of deposit to date of withdrawal," and "daily compounding of interest." Within the limits of the law, the first stage of the technological revolution brought on by the computer had begun. It was a small step, to be sure, but in the merchandising of money it was a fundamental innovation. And once begun, there was no turning back.

Looking back, we can see that in the second stage, computers and electronics were used to refine what was already in place, making it easier for financial firms to package complicated savings and investing plans. We also got access to automatic teller machines, debit cards, touch-tone 800 banking—technology that was both high-tech and self-help, and therefore cheaper for the bank. But the new banking also turned out to threaten customers' control over their money. People were asked to give up a human teller in exchange for a robot teller. This was a high-tech innovation, but not a "high-touch" one, and the public rejected it.

Now we are about to embark on the third stage. Microprocessors themselves will begin to create inventions and applications unimagined today. Ours is the last generation that will remember firsthand old-style banking, a system built on secrecy, rigidity, and a tradition dating from the Medicis, where every customer was important, most of the services were free, and each person was treated about the same as every other. Today, a growing number of banks are chasing the up-scale customer. In some of the new breed of boutique banks, you need a net worth of at least $1 million and an annual income of at least $100,000 to qualify as a customer. Yet those of us over 50 find it hard to accept this change. The more that high technology is evident in banking and investing, the less we want to use the services. And people of all ages want to be with people, not machines. It's one thing to have a computer do our daily ledger posting, it's another to find that it has replaced our friendly teller.

The introduction of computers in the 1960s was, of course, not limited to the financial community. Computers have had a profound effect on each segment of our society. What sets the financial industry apart, however, is that the computer actually freed it from centuries-old countinghouse methods and made its products come alive. In no other industry is that true. For that reason, the deregulated financial services industry now leads the pack in high-tech jobs. It has spawned a computer revolution in shaping its multitude of new financial products and extending these high-tech services to investors, credit card purchasers, and savers. With computers to keep track of hundreds of thousands of accounts, each individual account can be treated differently. The technology of the computer allows us to have a distinct and individually tailored way of paying our bills.

Two job categories, each topping a separate list of Labor Department projections for the year 1995, are emblematic of the direction in which the job market is expected to move in the next decade. The job world of the future belongs to the computer service technician and programmer (the skills needed to maintain high-tech systems are be-coming as important as the creative skills to design the systems) and to the custodian. The reason is obvious: Demand for people with high-tech skills will continue to soar, but people with low-tech skills or those who develop skills that become outmoded and are not flexible enough to switch to another field will be caught in a downward spiral. There won't be fewer jobs, but types of jobs will change drastically.

Let's take a look at the direction our nation is moving in with respect to jobs. Today, the information economy accounts for about 55 percent of the gross national product and for more than 60 percent of income earned. During the 1970s, as financial firms began to expand, almost 80 percent of all new jobs were in information, financial services, and knowledge. During the 1980s, a growing trend in America toward non-manufacturing jobs will continue. In the first half of 1985, *93 percent of all new jobs were in the service industry, while 168,000 factory workers lost their jobs.* The state of California provides a good example of the trend. Of almost 12 million employed adults, 10 million were in the service industries, and 8 million of them were in retail, finance, and government.

What has happened? Over the last short decade we've turned into a nation of "users," not a nation of "makers." And we'll continue to move toward a service-based economy as long as our basic needs and goods are provided by others. Take food. Fifty years ago almost 7 million American farmers tilled the land; now fewer than 2 million do. Land hasn't changed, yields have. Fewer farmers are growing more food more efficiently on the same number of acres. And farmers can produce more food than Americans need. In the 18 months ending in April 1985, the government paid nearly $1 billion for milk that no one wanted to drink. We have paid farmers not to grow crops, yet our storage bins overflow.

Between 1970 and 1980, 5 million blue-collar workers lost their manufacturing jobs, yet the total civilian labor force grew by 25 million. As imports continue to soar, more people will lose their jobs as makers, and more highly skilled workers will take their places as users.

Technology is revolutionizing our society. By 1990, 80 percent of all jobs will involve computers in some way. In 1984, almost 5 million new jobs were created in this country, but 80 percent were offered by companies less than four years old. Smokestack America is giving way to the innovation and creativity made possible by a high-tech society. The last time such a major shift occurred was when we moved off the farms and into the factories.

The most vivid example of the high-tech revolution is our emerging global economy. Today, the United States no longer dominates the world's economy. Our shoes and eyeglasses are made in Italy, cars and calculators in Japan, jogging suits in Taiwan, shirts in France. And for a vacation, we go to Mexico—it's cheaper than Florda. But I'm getting ahead of myself.

High-Tech Personal Banking Arrives

In 1969, an enterprising young executive of the Worcester Five Cents Savings Bank petitioned the Massachusetts Banking Department for permission to offer a "negotiable order of withdrawal" account. A "NOW account" was, in effect, a checking account with an interest-bearing balance. The executive knew he was skating on thin ice because it was, at that time, clearly illegal for federally insured banks and S&Ls to pay interest on any monies on deposit for less than 30 days. But the Massachusetts savings banks had their own insurance fund and Massachusetts law did not have the same tight restrictions as those that governed the federally insured banks and S&Ls. The state banking regulators, however, gave his suggestion a frigid reception and turned him down. But the enterprising executive believed he had found a formula that could pry open the regulatory gate, so he sued— and he won. Now it became possible for state-chartered savings and loans to offer checking accounts that paid interest. For the first time in history, banks faced competition for the "free" money their customers had been forced to keep in non-interest-bearing checking accounts.

To meet the new competition, Congress authorized NOW accounts for federally insured banks and S&Ls in the Northeast. Soon the new accounts spread nationwide. Just as scientists have a hard time predicting earthquakes, we can seldom predict exactly where and when new ideas will jolt our financial system; but once the quake begins, once a new idea gives consumers a better deal, the change can shake the foundations of our free-enterprise business world and set in motion a reordering to conform to a new set of realities.

Money Changes Forever

Bankers had talked about deregulation for years, but soon after the NOW account appeared, the need at least to abolish interest-rate ceilings took on a new urgency when inflation-bedeviled depositors began yanking their cash out of passbook accounts and putting it into the new nonregulated money market funds offered by brokers and mutual funds. In four years, between 1977 and 1981, money market assets climbed an astounding 17,200 percent, while bank savings deposits fell by 24 percent and those of thrifts by 35 percent. "The biggest problem facing commercial banking today," Walter B. Wriston, chairman of Citicorp, said in 1979, "is not the new competition but the old regulations. We are being forced to operate under rules designed for making horse collars, while the fellow down the street is selling horseless carriages."[2]

In 1980, banks and savings and loans were bogged down in a quagmire of Depression-era regulations. While Congress sat nitpicking about the rules of banking, hundreds of "quasi-banks" or "non-banks" were springing up nationwide, turning on the spigots full blast to capture a gusher of easy money. The loophole hunters had found that a "bank" could escape federal regulations if it was not a "bank." It was flimflammery of the highest order, but it worked. Federal regulations define a bank as an institution that takes deposits and makes commercial loans. After all, when the regulations were conceived, the big money was in loans made to businesses, not to consumers. But a "non-bank," or "consumer bank," which took deposits and made *only consumer loans*, presented a new wrinkle! And by the start of this decade, a growing pool of well-paid, highly educated consumers under age 40 was willing to buy now and pay later. Moreover, the postwar baby boomers were right in the middle of the "big bubble" in the 25-to-35 age range—the time in life when they are most likely to borrow. The battle for both consumer bucks and consumer loans was underway, so much so that in 1979 John G. Heimann, Comptroller of the Currency, forecast that "within the next three years, we could have a dramatically restructured financial system. And most of the change will be made by the market."[3]

A Revolution in Financial Services Begins

Unlike what we make or grow, knowledge is not bound by the laws of conservation. It can be expanded and, more important, it is synergistic—that is, the whole can be greater than the sum of the parts. Once financial institutions had computers with countinghouse capabilities, anyone with knowledge and creativity could merchandise money. What's more important, non-banks could behave in ways almost indistinguishable from banks by offering complete financial services to the consumer. America was quickly moving away from a tightly regulated banking system toward a new financial services system where, for the first time in history, the smart consumer could find a wide choice of savings and investment products.

As the decade of the 1980s began, mutual funds, brokers, and insurance companies jumped into the non-bank banking business with what came to be known as "limited service banks." Around these banks they built complete financial centers and, unhampered for the most part by federal regulations, they quickly spread nationwide. But if money was to be merchandised like Tide and Wonder bread, it had to be convenient to the public. Foot traffic would win out every time over empty money palaces. Suddenly everyone wanted a piece of the business. Sears, Roebuck and Co. assembled the first financial super-market for consumers, and between the garden tractors and the panty-hose, Sears Financial Network offered insurance, real estate, and the stockmarket. In California, where they already owned the eleventh-largest S&L in the state, they threw in the banking business as well. Next, K mart stores began offering banking, real estate brokerage, discount stocks and bonds, insurance, and consumer financing services. The new money players in the game could open a complete financial services center for $50,000, while across the street a $6 million money palace bank or savings and loan was being stifled by regulations that allowed it only to offer savings and checking accounts and make loans.

When I was a guest on a nationwide television program, a woman asked me whether I'd invest in a K mart CD. In her mind there was something that wasn't quite right about saving money in a discount store. The CD was marked with a big red "K" for K mart, and it was federally insured by the FSLIC, but she was sure it was not as good as her local bank's CD. I said that if K mart wanted to offer me a hefty boost in interest rates for the same CD, why yes, I'd put my money in an FSLIC-insured K mart CD. It's like selling television sets and sports coats with the discount in reverse: more interest, not lower prices. And since K mart's 2,000 stores are visited by an estimated 15 million people a week, the chain could become a major player in the money game overnight. In the years to come, 7-Eleven convenience stores and J.C. Penney will follow, since the giant retailers are increasingly lured by the smell of the profits to be made in selling money.

Backdoor Consumer Banks Enter the Marketplace

In a financial market that is rapidly running amok, banks and thrifts now face the mind-bending prospect of competing with every major corporation in America. For example, a financial supermarket has been operated for some time by the Boston-based Stop & Shop supermarket chain. Customers at "Super" Stop & Shops can pick up a quart of milk, a dozen roses, and 100 shares of stock. While they're shopping, they can have someone prepare their tax return, buy a life insurance policy, invest in mutual funds, or complete handy forms for a personal financial planning report. Stop & Shop isn't the first supermarket chain to enter the widening field of financial services, and it looks like more will follow suit and offer some form of one-stop financial shopping.

Non-banks like General Motors, AT&T, General Electric, and ITT are on the verge of coming up with what in McFadden's day was unthinkable: a way to become major players in the money game. GM could end up offering to give you a credit card, mortgage your house, lend you money, trade your stocks, or sell you a "red hot" insured CD. If a non-financial firm like GM transfers its marketing skills in selling cars to the financial services business, it could become a heavyweight competitor overnight.

When giants like Sears and General Motors put on their dancing shoes and let it be known that they wanted to tap their way into the glittering world of financial services, they threatened to demolish the retail banking business. In response, Congress passed the most sweeping overhaul of the nation's banking laws since the New Deal of the 1930s, the Depository Institutions Deregulation and Monetary Control Act of 1980.

In an all-out effort to make the banking industry competitive, Congress legislated a six-year phaseout of interest-rate ceilings that would turn various members of the financial community into direct competitors. Decisions as to the timing and speed of change were left to a new deregulation committee composed of the Secretary of the Treasury, the Chairman of the Federal Reserve Board, representatives of the FDIC (for the banks), Federal Home Loan Bank Board (for the S&Ls), and National Credit Union Administration (NCUA) (for credit unions), and the Comptroller of the Currency (non-voting). The committee was to meet at least once a quarter, in open session, and complete the job of deregulating the banking business by 1986.

But once unleashed, financial deregulation began to spread like wildfire, sweeping away interest-rate ceilings, boosting federal deposit insurance (FDIC for banks, FSLIC for savings and loans, and NCUA share insurance fund for credit unions) from $40,000 to $100,000, allowing thrifts to offer checking accounts, and making it easier for non-banks to buy or start up money machines of their own. In 1982, however, with regular banks and thrifts still bound by tight government control of interest rates and savings plans, investors again began to pour cash into money market mutual funds at the torrid rate of $300 million a day. Wall Street was in a deep slump. Gold and silver prices were on the skids. The money market funds were the only game in town in 1982, offering an average of 14 percent on short-term money. Concerned that banks and thrifts were falling off the pace as the nation's leading money gatherers, the new Depository Institutions Deregulation Committee moved up its deregulation schedule, and in December 1982 allowed banks and thrifts to introduce a new insured money market account with a $2,500 minimum deposit that ripped the ceiling off low-interest government-regulated passbook accounts.

Armed with the new insured money market accounts, banks and thrifts, in a blizzard of slick advertising, purchased deposits that cost them more than they could earn. I can still remember the hype and scramble to attract money when the interest ceiling on short-term savings fell away. To attract short-term money market accounts, some banks and thrifts offered yields on new accounts that were 3, 5, even as much as 10 percent higher than market rates.

By October of 1983, federal financial regulators voted to reduce minimum-deposit requirements and lift the interest ceilings on term deposits with maturities of 32 days or longer. The Depository Institutions Deregulation Committee then established the final wave of financial deregulation on the following schedule:

- Beginning December 1, 1983, minimum deposits were eliminated for all accounts used in tax-deferred individual accounts (IRAs).
- Beginning January 1, 1984, banks could increase the rate of interest they pay on passbook savings accounts to 5.5 percent— the same rate then offered by savings & loans.
- Beginning January 1, 1985, the regulated minimum deposit of $2,500 fell to $1,000 for all money market savings accounts, for deposits with maturities of 7 to 31 days, and for no-rate-limit "Super-Now" accounts.
- And the final act blew up banking regulations in one giant explosion: On March 31, 1986, the regulated deposit requirements were eliminated entirely.

Ironically, the banks and thrifts that had lobbied so hard for freedom from tight federal regulations were ill-prepared for the new, no-holds-barred competition that deregulation brought. Among other things, they were saddled with enormous and expensive buildings, money palaces built at a time when concrete and marble symbolized safety. Once grand gatherers of cheap deposits, these buildings have now become heavy cost burdens in a rapidly deregulated marketplace.

Many branches were haphazardly located. To cut costs, drive-up windows have been replaced by ATMs. Fancy lobbies are usually half empty. Bankers, preoccupied with creating new accounts and luring new customers with big returns, soon discovered that paying high rents as well as high interest rates meant that profits quickly disappear.

One of the great moneyshocks in this new era of financial deregulation occurs when your favorite branch bank or thrift closes its doors. Many banks are trying to get rid of what is known in the trade as "suction pumps." The pumps (branches) were great devices for sucking up low-interest deposits, but now they have become unprofitable when the same job is being done by a financial non-bank at a counter in a department store. The banks, of course, put their best face on their shrinking branch system by sending you a letter explaining that somehow you'll actually be better off if you have to go out of your way to bank with them.

But what scares federally insured banks and thrifts most is the repeal of the Federal Reserve Board's Regulation Q, which imposed interest-rate ceilings on savings accounts. Consumer groups say that Regulation Q cost $42 billion in lost interest between 1968 and 1978 alone, with most of the losses having been suffered by people over the agae of 65. The confusion of the money game in the fast-changing world of financial deregulation has, in spite of everything, meant a substantial source of relatively cheap money for banks and S&Ls—much of it paying 5.5 percent interest—which has kept many of them from going broke. In a very real sense, substantial numbers of banks and thrifts have been kept financially afloat on the backs of America's senior citizens who are deathly afraid to take their money out of their 5.5 percent insured passbook savings accounts.

For the first time since small-town banker Louis McFadden gave them a protected money machine, banks and thrifts are pinching pennies to survive. To make the kind of profits they previously enjoyed, they can no longer wait for the deposits to come in the front door. As a result, a new breed of money brokers now collects pools of funds from investors, breaks them into $100,000 lots (so they'll qualify for federal deposit insurance) and sells them to whatever bank or savings and loan offers the highest interest rate. That's why if a bank or S&L is offering a two-year insured CD to the "walk-in trade" at 9 percent, you can usually find a stockbroker offering a two-year insured CD paying 10 percent. On my local radio show, *Moneytalk*, I asked a broker how his firm could offer the same insured CD that banks and thrifts were offering, yet pay substantially more interest. "Because," he said, "we can bring in a lot more cash at lower costs and the banks and S&Ls are willing to pay a hefty rate for this fast cash." At some recently failed

S&Ls, as much as 80 percent of the deposits hadn't come in the front door, they had come from the higher yielding brokered funds.

And while banks and S&Ls pay sky-high rates to attract money, many depositors feel they don't need to be concerned about the risks being taken with their money because their investment is guaranteed by the federal government through deposit insurance. Plain and simple, the freedom of deregulation and the insurance for risk-takers attract gamblers to the money game. When the financial institutions go under, the taxpayers effectively inherit the loss through the U.S. Treasury, which has guaranteed its full faith and credit to repay the depositors.

As we enter the second half of the decade, the term "consumer bank" has a down-home ring, but of the hundreds of giant firms set to leap over the barriers to interstate banking as "consumer banks"—some of the most impersonal multinational corporations in the world—none are hometown bankers. They are not even bankers at all. The new financial players in the money game are Gulf & Western Industries, Parker Pen Company, Prudential-Bache, Dreyfus Fund, Sears, and American Express—just a few of the companies that have opened consumer banks. And with deregulation almost complete, the big regulated banks don't want to be left behind. To skirt the McFadden Act, they are buying thrift and loan companies that can quickly be converted into chains of consumer-oriented banking offices when the ban on interstate branching is finally lifted.

Bankers are beginning to learn just how bracing competition can be. Because their own thrift and loan companies are free from banking regulations, they offer much higher interest on passbook savings accounts and as much as 1 percent more interest on certificates of deposit than the parent bank itself. Having thus jumped through the non-bank loophole, the big banks themselves are caught in the middle of a shift from regulated to free banking. Until they can offer a better deal at their existing, heavily advertised banks, they have to find ways to keep their current customers from flocking to their own non-bank money stores. So they throw out a bewildering number of savings and investment plans to mask the fact that, in hundreds of their own non-banks, the same financial products are available with a far better rate of return.

Regulated Banking Is a Thing of the Past

Most small community banks are terrified. They fear they'll be whacked by the Chase Manhattans of the world, who will invade their markets and suck up their deposits by offering better rates. Their fears are much the same as those of Louis McFadden when he became president of the First National Bank of Canton, Pennsylvania, at the turn of the century. "What we'll get is the Citicorp equivalent of a McDonald's on every corner," says the director of the Independent Bankers Association, which represents the smaller banks. In fact, the small banks and savings and loans only have to look at the shakeout that's going on in the airline business to learn how an industry can be torn apart by rapid deregulation.

When the regulations were lifted in the airline industry, new players in the game charged onto the field. Being new, they could hire non-union people, and, unlike most older airlines, which were saddled with massive debt, they were able to expand nationwide, cutting their costs to the bone. With deregulation, they were free to offer any price they chose, undercutting the prices of the older, well-established players. The result: Half of what used to be the airline business is in danger of collapsing.

Now imagine the moneyshock of the 14,800 commercial banks and 3,200 thrift institutions across the country when the giant corporations—in banking, in retailing, and on Wall Street—introduce their one-stop money centers into cities and towns in every state in the nation. The smart players in the money game, with their consumer banks, will take advantage of the new technology. They'll offer banking, insurance, mutual funds, discount stocks, real estate, and an array of new savings products to lure consumers into their money stores. After all, with their well-known names, they won't have to put up an imposing marble palace in your hometown to impress you with how solid they are. They'll use the ultimate tactic: They'll offer you a better deal.

Steve McLin of BankAmerica Corporation may have summed it up best when he said, ". . . a blurring of distinctions may mean that there will be no banks at all within the next few years. The services offered by S&Ls, commercial banks, brokerage houses, and other companies such as Sears and Shearson/American Express will overlap to such an extent that a new appellation will have to be coined to describe the bank of the future."

Part of the problem today is that we're bewildered about money: It no longer works in the simple old-fashioned way. Fixed-rate savings have been traded in for widely fluctuating money market accounts. We flounder in a world without stable reference points, where, no matter how much we earn, we sense that what the tax man does not get, the high-commission salesman will. The old values of working hard, being prudent, exercising self-denial, and hoping for an occasional piece of good luck along the way are no longer enough. But for millions of

Americans, old habits about money die hard. Those people feel they've lost their grip on the present and that whatever is being done with their money is strange and unsettling.

When I went to rent a car recently, the man ahead of me was asked, "Do you have a credit card?" The man shook his head and held out a wad of 20-dollar bills. "I'm sorry," the smiling young woman said, "company policy forbids renting cars without a major credit card." The man began frantically waving money in her face, but I sensed she wouldn't rent him a car even if he put up the deed to the Empire State Building. When I stepped up to the counter, this pretty young creature of corporate decree informed me, "It's people like that who are always disrupting the system."

It's important to recognize how the financial marketplace is changing, how it will operate in the future. Economic and social trends used to change so glacially that anyone could predict them. That's no longer true. In 1981, interest rates rose higher than in the entire century between 1870 and 1970. Today, with loopholes in our banking laws widening, the old regulations can no longer hold our financial system in check.

Banks and S&Ls Are Not Dead—Just Dying

Victims of a fast-changing marketplace to which they are no longer able to adapt, banks and savings and loans need to redefine what business they are in or they will be out of business. Like the gas stations of the 1970s, large numbers of banks and S&Ls will soon disappear, their brick-and-mortar buildings replaced by McDonald's-type money centers with Big Mac savings plans and 800-banking.

Even so, in a financial banking climate aboil with change, the present banking system differs little from that of the 1920s. Now, as before, banks are deeply invested in foreign loans, in leveraged buyouts. They're getting back into the securities business by buying discount stockbrokers and fighting for the chance to underwrite certain bond issues. Some federally insured money players even sponsor real estate syndications for sale to the public, and invest depositors' money in any kind of business they want. In many respects, we've come full circle to the bargain-hunting 1920s . . . except for one big difference: The risk-takers today are playing with money that's federally insured.

2

From Hand Ledgers to Electronic Banking

How High Technology Is Changing Our Conception of Money

In Renaissance times, the Medicis knew the satisfying feel of gold pieces weighing heavy in the hand. The Morgans, the Rothschilds, and the rest of us have been content to part with gold coins and let crisp, quiet paper money nestle in the folds of our wallet or purse. Although both gold and paper are symbols of the idea we call "value," they are nevertheless tangible objects. We can see them. We can count them. We can hold them in our hands.

Today, however, money is mostly composed of electronic impulses moving at the speed of light. Hundreds of billions of dollars worth of impulses are blips that make their way through the banking system each day. Yet, while money flies invisibly through the high-tech world of banking, banks remain direct beneficiaries of the built-in inefficiencies of the past. Banks count on the "float," which today makes up a big part of their profits. Float is money in transit, a concept that is anachronistic now that "in transit" can now be measured in millionths of a second. In 1985, the U.S. Public Interest Research Group, a nonprofit consumer advocate and lobbying group, surveyed 669 banks and savings and loans to gauge the size of the float. It found that 52 percent of the banks put holds of three to five days on local checks, 75 percent put holds of over a week on out-of-state checks, and 20 percent held out-of-state checks for more than two weeks. The survey also found that a third of the banks even held local cashiers' checks for three days! By keeping the checks on hold and by denying depositors the use of their funds (90 percent of which actually clear within one or two days), banks and thrifts use roughly $3 trillion of checking-account deposits as interest-free loans. If we assume that there is a delay of only five days beyond the date when the Fed makes the money available to the bank presenting the check, then depositors are prevented from using $60 *billion a day* of their own money. On a 10 percent return, that's $6 billion a year of free money—two-fifths of the estimated cost of operating the banking system.

When computers became available, they were sold to the banks on the basis that they could provide daily printouts of the float and help maximize the bankers' interest-free loan portfolios.

Computers Evolve—And Offer Banks New Possibilities

As we have said, from the beginning of banking financial firms were really nothing but huge countinghouses. To get money to lend at high interest, they had to first attract deposits, on which they paid a lower interest rate. And to keep track of their income and expenses—that's the magical "spread" that determines a bank's profits—they had to post each ledger, each month, by hand. It was a clumsy way to manage money. Only the simple passbook savings account could possibly work in a hand-posting era.

Then in the 1960s the computer arrived.

I remember a tour of a new computer operation in the early 1960s. At that time the system was the newest wonder of the banking world. The computer itself was located on an elevated platform in a separate, air-conditioned room with walls painted in soft pastels. This marvel of computerized banking was viewed through large glass windows. For sucking information into its brain, it ate IBM punch cards. When installed, the machine had a memory of 16 thousand bytes of information (called 16k for short), and a year later its memory had grown to an unthinkable 32k.

By 1978, the electronics industry was making a microcomputer that could handle 64k bytes of information. This was no massive room-size machine, but a compact device with working parts not much bigger than a fingernail.

By 1985, a little MacIntosh small enough to sit on a corner of your dining room table had 512k of memory. Today's inexpensive personal computers can have 8 to 40 times the power of the giant computers that rested in the pastel-colored rooms of the 1960s.

The technology is now available to move big banks even faster from human touch to high-tech touch. In only two decades we have gone from a manual system of posting records to a high-tech system whose speed approaches the speed of light. The problem is, the high-tech system of financial services is being imposed on people without any high-touch tradeoffs.

During 1985, the Cary 2 (at this writing the world's fastest computer), with a bargain-basement price of only $17 million, began to crunch out the numbers for business. The Cary 2 can perform one mathematical operation every 4.1 billionths of a second, or up to 250 million mathematical operations a second. With something called half a gigabyte of memory, it has about 1,000 times the capacity of the maximum memory in a big IBM computer and about 40,000 to 50,000 times that of a personal computer. "Now," says a computer operator, "we can carry out vast amounts of work at incredible speeds. What took a year in 1952, we can now do in a second." The supercomputer, which is doughnut shaped and is about the size of a large industrial washing machine, is immersed in a tank of colorless, odorless fluorocarbon fluid that, incongruously, is also used as an artificial blood plasma.

Even more impressive will be the Cary 3, which is expected to be in place in 1986 or 1987, with a computing capacity that is a staggering 40 times faster than the Cary 2.

Currently, a quiet breakthrough in the creation of ultra-powerful silicon chips is propelling the computer revolution into new realms. For example, until now computer technology has been unable to make use of radio waves. To do so requires that speed-of-light signals be translated almost instantaneously into the digital pulses that are the language of computation. But today, computers are capable of transmitting data over radio waves, using the first superchip that can do that and more. The computer chip has evolved from what was once an incredible thousands of transistors on each tiny square of silicon, to tens of millions of transistors. The creation of superchips with fast clock rates (the speed at which they can process data) of 100 million hertz, or cycles per second, will open up vast new areas to computers. (By contrast, most home computers today run at 1 million or 2 million hertz.)

Computer chips that can process radio and television signals will open a wide range of new possibilities. Instead of using phone lines to link up computers, we'll be able to use radios and television sets. In the computer age we must conceive of space in a new way—not in miles an automobile can travel, but as a distance connected by the electromagnetic spectrum, where television waves vibrate many billions of times faster than waves generated by the human voice. Imagine, if you can, an object so small that two of them could fit on the head of a pin, each of which contains more than a million transistors that are less than one-hundredth the thickness of a human hair. A single one of these new chips has the capacity of one of today's big mainframe computers. By the 1990s, designers will be packing more than 4 million transistors on a single chip. The result: The desktop or home computer will become a supercomputer.

To understand just how fast these new computers will overtake us, confuse us, and do our financial planning for us, here's what's ahead: As early as the mid-1990s, a single integrated circuit will pack more raw computing power than a dozen of today's giant $4 million supercomputers. And the new "superbabies" will probably sell for just a few hundred dollars each! But, again, I'm getting ahead of myself.

Where is electronic banking headed tomorrow? When computers came to banking, the first thing the bankers used them for was to bring order out of chaos. Financial firms had grown so large that without the invention of the computer they would have drowned in a sea of paper. The banks soon found that it was easier to run the entire bank customer list past the computer than to hunt through the records for just those accounts that needed updating. Now it became possible to post interest every night, not just once a month or once a quarter. Computers made possible interest-bearing checking accounts. In fact, by the 1970s the electronic tide was rising so fast that insurance companies, brokers, and mutual funds were all developing high-tech money systems to manage the complex record keeping of their high-touch consumer products. The continued development and use of computers spawned new savings and investment plans, consumer services, and superbanks, all of which have sent shock waves through the once tightly regulated banking industry. By the start of the 1980s, the information explosion was moving so fast that the people in Congress who oversee money were being left behind. Congress wants to direct the movement of money, but it's no longer in charge of the deregulated marketplace. And as the power of computers grows, changes will come even faster.

Banks Didn't Know How to Work with Something "New"—But Other Institutions Did

Before deregulation, bankers claimed that they would like to offer better savings plans and join the world of the non-banks, but the McFadden Act prevented them from doing the kind of banking that would benefit the consumer. Yet they defended the Act as the last bastion of competitive individual banking and claimed that it allowed them to deliver personalized services at a local level. And so, to keep the superbanks away from the neighborhoods, banks and thrifts, mired in regulations, sat on their hands.

But as banks remained behind the McFadden wall of protection, non-banks began to offer a dizzying array of financial services. Banks found that their bread-and-butter customers, the blue-chip corporations, were deserting them in droves. To obtain short-term financing, corporations began selling their notes to investors by going directly to the less-expensive commercial-paper market instead of to the local bank. In the new pecking order of money, the bank's customers had now become their competitors. Without the big corporate pocketbooks, the banks were forced to scramble for deposits from consumers—the very group they had originally ignored under the McFadden Act. And yet banks and thrifts still sat on their hands.

Many Americans were also undergoing a fundamental change in their banking habits. No longer content to deposit all of their money in a bank, they wanted to keep the smallest possible balance in their checking accounts and move their money from one financial institution to another in search of the best deal. And as financial deregulation began to spread, finding the best deal fast became the highlight of car-pool conversations.

In 1975, Merrill Lynch executives sat around a table and asked themselves what people might want and expect from a super money store in the 1980s. The result of the brainstorming sessions was the "cash management account" or CMA. The cash management account allowed customers to borrow against their assets by writing their own checks or by using credit cards. A CMA was like an interest-bearing checking account—except that customers earned interest on their funds up until the time that check actually cleared the bank.

What made this "checking account" so successful was a new invest-ment called Ready Assets—a money market mutual fund. The idea of the CMA was to help brokerage customers earn interest on their idle funds between stock and bond investments. When a stock was sold, the money would automatically be swept into the Ready Assets money fund. If the customer wrote a check, the funds would be withdrawn first from the cash in the account. After the cash reserves were used, the CMA pledged the customer's securities for a loan. The customer could write checks not only for the cash amount available, but for the total margin value in the brokerage account.

The success of Merrill Lynch's cash management account sent the banks, still mired in their passbook savings accounts, into panic. Paul Volcker of the Fed called it "a complicated form of overdraft." John Heimann, then Comptroller of the Currency, said it was the kind of financial service the public wanted. The banks and thrifts called it unregulated banking. The public called it just what it was, a better deal for saving and spending money. But Bank of America's President Samuel Armacost may have made the most accurate assessment of all when he said, "We've already got the nationwide banking of the future. It's called Merrill Lynch."

The other stockbrokers quickly began to offer their own brand of cash management accounts and money market funds. Then came the mutual funds. Fidelity Fund, which already had offices nationwide, set out to make your checking account obsolete. They came up with Fidelity USA, a single account that takes care of everything to do with money. The USA account provides unlimited checking, a credit card, nationwide automatic teller machines, electronic funds transfer, direct deposit, discount brokerage, automatic bill-paying, and, of course, mutual funds. One single statement keeps you up to date each month.

The federally insured banks and thrifts—clinging to McFadden, yet hopelessly snarled in regulations—watched the non-banks aggres-sively elbow their way onto their home turf. Between 1980 and 1981, bank demand deposits dropped by almost $100 billion. It was, as one bank officer explained, "like a fish-feeding frenzy, and the banks were being eaten alive." Banks and thrifts could offer only ideas whose time had gone.

The Reagan administration, the Treasury, and the Federal Reserve Board believed banks and thrifts needed more freedom to compete with the money supermarkets. Their plan, which became the Depository Institutions Deregulation Act, drew new boundaries within the finan-cial services industry by allowing banks and thrifts to ultimately compete head-to-head with other financial firms. But the banks, and especially the thrifts, were vulnerable to something more dangerous than cash management accounts: interest-rate risk.

One thing they did understand with the introduction of deregulation was that paying higher interest rates and carrying losses from bad loans can all but eliminate profits. Many bankers feared they might be drawn into the kind of pricing rivalries that led to bankruptcies in the deregulated airline industry, where long-time carriers like Braniff were blown right out of the sky. "Banks can't be counted on to discipline themselves," says Albert Wojnilower, chief economist for First Boston. "Deregulation gave the banks enough rope to kill themselves, and they almost have."[1]

Borrowing short and lending long had left them naked should interest rates rise. And inadvertently, Paul Volcker, Chairman of the Federal Reserve Board, came close to doing in the thrift industry. He allowed interest rates to rise to levels previously undreamed of in the United States. Between 1982 and 1983 the thrift industry lost a total of $12 billion as they paid higher rates to depositors to attract money than they earned on their old, low-rate, mortgages. Almost overnight, so many thrifts looked like they were going under that they were sending out lifeboats.

The industry's answer, again, was to seek broad new powers. The beleaguered savings and loans were granted new freedom to bolster their sliding deposits by the Garn-St. Germain bill of 1982, which included the right to offer checking and trust services and to make consumer and commercial loans. The bill also allowed thrifts and commercial banks to pay whatever rate was necessary to attract deposits. The upshot of these new powers was to gradually blur the distinction between a bank and an S&L.

The Shift from Low-Cost to High-Cost Banking Began

One of the biggest losers in the battle for consumer dollars has been the "Super-NOW" checking account. (NOW stands for negotiable order of withdrawal.) Unlike regular zero-interest checking accounts and regular NOW accounts, which pay a maximum of 5.5 percent, Super-NOW accounts are subject to no legal limit on the amount of interest banks and thrifts can pay. Instead of offering toasters and piggy banks, banks can offer high interest rates. Theoretically, that sounds like a good deal. But on some deposits, reserves equal to 12 percent of deposits collected in the new accounts must be set aside. That means that 12 cents out of every dollar in deposits will not be available for making loans—or, from the bank's point of view, for each dollar on deposit on which interest is paid, only 88 cents can be loaned out again. From the customer's point of view, what's not so super about Super-NOWs is that they have lower-than-usual interest rates because checking accounts are expensive to operate. What's more, many banks and thrifts also slap on hefty service charges and fees to cut the effective yield even more.

Banks and thrifts had to design savings plans that protected their high-profit, low-interest passbook accounts, so they demanded and got a $2,500 minimum on the Super-NOW accounts. Instead of selling what they really had that the new money stores didn't—federally insured money—they launched slick advertising campaigns to make their Super-NOWs look competitive. "People have a vague idea that if you have $2,500 you can get a hell of a lot better rate than you are getting now," a bank officer told me when the new accounts first burst on the scene, "but they don't know much more. What they don't know," he went on, "is that we were afraid we'd lose a lot of money if consumers transferred their money from zero-interest checking and passbook accounts to high-interest checking, so we loaded the new Super-NOWs with service charges, penalties, and clauses that drastically cut back the actual interest earned in these new accounts."

Watch Out for Computer-Driven Fine Print

By establishing a $2,500 minimum for their money market accounts (MMAs) and for their Super-NOW checking accounts, most banks and thrifts were able to keep the low-income savers locked into their 5.5 percent passbook accounts, whack the middle class with the fine print, and trim the annual return for those with hefty balances on deposit.

Consumers have to be careful, because a blunder can be costly in an era of financial supermarkets. For example, on some Super-NOW checking accounts, the fine print shows a $6-per-month service fee, which really means you get a 3 percent annual return on your $2,500 balance. If the account is paying 8 percent, your net interest is only 5 percent, which is less than the 5.5 percent on the old NOW account or the passbook savings account. But what really made bankers' eyes dance with visions of riches was the $2,500 minimum balance requirement. The banks could make money on Super-NOWs, not by offering a better deal to the consumer, but by paying 5.5 percent on the accounts that fell below the minimum. On money market accounts and Super-NOW accounts, some banks and thrifts leaped at the chance to pay 5.5

percent for the entire month if the minimum balance fell below $2,500 for even one day. Others used an average monthly balance. To bolster their income even more, some banks and thrifts boosted the service fee from, say, $6 up to $10 when the balance fell below the minimum. And that could happen several times a month!

Super-NOW checking can be summed up best by the comments of a banker for a large state-wide California bank. "The fees will make Super-Checking unattractive to about 80 percent of our customers. They just don't have enough money. People who write a lot of checks (more than an average of 22 a month) and who keep less than several thousand dollars in their checking account are unlikely to gain with Super-Checking."

But small investors theoretically got a break on January 1, 1985, when financial institutions were allowed to lower the minimum deposit on money market accounts and Super-NOW accounts from $2,500 to $1,000. The bad news is that most banks and thrifts are simply ignoring the lower minimum balances. Many bankers fear that if they lower the minimum deposit for money market accounts, any funds that flow into these accounts will come from their own profitable low-interest savings accounts. And with an astounding $300 billion still deposited in low-interest passbook savings accounts, bankers are anything but eager to spread the word. Why should they be? The $300 billion of cheap money adds up to about one-fourth of the total of $1.3 trillion in deposits held by banks and savings and loans. The money-shock of all of this is that 76 percent of American households continue to hold low-interest passbook accounts even though deregulation has made higher yielding insured accounts readily available. In fact, passbook savings accounts are one of the few things that have never kept up with inflation. Twenty years ago, S&Ls were paying 3.25 percent; today they are paying 5.5 percent. And when you are earning hundreds of millions of dollars in service fees and paying only 5.5 percent interest when accounts fall below the account minimum, you develop an enormously greedy appetite.

In the years to come, as the Sears and Merrill Lynch money bazaars attract more bank customers, banks and thrifts will offer lower minimum deposits to attract new accounts, and then will significantly reduce the effective interest yield of the money market accounts by linking the interest yield to the amount of the account balance. The moneyshock of the future will occur when high-tech computers bounce our interest yield up and down on a monthly or daily basis. Say your bank has a four-tier structure with interest rates paid on the size of the daily balance of your account. As you make deposits and withdrawals, the size of your account could shift daily from Tier I, 5.25 percent (the interest floor), to Tier II, 6.75 percent, then to Tier III, 7.15 percent, and then back down to Tier I, 5.25 percent. And the high-tech banking specialists have another surprise waiting for you: Every time your balance falls below the minimum—which can be anywhere from $1,000 to as much as $25,000 on jumbo accounts, you not only drop to Tier I, but you get charged $10. If your balance bounces up and down near the minimum—whatever that is—you could very quickly find that you're earning a negative interest return!

Today, computers search out the daily movement of our money and slap on an almost endless number of service charges, penalties, and fees. For example, the cost of bouncing a check has skyrocketed. A 1984 study by New York State officials concluded that a bounced check costs a bank less than $5—sometimes a great deal less. Yet in the New York study, banks charged the average customer $10 for a returned check. In Philadelphia the average charge was $18, in Boston, $12, and, in San Francisco, as low as $8.

The House Committee on Banking reported that bank charges for the average American household have more than doubled in the past five years, to about $200 a year. A 15-state consumer survey of banking charges by the Consumer Federation of America, released in May 1985, indicated that the cost of bank and thrift services was far outstripping the nation's inflation rate. According to the survey, the annual cost for a simple non-interest-bearing checking account rose by an average 25.49 percent over the previous year. Service charges on savings accounts at the five S&Ls surveyed rose a hefty 61 percent, while the national inflation rate for the same period was about 3.7 percent!

"Inflation may be licked in some areas of the economy, but it remains a raging monster in the financial community," House Banking Committee Chairman Fernand J. St. Germain (D-R.I.), said. "Today, the alert consumer must take a look at the nickles, dimes, and dollars that are being grabbed in the form of fees."[2] To gauge the speed with which fees are rising, the House Committee report said that small depositors will have to pay more in 1985 than in 1984 for a standard checking account, and substantially more for a Super-NOW interest-bearing checking account. "What's happening," a bank executive told me, "is that in the not-too-distant future, bank fees and charges will eat up almost the entire earned interest for most small and medium depositors." And fees for cashing Social Security checks—the most profitable bank operation—can run high as $3, which sometimes represents as much as 1 percent of the amount of the check.

With banks and thrifts able to set their own fees, many have become merchandisers of services and not banking. After all, it's easier to fleece the sheep you already have than to attract new ones to an old shop. One banker told me, "We keep all the low-balance customers and then service-charge the hell out of them. We give them a package, I think we call it a consumer package. For $10 a month you get ten checks, unlimited electronic transfers, cash machines, and a lot of other stuff. But you're happy, you stay with the bank. It cost me six bucks, I'm happy." This attitude of nicking customers' accounts and cutting back on service has many consumers believing all bankers are cold and greedy. During my televison show, I asked a middle-aged man how he liked the modern way of banking. "I no longer feel as though I'm treated like a human being," said he. "The banks in our area keep saying they're warm and understanding, but the truth is, you walk in and look for the same happy faces you see on TV, and they usually aren't there."

Competition with financial supermarkets, which spelled the end of a life of 3-6-3 (pay depositors 3 percent interest, lend money at 6 percent, and tee off at the golf course by 3 P.M.), should have forced banks to rethink what business they were in. Yet many banks are still in the same old business of making money on the fine print, not offering the consumer a better deal. Take, for example, the latest credit card gimmick. Some banks and savings and loans are now assessing interest charges when the purchase is made. Others start interest charges when the purchase is posted to your account. You'll pay interest charges to the bank even if you pay your bill in full upon receipt. Why do banks go on using the fine print to suck up profits when the money centers springing up around the country are not only offering a better deal on bank charges, but also on credit cards that pay a hefty interest on a positive balance? The answer is, of course, because they can't. To stay alive in the years to come, most banks and S&Ls will have to learn more efficient ways of doing things and to become more consumer-oriented. Inflation and electronics have made old-time banking obsolete virtually overnight, but many bankers continue to look inward, boosting service fees and penalties and trimming service—and then head out to the golf course at 3 P.M.

The moneyshock that lies ahead is that banks as we know them today will be unnecessary for most consumers. In the past, bankers built branches to offer us convenience, but how important is this convenience if even more banking services are available closer by at K mart? Banks and thrifts built huge money palaces to symbolize safety, but what we rely on now is federal deposit insurance. Bankers gave us checking accounts, but these are now available from mutual funds and stockbrokers who have acquired a federally insured bank on the cheap.

High Technology Spawned Myths and Marvels

We are living in a time of transition, moving away from the shackles of regulation to a free marketplace where every variety of financial service will be offered in one place. Computers are both causing and accelerating this transformation, and they are pulling us farther from our old ways of saving and spending money, shoving us from an industrial society to an information society. Bankers have allied themselves permanently with computers, using them to cut costs, hunt for our savings dollars, and lure us with high-tech services—services that threaten to distance us even more from our money.

Whatever Happened to the Checkless Society?

For at least 20 years, "experts" have been saying that the personal check was headed for obsolescence, doomed to become the dinosaur of banking. The banking world was drowning in paper. The public's enormous appetite for checks had leaped to over 20 billion a year by 1970, and the number was rising. Here was just the job for the computer. The traditional clearing of paper checks would be replaced by electronic funds transfer (EFT).

In a banker's heaven of electronic transactions, when a father in Boston mailed a birthday check to his son in San Francisco, who cashed it at a local bank, the check would never leave San Francisco. At the end of the month the check would show up on the father's statement only as a line typed by a computer. If the depositor wanted to finger his cancelled checks every month, he'd have to pay a hefty fee to look at photocopies. People would also get paid more efficiently by direct deposit and never see their pay checks. They would pay their bills more efficiently by pre-authorizing their bank to pay them. And all this would be done by banks and thrifts spinning around reels of magnetic tape rather than millions of paper checks. It was a great idea, it was going to save the banks millions in check handling and postage. Electronic funds transfer was going to eliminate the traditional clearing of paper checks and save the banks a bundle.

A funny thing happened en route to the checkless society. The number of checks has been multiplying instead of declining. The Federal Reserve Board estimates that around 40 billion checks are now written each year, twice the number written in 1970 when electronic banking first hit the market. The banks' efforts to lure consumers away from paper and into reels of magnetic tape, in fact, never got off the ground. The reason: The banks had cut themselves off from the concerns of the end users, and the public wouldn't buy the idea. The banks, unlike almost every other business, had considered their own internal operations first and the customer second. Because electronic funds transfer was seen by the banks as a substitute for checks, the system was organized around the efficient transportation of information. But the customer didn't give a darn about efficiency. The customer wanted his or her own method of paying bills, physical evidence of payments, something that could be fingered and filed as cancelled checks. The banking customer didn't care how the money was transported between banks and the Federal Reserve system.

And the public was getting smarter about banking. Another reason electronic funds transfer drew a less-than-enthusiastic response was that the public wanted to keep the float on the checks they wrote. If the bank could sit on interest-free money, why not the consumer? You could write a check and put it in the mail on Friday and not scramble to cover the check until as late as the next Monday. With electronic funds transfer, on the other hand, the payment would be deducted from your account at the speed of light. (While E.F. Hutton pleaded guilty to fraud stemming from illegal use of the float in handling checking accounts, individuals can make use of the float profitably and legally.) Dreyfus Liquid Assets, for example, has an arrangement that when you withdraw funds, you continue to earn interest on those funds until your check has cleared. When you deposit funds, you earn interest immediately—they don't wait for your check to clear.

Electronic funds transfer has shown us that if high-tech banking is to be successful, it must be accompanied by a corresponding high-touch positive gain, or the technology will be rejected. There must be a balance of what's good for the bank and what's good for the consumer. The people who run the new money bazaars know this. The financial centers run by mutual funds, department stores, and stockbrokers continue to attract thousands of bank customers with lucrative new high-tech, high-touch services.

To drum up more support for electronic banking, banks need to develop a system that lets the customer, in a hands-on, high-touch environment, do as much of the processing as possible and at the same time get breaks of lower costs or higher interest. People want to feel that they are in charge of their money. They're not interested in becoming involved in an electronic process where they believe they cease to exist or become unimportant. But the banking industry has not been able to change. As one Manhattan banker told me, "Banks hate to get into a new business. It all goes back to how banks think—and that's why the new non-banks will eat them for lunch."

Computers Made the Iron Monster a Reality

If high-tech electronic funds transfer wouldn't work, then how about using automatic teller machines (ATMs)? When people say banks leave them cold today, they are often talking about what I call the "iron monster"—the automatic teller machine. Banks and savings and loans installed ATMs everywhere in an effort to get customers to use them. In their rush to cut costs, banks increased the number of ATMs from 1,935 a decade ago to something over 50,000 by 1984. It was the self-help idea of all time. Remove the expensive human tellers and replace them with a high-tech video screen. When customers didn't flock to the new iron monsters, many banks, like New York's Citicorp, began to tighten the screws. Citicorp tried to force customers with less than $5,000 in their accounts to use an ATM rather than a more expensive human teller. What the banks didn't consider, with all their high-priced marketing help, was that their customers were mostly mature Americans who were not about to use ATMs. For those unskilled in electronic funds transfer—and that's almost anyone over the age of 50—there is no high-touch in high-tech banking. Most people want to write their own checks, to be in control, to know the job will be done. Offering complicated machines, where people have no part to play in the transaction, leaves most people out of control and they reject it. Caught up in its own cost-cutting programs, Citicorp found this out and dropped its "must use" ATM program.

Some bankers have tried to give cold ATM machines traditional banking qualities—called in the trade "warm and friendlies"—by putting a Santa Claus costume on ATMs during Christmas. Then customers, deprived of the chance to talk with tellers, put get-well cards in deposit slots when the machines broke down.

Money hung on the outside of banks and thrifts became an easy target for crooks. Automatic teller machines, like vending machines, can quickly be opened by burglars using hydraulic tools and one quick blast of an acetylene torch. In many cases the new machines put the customers in competition with the bank robbers—a frightening prospect after hours or on weekends. So it's not surprising that less than 30 percent of the people who have ATM cards use them. Bankers say that trying to boost the 30 percent level is like hitting a stone wall. Nothing gives. Not even the old toaster gift routine will get people to help cut costs at the expense of high-touch banking. Maybe, as someone suggested to me after I addressed a convention recently, you could give the bank a toaster and it would put $250 in your account!

The Debit Card Is So Rational, It Will Never Succeed

The next idea the banks offered was a debit card. It works like an ATM card, but it can also be used to spend your money immediately by authorizing instant payment from your checking account to the gas station or department store. Debit cards look like credit cards, but they are the equivalent of paying cash on the spot. Depriving consumers' of their float—which is sometimes as much as six weeks on major credit cards—debit cards have met the same stone wall as ATM cards. Yet debit cards have spawned a whole new industry and the banks are betting billions of dollars that they can change the way America pays its bills. For most of us this whole exercise seems unnecessary—we already have enough ways to part with our money. But to banks and retailers, ever charging toward the checkless society, the usual methods require tremendous paperwork. Debit cards hold out the promise of getting the customers' money out of the banks and into the merchants' accounts quickly and at the lowest cost.

Over the years, the high-tech way of paying the tab has become a hodgepodge of confusing technology lumped under the term electronic funds transfer. But one thing is sure: In high-tech banking of the future, computer networks will become more important than vaults and fancy offices.

Information about Money Will Replace Money Itself

Up until the decade of the 1980s, banking and financial services could be personal. You talked with your banker, insurance agent, or stockbroker, and anyone who had any amount of money to manage had his or her own financial adviser. But electronic funds transfer threatens to replace human contact with machines. It is set to take over the way we spend our money if only we will let it. For the immediate future, it has allowed non-banks to elbow their way into the financial services industry. William Moroney, president of the Electronic Funds Transfer Association, says, "Now anyone with a good network and computer can get into the money business—and is."[3]

For instance, Sears has a new financial card, "Discover." The Discover card will combine a credit card with a wide range of financial services to compete with MasterCard and Visa. With 28 million active credit card accounts, Sears' new black and orange Discover card will include a family savings account, access to ATMs, financial services from Sears' Dean Witter Reynolds brokerage subsidiary (which can sell you IRAs and stocks), check-cashing services, loss and theft protection, emergency cash, . . . and what could turn out to be the biggest lure, a variety of merchant-related discount programs, including discounts on Sears merchandise.

These new financial cards, putting a one-stop money center in your wallet or purse with a smart-card computer built into the card to record your transactions, will let non-banks and limited-service banks develop bank-like relationships with banking customers. Full-service banks and thrifts are left with the job of fighting back time, of offering one-function cards to protect their turf. More and more, it looks as if they're going to fail. The new money services industry threatens to erode the very foundation of their relationship with their customers.

But life can be risky when you rely on electronic money in the form of an ATM or a debit card. With credit card crime rampant in the United States (reported losses on bank cards alone rose from $85 million in 1981 to over $200 million in 1983 and projected losses by 1986 are a mind-boggling $350 million), petty thieves are giving way to big-time crooks. An ATM (or debit card) works only when you enter your personal identification number, or PIN, into the machine. In theory, only you know this number and only you can use your card. But you run some risks just carrying one.

More and more reports are coming in about people being attacked after hours at ATMs and forced to take money out of their accounts. For the crooks, it beats robbing the bank when they can rob a single customer. If a thief gets your card or if you lose it, theoretically you have some protection. Federal law limits your liability to no more than $50 if you report the loss of your card within two business days. If the bank is told within 60 days, maximum liability is $500. Past two months, however, your losses can be unlimited. Remember, to gain access to your cash, someone needs both the debit card and your PIN. If you keep your personal identification number on your card or in your wallet or purse, the thief has all that's needed to get into your account. A favorite trick used to fleece the unwary is for someone to ask for help in working the machine. The "helpless" person may have an accomplice who notes your identification number as you tap it in, and then snatches your card and helps himself to your cash. Make sure you keep your card in your own hands.

With the rising number of ATM and debit card thieves—and to a smart operator the cards are as good as cash—banks and thrifts have been increasingly forcing customers to eat their losses. If you lose both your debit card and your PIN, many banks are taking the position that you have been negligent and aren't entitled to the protection of the law.

That's simply not true. Regulations for the use of debit cards have no exceptions for negligence. One cardinal rule remains: If you report the loss of your ATM or debit card within two business days of discovering its loss, you should not be charged for more than $50.

But what gives bankers recurring nightmares is knowing how easy it is to steal the information stored on the magnetic strip of a bank card. Computer magazines regularly offer a gadget called a "swipe reader/writer" that can copy the magnetic data on the back of the card onto another strip of tape. This is called "skimming." The $30 hand-held device can transfer a valid card's magnetic strip and re-record it on another card or piece of paperboard—and presto, the crooks have outwitted the machine. In the world of high-tech electronic fraud, it doesn't take much to fool the cash-dispensing machine. If the PIN belonging to that card number is known—and as I've already said, many people write them on their cards because they have trouble remembering the code—a piece of ordinary paperboard becomes a perfect substitute for the skimmed ATM or debit card.

Forced Technology Can Bring Its Own Backlash

It's widely believed, just as it was for electronic funds transfer, that debit cards, ATM cards, and high-tech machines will replace personal banking. The retail-payments industry (made up of the people who make and sell the gadgets) is confident that debit cards, ATM cards, and point-of-sale terminals will eventually gain wide acceptance. From the banks' point-of-view, "everyone knows it's going to happen," says Walter Miller, executive vice-president of the Northwest Corp., which owns 82 banks. "It's going to take some time, but it's going to happen."[4]

If an opera isn't over until the fat lady sings, the fat lady of electronic money is still waiting in the wings. According to the League of Savings Institutions, a typical household in the United States makes use of an automatic teller machine only once every three months. Despite the fact that banks and S&Ls have installed over 60,000 ATMs around the country, well over 90 percent of all consumer transactions continue to be made by traditional methods. The outlook from the League: "To make a drastic impact on the huge amount of cash transactions will take an enormous amount of promotional expenditures to gain a marginal increase in usage." For automatic teller machines and debit cards, the fat lady clearly hasn't sung.

Forced high technology without corresponding high-touch interactions runs against most people's inner nature. To be successful, high-tech innovations must let users participate in the act. The banks' self-interest must be counterbalanced with a reward for the user. People need time to respond to high-tech changes, to rethink old habits, and to move closer to accepting it in stages as innovations flood the market. Human nature being what it is, we need to feel a positive gain and remain in control before acceptance on a wide scale is possible.

The Smart Card May Be the Answer

The earliest reference to a credit card was in the 1880s when a move was underway to replace paper currencies and checks with credit. Installment credit, however, was pretty much invented in the 1920s, and it was little used until after the Depression and World War II. The Depression and the war created a huge backlog of unsatisfied wants. Consumers gradually came to believe that their incomes would continue to rise, despite a few interruptions by recessions. As Americans felt more secure about their prospects, they became more willing to borrow from future income.

The historic evolution of plastic money, as we know it today, began with the first computers in the 1950s. The early card was used as a way to make impulse buying easier, and the first major issuers were the airlines and the travel and entertainment industries. The first plastic credit cards with embossed names and account numbers allowed merchants to imprint this information on a sales slip at the time of sale. By the 1970s, the magnetic stripe on the back of the card had gained wide acceptance as a way of transferring information on the card to the more sophisticated card readers. By the start of 1985, American cardholders, hopelessly snarled in a life of credit, had $108 billion in unpaid charges, averaging $1,092 per cardholder. (Henny Youngman had a favorite joke about the time his wife lost her credit card. He said he was not going to report the loss because the person who found it was spending less than his wife had.)

Today, the traditional savings and loans and banks, which were supposed to be helped by deregulation, may be exchanging their birthright of protected turf for the right to lose the battle in the technology war. Meanwhile, J.C. Penney, American Express, and Kroger supermarkets use their creative ideas to run away with the prize. American banks and thrifts have neglected the most interesting high-tech, high-touch innovation now available, an innovation that could help them and their customers manage money better. The new technology could thwart the credit card crooks by registering each user's password on a computer chip, so it can't be copied the way information encoded on bank cards' magnetic stripe can be. This invention can follow instructions, make logical choices, and follow alternative decision paths. It's called the "Smart Card."

The Smart Card is a credit card (a "financial transaction card," in the language of the 1980s) with an integrated-circuit computer the size of a quarter built into the card. The chip can contain up to 128k (128 thousand bytes) of information. This mini-computer acts like a memory device that can store as many as 600 lines of print—the user's financial records for a year—within the plastic card. And the computer revolution in money is just beginning. Before the end of this decade, Smart Cards are expected to contain 512k of logic memory. They will be considerably easier for the public to use than personal computers are. No hunt-and-peck keyboards, no programs to write, no complex access procedures. Most experts I've talked with believe that Smart Cards will achieve the same level of public acceptance now enjoyed by the television set.

Smart Cards were developed in France and Japan. They will be test-marketed in Washington, D.C., and Miami, Florida, in late 1986 by the two current makers, Japan's Casio Microcard Corp. and France's Bull Micro Card Technologies, Inc. You can expect Smart Cards to be used as ATM cards, as debit cards, as credit cards, as cash cards—any place money is spent or records are kept. American Airlines, for example, has launched a Smart Card program to help passengers keep track of their mileage bonus points. Outside the business world, Smart Cards have health care applications. Called Life Cards, they can contain a patient's complete medical record, medications, insurance data, and just about anything that would be handy to have when going to the doctor or hospital.

But even as I write this book, we are told that the next generation credit card is about to revolutionize the way we use plastic money. Called the Super Card, it's a smart card with a built-in computer chip (with more memory than a personal computer) and a calculator-like keyboard and display unit. Super Card holders will literally carry their banks around in their wallets or purses. They'll be able to initiate off-line transactions, authorize transactions in their checking, savings, and credit card accounts, and update their balances—using the Super Card and without the need for ATMs or terminal equipment at banks or merchant locations.

Visa plans to introduce the Super Card in early 1987. Charles T. Russell, President of Visa, stated, "We believe the super card represents the most significant development in consumer banking since the ad-vent of the automatic teller machine."

Smart Cards Leave People in Control

We all know the high-tech world is here, and we can see the way it already affects how we spend and keep track of our money. We can't stop it, or the changes it will bring, in spite of the failure of ATMs and debit cards. But, we need to keep control of our own affairs, to protect ourselves from an avalanche of high-tech changes whose sole purpose seems to be to confuse us while they save financial firms a bundle of money.

Using ATMs meant having to rely on the bank's computer rather than on ourselves and a teller. If the unit wasn't working, we were often left stranded—with the checkbook sitting at home. The bank may have all its records, but we were stuck with a plastic card. The people who told us electronic marketing would change our lives are the same people who told us that we would all shop at home and that stores would become extinct. What we really wanted was a way to simplify what we were already doing. We didn't want a substitute for the high-touch of banking, shopping, and meeting people. In short, we wanted a human factor built into high technology before we would accept it.

Smart Cards seem to be the answer. They are the forerunners of changes in our financial habits—changes that are not forced upon us. They offer:

- A way to remain in control, to interact with human tellers and salespeople, and then to update our own records as we do our banking or shopping.
- A simple, easy-to-learn procedure. When we use electronic bank-ing, the operation must be so simple that a customer watching another person using a Smart Card once can successfully repeat the operation without any assistance.
- A continually growing individual data bank that is updated every time we spend, invest, or deposit money. It's like having a personal computer without having to make entries or learn how to operate it.

Smart Cards will, for once, provide a self-help option for the customer. With a low-cost terminal, you'll be able to read the Smart Card on your personal home computer or television set. You'll be able to keep track of your bank balance and purchases, and you can even sort them out for tax purposes. Every time you make a purchase by paying cash, using a credit card, using a debit card, or putting the purchase on your store account, your Smart Card will automatically be updated. You can even pay your bills using the information from your Smart Card shown on the screen.

Consumers Must Read
the Computer-Generated Fine Print

No chapter on electronic banking would be complete without some reference to the way computers have been able to fine tune the interest rates financial firms offer on their savings plans. We are drowning in a sea of splashy advertisements, yet are starved for facts. In defense of the banks and S&Ls, the ads don't lie outright, but with the fine print buried at the bottom of the pages, their claims can be thoroughly misleading. And your mistake can translate into thousands of lost dollars over the life of the account.

Richard Lehman, a Democratic congressman from California— where the interest hype is in full swing—is sponsoring a "Truth in Savings" bill designed to force banks and S&Ls to clean up their act. "The banks are out there competing, not with the actual amount of money they're going to give someone," says he, "but with tricky advertising."[5] In fact, you can often earn a higher net return with a lower interest rate because banks can use computers to calculate interest rates in a lot of different ways. Different banks offering the same rate of interest may pay different amounts; the one promising a higher rate may actually pay less than one with a lower rate.

Even more difficult to evaluate is the way banks calculate the real return you will get from money in a certificate of deposit. When you see CD interest rates advertised, the bank is usually referring to the "annual effective yield." But knowing the annual effective yield doesn't always provide a true picture of how much you'll earn on a CD at maturity. The best way to compare certificates of deposit is by using the "average annual yield." Annual effective yield factors in the bank's or S&L's method of compounding and tells you what you'll earn over a one-year period. The average annual yield, on the other hand, is the annual effective yield averaged out over the number of years of the CD. To find the average annual yield, you'll need to understand how bankers calculate what they'll pay you for the use of your money.

Take the rate you usually see in the newspaper. Say you're offered a five-year CD at 12 percent interest. You want to know how often the interest is compounded. Daily? Monthly? Quarterly? Or is the bank offering simple interest without compounding at all? One bank may offer 12 percent compounded daily, with an effective annual yield of 12.75 percent. Another may offer a splashy ad for a CD paying 12.75 percent simple interest (no compounding), so the annual effective yield will be the same amount: 12.75 percent. Which deal is best for the five-year CD? The average annual yield for the first bank's CD turns out to be a whopping 16 percent; at the other bank it remains at 12.75 percent. Why? Because the first bank pays interest every day on all your money, earning interest on interest, while at the other bank interest earnings start over at zero each year.

You could deposit $1,000 in a five-year CD paying *13 percent* simple interest to maturity, and at the end of five years collect $1,650. But if you invest in a five-year, *10 percent* CD on which interest is compounded daily and subjected to a high-yielding 365/360 formula (where 1/360 of the interest is compounded for 365 days of each year), your $1,000 would be worth $1,660 after five years. In this case you'd actually earn $10 more on a five year CD paying 10 percent than on one paying 13 percent!

But it's with the passbook savings accounts that many banks really hit pay dirt. First the banks take advantage of older Americans' fears about financial deregulation by keeping them locked into low-paying 5.5 percent accounts, then they drain away whatever earnings depositors accumulate by fine-tuning their computers. Here's an example of how banks sweeten their own pot at the expense of the depositors: Suppose you had $100 in your passbook savings account on the first of the month. On the second, you deposit a $1,000 pay check, for a total of $1,100. In the middle of the month, say on the 15th, you deposit $5,000 from the sale of some assets, and you keep the total $6,100 on deposit until the last day of the month, when you withdraw $1,000 for some repairs on your home, ending the month with a balance of $5,100. If your bank pays interest every day (daily compounding) on all your money, you'd earn $16.60 of interest for the month. But if your bank wants to extract all the blood out of the turnip by using the "low-balance" method, *you'd earn interest only on the $100* (your low balance for the month), for a grand total of 45 cents. Other banks, using different methods, can pay you somewhere in between these figures.

Deregulation is also about to kill one of the darlings of the 1970s, the money market account, because mandatory penalties of one month's interest for early withdrawals from insured CDs of 32 days to one year and three-month penalties for insured CDs of over one year will fall victim to the invasion of the free marketplace in financial services. The FDIC (for banks) and the Federal Home Loan Bank Board (for thrifts) lifted the requirement that banks and thrifts impose a penalty for early withdrawals from time deposits because they were no longer needed to ensure compliance with the prohibition against paying interest on demand deposits.

Steadily but cautiously, savers will boost their income by junking the low-paying money market accounts in favor of the one-year CD. Banks and uninsured mutual funds are watching with horrified eyes as more and more deposits slide into high-yield CDs. Say you have an uninsured money market fund paying 7 percent and I have a one-year insured CD from a bank paying 9 percent, yielding a fat 9.5 percent. I have two hefty advantages: I've got federal insurance, and I'm earning about 2.5 percent more interest. I can also have a one-year CD where I can make deposits without changing the term of my CD, much like a money market account. But, you say, "I've got you! What if you need some of the cash before the one-year CD term matures?" I just dip into my one-year CD and pay the early withdrawal penalty of one month's interest on the money withdrawn. Since I'm already earning about 2.5 percent more interest than you are with your money market account, I can easily afford to pay the slight penalty, if necessary, for the quick access to my money. And if I don't need the money, I come out a big winner.

My contention that I can earn more interest income on short-term money in an insured CD than in a money market account is based on the premise that the bank or savings and loan will either not impose early withdrawal penalties as requested by the federal agencies or stick with the minimum one-month interest penalty for early withdrawal. However, numerous banks and S&Ls that have the freedom to set their own policies will continue to slap hefty early withdrawal fees on unwary depositors. My own sense of it is that not many of us will be aware of where the best deal is, believing that bank and savings and loan rules are the same for all. Some hungry banks and savings and loans have been offering a 364- and a 366-day insured CD. For the former, the early withdrawal penalty is one month's interest; for the latter, it's a hefty six month's interest. On some two-year CDs, a 9-month and even a 12-month early withdrawal penalty is not uncommon. But all this pales by comparison when you discover that some banks and S&Ls also charge an early withdrawal "fee" on top of the interest penalty. The fee can be as much as 2 percent of your original investment in the CD. The banks and S&Ls grow testy when you ask about this rip-off. They try to brush it off by offering to loan your own money back to you. To avoid these hefty early withdrawal penalties, you can usually borrow up to 90 percent of your own money back at 3 percent over the market interest rates.

But the arithmetic often obscures that fact that sometimes you can get back less than you deposited in a federally insured CD. Say you open a 366-day CD. After four months, you have an emergency and need the cash. The bank or S&L could deduct the four months' interest you've earned and then deduct a penalty of two more months' interest from your principal. If you add the early withdrawal fee of 2 percent of your investment, your money shrinks again. Bank executives I've talked with tell me that, eventually, some early withdrawal penalties will probably become either the monthly interest penalty or the cost to the financial institution of replacing the funds, whichever is greater. For example, say you have a two-year CD earning 8 percent interest. After one year, interest rates have risen to 10 percent and you'd like to grab the higher rates by opening a new CD. The replacement-of-funds penalty could cost you 2 percent for the year left on your old CD paying 8 percent, since new money is now earning 10 percent. Before you invest your money, find out how the growing trend in early withdrawal penalties and fees will affect you should you need the money before the term of the account.

And when you are shopping for interest rates, remember that financial firms can now fine-tune your money almost any way they want. Insist on daily compounding of interest; the shorter the compounding period, the more interest you'll get. Most bankers won't tell you how high your rate can zoom with daily compounding of interest. If they can get away with a longer compounding period, they will— they want the pain in your pocketbook to go unnoticed. Comparison shop. Ask your bank and other banks, stockbrokers, and S&Ls, "If I give you my money today, how much money will I have in my account when the CD matures, after subtracting any fees and charges?" If your bank can't or won't answer your question, take your business elsewhere.

We Are Moving from a Generation of Savers to a Generation of Money Managers

In 1984, the Federal Reserve Board's *Survey of Consumer Finances— 1983* (described as the most comprehensive analysis of the American family's balance sheet since 1977) showed that with financial deregulation, the rich were getting richer, the middle class were getting a little poorer, and the poor, to no one's surprise, were already poor. What was a surprise was the growing number of people who are turning their backs on a staple of American thrift—the bank and savings and loan savings account. In the past 13 years, according to a survey of consumer businesses, through the end of 1983, there has been "a substantial reduction in the proportion of families with savings accounts, savings bonds, and stocks." The decline in old-fashioned savings accounts could be explained by the surge in IRAs and the growing number of new, safe investments that we'll cover later in the book, but the decline in stock holdings is more puzzling. According to the report, 25 percent of American families held stocks in 1977 and only 19 percent held them in 1983, while 77 percent of American families held savings accounts in 1977 compared to only 62 percent in 1983.

Today, we still have the Main Street Savings & Loan or the small-town bank, but it's perched on the brink of oblivion. Tomorrow it will be the superbank, the one-stop shop for insurance, banking, real estate, stocks and bonds, and financial services. The money bazaars will tout a bewildering number of new and exciting savings and investing plans. For banks and thrifts unwilling to adapt, it will be a time to fail. An American Bankers Association's study released in late 1984 tells us that "after 50 years of heavy regulation, most banks have little experience" in marketing money. The good news, the study tell us, is that we can "expect banks or other financial services providers to be more responsive to our needs." "The public is more aware of things than they used to be," a banker told me, "and we can expect people will either find a bank that can fully address their needs or they will go out and shop for another bank." That is the really good news of deregulation.

3

How Safe Is Our Money?

Why There Is A New Yearning for Protection

Going to the bank nowadays is more "fun" than it used to be. I never know whether the bank will run out of money before I get there. The way bad loans are depleting the banks of cash, I sometimes think that the vice-president in charge of investments would do better by reading the daily racing form.

The current savings and investing system—partly free and unprotected, partly government guaranteed—is a hybrid of deregulation and it's coming unhinged. Americans are pouring billions of dollars into uninsured money market funds because they believe them to be safe. But an even greater number of American savers believe that anything fancier than federally insured savings is too dicey in these turbulent times. For those savers, we've shifted the losses generated by bank and savings and loan deposit guarantees from the backs of depositors to society as a whole. This hybrid system worked well under tight financial controls, but when the system began to break apart under deregulation, most people—and especially those in Congress—failed to see the psychology that has been inspired by federal guarantees of absolute safety. Competing in a new era of cutthroat competition and needing to attract money by paying high interest rates, many financially wounded banks and S&Ls made a crucial psychological shift from "safe" investing to "risky" investing under the protection of federal insurance. As more weight was placed on the guarantees, the banking system began to unravel. This happened because the cost of keeping part of our financial system protected by guarantees further weakens the competitive position of the strong banks and thrifts—the financial firms that pay the hefty insurance premiums.

To Save One Financial Industry, We Gave Special Powers to S&Ls

Under the post-1982 rules granted by the Garn-St. Germain bill, thrifts had the right to offer checking and trust services and to make consumer and commercial loans. The bill also allowed thrifts and commercial banks to pay whatever rate was necessary to attract deposits. Many savings and loans, for example, found they could raise cheap money by selling deposits through brokers. By the unusual accounting rules that apply to the savings and loan business, S&Ls can use deposits to leverage their stockholders' cash investment 200 or 300 times. It is unique to S&Ls and they were given this power because they were presumed to be safe, and the higher leverage would help them help Americans buy homes. What the new rules did, however, was give many S&Ls a way to raise relatively cheap money (that is, Other People's Money, or OPM) under federal guarantees, and move away from the home mortgage market into the higher risk commercial real estate and securities market.

One of the moneyshocks of the 1980s is that the capital markets are on the verge of replacing savings and loans as the primary source of mortgage funds. "We are well into the era of the securitization of mortgages," said a leader in the mortgage banking industry, "and the savings and loans and banks are the least equipped to be in the loan-origination business." With deregulation, many S&Ls can no longer afford to be primary housing lenders because of the growth of mortgage sales in the secondary market. Lenders no longer let their mortgages sit on the shelf. Instead, they repackage groups of them and sell them in the secondary market as real-estate-backed securities. These mortgage-based securities not only attract money from the national securities market, but from the world-wide capital markets as well.

None of this comes as a surprise to banks and S&Ls; they are too busy buying Other People's Money to make traditional long-term mortgage loans. But in buying OPM in a deregulated environment, they came up with what at first appeared to be an unlikely scenario: Let someone else collect the funds. Accordingly, successful S&L managers, who understood capital markets and knew how real estate mortgages were sold, now understood how savings could be bought. By pushing transactions that generated fees rather than interest income, and by letting stockbrokers raise their federally insured money for them, they no longer needed expensive money palaces to attract cash. At about $1.50 on $100, raising the interest rate on brokered deposits turned out to be far cheaper than renting a marble money palace, filling it with employees, and offering free toasters and piggy banks.

Take the case of Homestead Financial Corporation of Burlingame, California, which in 1984 grew 120.6 percent in revenue—to $295 million—without a single acquisition. It jumped from number 72 to number 56 on the list of diversified financial companies by boosting its assets by 114.7 percent to a whopping $3 billion. Homestead's meteoric growth is based on the California housing market and the surging demand, in a high-interest environment, for adjustable-rate mortgages. To grab a share of this market, Homestead Savings needed cash. Rather than beat the local bushes for new savers, it collected $1.4 billion in new deposits from New York brokerage houses. Called "brokered deposits," these are insured CDs that brokers place for their customers in commercial banks and thrifts. By offering a higher rate of interest— sometimes as much as 1 to 1.5 percent higher on the same insured CD than the banks and S&Ls themselves—brokers find this a safe way to park their clients' money. An S&L executive summed it up best when he said, "It's cheaper and faster to buy the deposits than to wait for them to trickle in our front door." One big S&L, Butterfield Savings in Santa Ana, California, did away with its branches and simply went into what it calls 800-banking.

With all the money from non-traditional sources flowing in, some S&Ls began to go for the quick profit. They bought restaurants, purchased junk bonds (older bonds sold at a discount to reflect the current interest rate), and bought stock in leveraged buyouts. Many of the new "diversified S&Ls" are using profits from these ventures to subsidize their mortgage business. Those bankers say that they finance mortgages only because if they were to stop altogether, a government regulator might say they aren't really S&Ls and take away their charters.

But buying money in huge amounts can lead to trouble. In 1985, regulators took over Beverly Hills Savings & Loan in the Los Angeles area, after the thrift had lost $100 million in the previous year by investing its brokered deposits in bad real estate and other risky loans. Representative Ron Wyden (D–Ore.) said that the Federal Home Loan Bank Board was guilty of a "pervasive level of lethargy and inertia." The federal regulators "stood by doing nothing." Bank Board chairman Edwin J. Gray defended the actions of his agency, which regulates federally insured S&Ls. He testified that the problems at Beverly Hills Savings weren't occurring in a vacuum. The Bank Board, he told a House subcommittee, was faced with numerous problems at other thrifts. Several failed S&Ls were indeed found to have as much as 65 percent of their total deposits in brokered funds. The Federal Home Loan Bank Board has now moved to keep thrifts from gorging themselves on brokered money by linking the amount of money they can buy to their net worth.[1]

What we have today, then, is a special savings and loan industry, with special subsidies and powers, that in many cases is no longer clearly distinguishable from other financial institutions. We're in the midst of a large-scale shift from local deposits to national deposits. With the major capital markets flush with cash, S&Ls, and, of course, banks, can raise money more efficiently through a Merrill Lynch than through their own branch offices.

We are, in fact, in the process of reinventing the savings and loan. High interest rates and the diminishing spread between the interest banks earn on home mortgages and what they pay for the money have made the one-business money shops obsolete. The moneyshock is that, unless the nation's savings and loans expand their financial services and compete on a low-cost basis, they will die by the end of this decade.

Reversing the Trend Toward Federal Guarantees

As I speak around the country to audiences concerned about their money, people tell me they expect that all their savings and investments should somehow be protected by federal insurance.

For most of our history, the United States had a financial system in which businesses flourished or failed without government props. But they did so in a stable economy. From 1790 until the 1930s, long-term interest rates oscillated between 3 and 6 percent. Based on the expectation that such a situation would continue, our financial institutions were established and they prospered. Then, after the Second World War, during which most of us were denied the good things of life, Americans threw off their fear of debt and plunged in on a grand scale.

Inevitably the mounting debt led to inflation. Interest rates were pushed to levels our financial institutions were unprepared to deal with. Banks and thrifts, most vulnerable to escalating interest rates, were stuck with federal ceilings on interest they could pay depositors. For a while this was a blessing. They could loan out money at very low rates because it was impossible for them to pay high rates. But it couldn't last. In the long run they watched deposits hemorrhage out of their system until they were on a financial critical list. Congress's answer was deregulation. Banks and thrifts were to face up to free-market competition by paying any interest rate they wanted. The problem was, they could go broke chasing after the consumer's savings—and many of them have.

To a large extent, the problems of the banks and thrifts are mirrored by the life insurance industry. Life insurance was wounded when deregulation freed the amount of interest banks could pay, and it will probably walk with a permanent limp. For a century, whole life policies were built around guarantees. The public never noticed how little they got for their money because it was the only guaranteed game in town. But as deregulation allowed interest rates to soar, a wiser public began to turn the tables on the life insurance companies. Americans borrowed money from policies that allowed cash value loans and that had guaranteed 4 and 5 percent simple-interest loan rates built into them. Those people then reinvested the cash on the outside at two or three times the policy loan rate. As competition heated up, the need to guarantee high-cash-value interest rates on new policies, as well as to offset the looting of the old cash values by savvy policyholders, forced the insurance companies to make risky investments.

It became even harder to sell life insurance when companies starting pushing new products. "Universal life," for instance, resembled a term life policy tied to a money market fund. Then insurers found that they could sell life insurance more economically by using stockbrokers and mutual fund salespeople than by using the old agency system. To meet the competition, life insurance rates have fallen—for non-smokers by as much as 75 percent over rates of just five years ago. The high cost of servicing the new policies (computers now update records on a daily basis, not an annual one as before) and profit margins made lower by the hot competition, mean that life insurers face tough going. It will be difficult for small- to medium-size companies to survive the deregulation that lies ahead. With the last few years several life insurance companies have gone bust, something that was unthinkable just a decade ago.

If we are to have financial deregulation, maybe it's time to go back to our historic system in which all financial firms had the freedom to fail, where savers and investors alike had to use their own judgment about whom to trust. We could start by shifting the financial burden of federal guarantees to those banks and S&Ls that are most likely to fail and use the insurance. Under the current system of federal deposit insurance, every bank or S&L pays the same premium—a flat one-twelfth of 1 percent of their deposits for $100,000 per account of federal protection. But William Isaac, former chairman of the Federal Deposit Insurance Corporation, wanted to stop bankers from playing fast and loose with federally insured money. He'd have based the insurance premiums banks pay on the risk they run of going broke. A Washington attorney agreed with Isaac, noting, "What started out as insurance to protect the small depositor has grown into a system where no one is at risk except the federal insurance fund."

But not everyone agrees that by increasing insurance premiums we can rein in the risk-takers. "It's a rotten idea to think that a $2 million hike in deposit insurance premiums will make any difference in the way banks act," a bank executive told me. "A $2 million fine is like a $2 parking ticket to a big bank. You need to change the way banks act, not how much insurance you provide, if you want to get at the real problem." While Isaac favored financial deregulation that's similar to airline and telephone deregulation, he realized that the transition will create a new set of problems. He believed that the present federal deposit insurance system, designed for tight controls, will not be able to cope with the unravelling of the old banking system. "Change in the deposit insurance system," he said, "is central to the whole issue of deregulation."[2]

One idea is to return to the original form of federal deposit insurance and limit coverage to the first $10,000 of deposits and to only 75 percent of the funds over that limit. Another idea is to provide a basic amount of federal deposit insurance and have investors pay for any protection they want over that amount. To be sure, if recent trends continue, something will have to be done.

Take the case of the ten largest American banks. Nearly half of their deposits are overseas, where, according to the FDIC, the banks don't pay federal deposit insurance premiums. But those funds are protected. The system of protecting our savings is already unfair and growing more so. In 1984, Bank of America paid the FDIC $40 million; Citibank, with more deposits, paid $18.5 million. Citibank has more deposits overseas. Yet when a crisis develops in one of the nation's major banks—like the one that occurred at Continental Illinois National Bank, the nation's eighth-largest bank—the FDIC is forced to guarantee all of the bank's deposits—domestic and foreign—to prevent a run on the bank and a spreading financial calamity.

Continental bet heavily on loans to energy firms and other domestic borrowers in its quest to become the nation's biggest commercial lender. But much of its billion-dollar loan portfolio, including a big chunk of loans from the Penn Square Bank of Oklahoma City, went sour. By May 1984, the bank that wanted to become the biggest was dying right in front of the startled eyes of federal regulators.

The scramble to avert the collapse of Chicago's largest bank also led to the frightening knowledge that the collapse of a leading money center bank closely tied to the national and international money markets could damage the entire banking system. "The bank would have failed," said William Isaac, "if the run had continued." To bolster Continental's net worth and keep it financially solvent, the Federal Reserve loaned the bank more than $4 billion. The FDIC, together with a number of private banks, pumped in another $2 billion of cash. As the former U.S. Comptroller of the Currency, C. Todd Conover, told me, "It's now the safest bank in the country. The federal government owns most of it."

But in the FDIC's rush to put a safety net under Continental, the corporation was forced to provide deposit insurance to all customers, regardless of the amount on deposit with the bank. Why? Because the regulators knew that if the big depositors—both foreign and domestic—yanked out their deposits, the bank could collapse overnight. Here's a transcript of a conversation with a federal regulator of deposit insurance, which took place on one of my recent radio programs:

"Let me see if I understand you," I said. "The banks aren't paying premiums on as much as half of their deposits parked overseas, is that correct?"

"Yes," was the response.

"And, if one of the major American banks threatens to go bust, federal regulators will rush in and give every depositor full federal insurance protection no matter how much each depositor has in each account in the bank. That's correct, isn't it?" I asked.

"Yes."

"So what you are really telling me is that the government is not collecting premiums on half of the deposits it's really insuring."

"That's right," the beleaguered federal official said, "but hopefully the guy in the failed small-town bank where deposit insurance is limited to just $100,000 per account won't find out about it."

Representative Fernand St. Germain (D–R.I.) charged that federal regulators were bailing out the big banks, and indeed they were.[3] In the first six months of 1984, almost 30 federally insured banks—all of them small institutions—were allowed to fail. But why are some depositors protected in full while others are protected for only $100,000? It's not a question of equity, it's a question, pure and simple, of survival of the nation's banking system. You can be sure, however, that if the unthinkable—a major bank failure—is about to happen again, the jitters will send the regulators out to protect all the deposits, foreign and domestic, regardless of amount, while small American depositors with their cash in small banks in similar circumstances will have to take the loss over the limit of federal insurance. The federal deposit insurance system is now perceived as an insurance system for the big, but not for the small.

If we really believe in financial deregulation and fair competition, we should make part of the federal deposit insurance program optional, based on individual responsibility. We already have such a dual system with municipal bonds, where private insurance is available for an additional premium. In this new era of deregulation, we could take the high risk along with the yields on our savings and investments or we could buy insurance and cut our yields. Granted it's a new idea, but it's in the best American tradition: We make our own choices.

Financial Deregulation Means We Must Understand How Banks Work

To start a bank, you have to raise capital. This is the stockholders' equity, the money people invest in the bank to make a profit. Then, once the bank is in business, its first job is to attract depositors who, in a real sense, loan their money to the bank in return for interest income. But a vault crammed with money on which the bank has to pay interest must be loaned out to businesses and individuals at a higher rate of interest. The difference between what the bank pays depositors to get their money and what the bank earns on its loan portfolios is known as the spread. From the spread comes the money to pay rent, salaries, and taxes; what's left over is the profit for the stockholders. Eager for greater profits, bankers were soon asking how much money they could loan out and still stay solvent. The answer: They just had to meet the net capital requirements (equity-to-assets ratio) established by the federal regulators. The best way to gauge the health of a bank or thrift is by its net worth, which is the amount of capital (the money the stockholders paid in plus profits minus losses) it has on hand for every dollar of loans and investments on its books. The lower the percentage of its net worth against its loans, the riskier the bank and the less likely that it will be able to survive rough times.

In the 1970s, banks and thrifts were heavily protected by regulations, including a cap on the interest they could pay for deposits, and thus they controlled their costs. Regulators made a fuss if any financial firm's net worth dropped below 5 percent (every $100 of loans and investments would be offset by $5 in bank equity and $95 in depositors' money). Today, the regulators would like to see a mere 3 percent of net worth. Many savings and loans lost money by the bucketful during the early 1980s, so that the FSLIC was forced to redefine the word "insolvency." With over 800 federally insured S&Ls shut down in the past five years, an S&L can now be considered insolvent when its net worth drops to zero.

On March 31, 1984, the S&Ls insured by the FSLIC reported $34 billion of net worth. When the regulators subtracted deferred losses and other bookkeeping gimmicks designed to puff up their balance sheets, the industry's capital was cut to about $27 billion. Now, if you exclude the hefty goodwill (the loyalty of customers and the established name of the institution, which won't pay off a single depositor when push comes to shove) of about $20 billion, what's left for the nation's savings and loans is a tangible net worth of about $4.5 billion—about .5 percent of S&Ls' liabilities at the beginning of April 1984. Most of this capital is concentrated among relatively few large institutions, and some of these same large S&Ls have a negative net worth.

In fact, the moneyshock today is that some savings and loans are effectively bankrupt—but are still allowed to stay open. Their number has increased fivefold since 1981, to more than 400, and another 400 are teetering toward disaster with assets that barely exceed their liabilities. In 1985, it was disclosed that one out of 16 banks is on the FDIC's "problem" list—a staggering 2,268 federally insured banks. The Associated Press, in a story for June 1, 1985, said, "Federal and state bank authorities shut down six banks in three states, all because of shaky loan portfolios that threatened the institutions' survivability and their customers' deposits. All the banks were insured by the FDIC and depositors were protected up to $100,000 per account."

These were some of the worst cases. Banks and thrifts are allowed to stay open because federal authorities have to avert any abrupt shakeout that could deplete the insurance fund and send nervous depositors flocking to smaller institutions to yank out their money. The General Accounting Office has warned investors and savers that government-released financial statements (from the FDIC and the FSLIC) for financial institutions can be misleading (and presumably harmful to your financial health) because they do not follow generally accepted accounting procedures. A former chairman of the Federal Home Loan Bank Board says the current accounting system for S&Ls deals "in shadows. It has no relation to their real financial health." As it has done with cigarettes, the government has agreed to put a warning on future reports, to tell the public, in effect, that the regulators know these reports of the financial health of the nation's banks and S&Ls are misleading.

The FDIC's and FSLIC's cost for failures for 1983 ran about $1.7 billion, well within the insurance funds' reserves. But with a sinking banking system in a world of mushrooming non-banks, regulators have few options. They can't bail out the banks and thrifts en masse; the $25 billion in the nation's deposit fund won't begin to cover the tab. Yet regulators are required to protect a banking system that is unable to die without taking the depositors for a ride, so they go on sanctioning accounting gimmicks that make weak balance sheets look almost healthy and keep the public in the dark. Banks thrive on secrecy, and the regulatory agencies help by hiding their misdeeds, on the theory that anything is better than a loss of confidence in the banks.[4]

Regulators have nightmares about executives of a bank or thrift who try to save their institutions in the face of rising debt by betting a hefty chunk of the firm's assets on a big win with a risky investment. As we have seen in the last few years, this high-stake gamble can easily bring down the whole house of cards. Former FSLIC chief David W. Glenn believes that "a lot of people are going to be encouraged to take desperate gambles. If they lose, the government will have to pick up the tab. And if they win, they get to keep their jobs and their stock options."[5]

In a Chaotic Period, We Have Nothing Left but Blind Faith

In the end, it's not what's inside the bank, or how fat or slender the S&L's balance sheet may look, it's the confidence of the depositors and investors that will be decisive. As long as the safety net of federal deposit insurance is working, as long as the scent of danger does not fill the nostrils of scared depositors, banks need very little money—their own or their depositors'—to handle day-to-day banking business. As long as there is no run on the bank, regulators can stall closing a shaky bank or thrift for a long time, keeping the institution alive with funny-money accounting and dubious bookkeeping items, such as counting substantial assets in the form of good will.

But what if there were no regulators, no federal deposit insurance, no accounting gimmicks to keep the money stores alive? This situation exists today. In this strange financial world there's another set of mostly uninsured, unregulated, yet apparently successful institutions available that look and sound just like banks. These are the thrift and loans. Most of them don't come under federal regulations and the states haven't seemed particularly eagle-eyed either. They promise depositors "thrift certificates" or "investment certificates" with sky-high interest rates and "state insured" safety. But some promises are too good to be true. You might think savers would question interest rates running as much as 2 percentage points higher for a state-insured money market account than for a federally insured money market account. Not so. A lot of savers believe that anything that looks like a bank must be a bank, and anything that looks like an S&L must be an S&L. After all aren't all banks and thrifts insured?

But Blind Faith Can Mislead

The problem is that our assumptions are rooted in the past, when government guarantees meant what they said, and consequently our decision-making has not caught up with the new reality. The larger story is only now becoming clear. The safety net that we thought protected banking is full of holes. We are now beginning to see where the holes are and, for the first time since the Great Depression, we are asking the question: Can you bank on your banker?

The moneyshock of deposit insurance began with Nebraska's largest industrial loan and investment company, Commonwealth Savings. In early 1985, "60 Minutes" told the tragic tale of depositors who thought they were insured for $30,000 each. If Commonwealth was a bank, it was supposed to be insured. After all, depositors could open an IRA, open checking and savings accounts and take out a loan. But when Commonwealth's insurance fund went broke in November 1983, almost 7,000 depositors, with $58 million in deposits, ended up empty-handed.

Nebraska's Depository Institution Guaranty Corp., or NDIGC, was typical of many state deposit insurance funds. When Commonwealth Savings failed, its $58 million of deposits were "protected" by a scant $2 million in the state deposit insurance kitty. Unknown to depositors, they were actually taking an equity position (becoming stockholders) in Commonwealth, not making deposits. As stockholders, if they are ever going to recover their money, they'll have to wait until all the other creditors are paid off. Worse yet, three states—Kentucky, Tennessee, and Oklahoma—allowed so-called non-banks to fail *without any state insurance at all*. Only in Colorado has the state insurance fund paid account holders in full up front. Hawaii is the only state that has taken action to control so-called non-bank state thrifts. Two small industrial loan companies failed there in 1983 with a total of $40 million in so-called state-insured deposits (so far only $14 million has been repaid). Hawaii now requires that all deposit-taking industrial non-banks have federal insurance.

The most vivid example of what can happen when people become confused and believe what a state government tells them occurred in California in April of 1984. Western Community Money Center (a non-bank) failed with $93 million in "state-insured" accounts. Its 12,000 depositors believed they were covered by a state deposit insurance fund up to $50,000 per account. The deposit insurance fund, The Thrift Guaranty Corporation of California, created by the state legislature, turned out to be a private insurer financed by the thrift and loan industry itself. The state of California, which set up the "state insurance fund" and led the public to believe that state deposit insurance was backed by the state government, did not actively oversee the insurance fund. It looked the other way when the thrifts boosted the individual deposit insurance coverage from $20,000 to $50,000 in 1982, without raising assessments to the insurance pool. Not only did the state allow its citizens to believe that somehow an insurance fund of only $14 million could continue to protect privately insured thrifts with combined deposits of $1.5 billion, but it failed to disclose that state law only allowed for the insurance fund to make up the deficiency after liquidation of assets, and that it was not allowed by law to quickly pay off the "insured" account.

The FDIC and FSLIC are designed to either merge a failed institution with another bank or S&L so the customer can continue to bank without interruption, or to pay out the insured amount of the account at once and then recover its funds as best it can. California's Thrift Guaranty—and many other state insurance funds—only make up the deficiency and are not allowed by law to promptly pay off the insured account. In fact, to the surprise of depositors, Thrift Guarantee is prevented from making payments from the insurance fund until all assets of the thrift have been liquidated—and that, the state says, could take up to five years.

The New Source of Safety Is Not Money in a Bank—It's Information

You might ask, how did Western Community Money Center go from $5 million to $120 million in assets in just two years? As financial deregulation opened up the competitive war for savings, Western offered one to two points more interest on savings than its federally insured competitors. For many people, it looked like a bank, it acted like a bank, and it was a good deal for weary savers. One depositor told me, "I opened my IRA, did my business checking and savings, and borrowed money for my house. How the hell was I supposed to know that state insurance wasn't worth a damn?" Jack Carlson, assistant commissioner of California's Department of Corporations—the state agency that took over the failed thrift—summed up the question of deposit insurance this way: "They (Western Community Money Center) said, 'It's protected by Thrift Guaranty Fund.' When an investor would ask, 'What's Thrift Guaranty?' the company would say, 'That's just like FDIC.' "[6]

Many depositors faced financial ruin. They claimed that the state permitted the Western Community Money Center to operate like a wolf in sheep's clothing: It was an uninsured thrift masquerading as a bank. Some depositors even called the state's Department of Corporations before placing their money with the Money Center and they received "an upbeat report" on the thrift—even after state regulators knew the thrift was in deep financial trouble. Worse yet, according to the depositors' group, the state allowed Western Community Money Center to open an office outside the gates of one of the state's bigger retirement communities, a place full of people who would move their insured money just to get a half-point more interest.

On my radio and television programs, state legislators acknowledged that they felt it was the responsibility of the state government to help the savers who relied on so-called state insurance. Yet it was October of 1984, six months after the collapse of the Western Community Money Center, before state officials acknowledged for the first time that the state was partly responsible for the failure of the state-insured thrift and loan. "The state lent its name, in effect" to guarantee deposits, said the Department of Corporations' chief. By November, depositors had received only $22 million of the $98 million of "insured" deposits. The good news, at least for these savers, is that a bailout bill was signed into law in July 1985, allowing the state of California to pay depositors the balance of their accounts up to $50,000.

California wasn't alone. In 1985 came the first bank holiday since the Depression. Home State Savings in Cincinnati found depositors lined up at its front door as rumors spread that it was in trouble from the collapse of ESM Government Securities, Inc., of Ft. Lauderdale, Florida. Home State Savings, like a score of other banks, thrifts, and municipalities, was caught with big losses when the Securities and Exchange Commission closed down ESM on March 4, 1985. Home State's loss of at least $145 million forced the thrift to close five days later and quickly wiped out the state insurance fund that backed deposits at 71 other state-regulated thrifts. Ohio Governor Richard F. Celeste, shocked and reeling, was forced to close down all the state's privately insured thrifts until he could get legislation to sort out the mess. By March 27, only 22 of the 72 institutions reopened for full business after the state found them sound enough to qualify for federal insurance.

Then in May of 1985, long lines of anxious depositors once again camped outside state-insured thrifts, this time in Maryland. The state's second biggest S&L, Old Court Savings and Loan, was felled by a run on deposits. What may make Old Court's failure different from the rest is that it advertised heavily in newspapers across America, offering money market accounts and CDs guaranteed by imposing-looking state insurance (Maryland Savings-Share Insurance Corp.), and paying hefty interest, often 2 percent or more above that of local, federally insured banks and S&Ls. Maryland's Fairfax Savings Association, which was also caught in the May panic, had previously advertised its state-insured Preferred Money Fund in newspapers and by direct mail across the country. When federally insured banks and S&Ls were paying 12 percent interest, Fairfax ran bold headlines telling you how you could earn 15.25 percent in a money market account. Maryland residents began to panic.

With 100 of the state's privately insured S&Ls facing a run on deposits, governor Harry Hughes was forced to limit withdrawals to $1,000 a month per account. Hughes, in a plea to the state General Assembly for new laws to allow him to call a bank holiday, said it was the state's moral obligation to insure all accounts up to $100,000, even if there were state-insured institutions that could not qualify for federal insurance and thus might be forced out of business.

The collapse of California's, Ohio's, and now Maryland's private deposit insurance funds sounded a death knell for nonfederal insurance. Governor Hughes turned his back on years of protecting deposits by state insurance, and ordered the state-insured institutions to seek protection from the FSLIC as a condition for staying in business.

Feeling the new wind of change, privately insured institutions in North Carolina, in a move to keep their depositors from lining up to yank out their deposits, began to seek shelter under the federal insurance umbrella.

As I write this book, hundreds of financial institutions escape federal regulation because they fall through the regulatory cracks by insuring their deposits with a private fund rather than a federal agency. Many will remain outside the protection of federal deposit insurance because they want to continue to escape strict federal regulations that would prevent them from making the high-profit deals that they feel are necessary to attract depositors from the more established banks and thrifts.

Most people don't understand the difference between a federally insured bank and a privately insured thrift and loan. Unfortunately, the old, the poor, and the trusting, who should benefit the most from federal and state regulations, are the ones who are the most oblivious to the distinctions. A bank president gave me the banker's point of view: "It's obvious thrifts and loans are not banks, and their deposits are not protected the way a bank's deposits are. The vast majority of people that put their money in a thrift and loan are looking for a higher interest rate. Sure, some little old ladies were hurt by the failure of these privately insured thrifts, but a lot of depositors were middle-income executives who know darn well what a thrift certificate is. . . . It's an investment, not a deposit. We all have a lot of alternatives in where to place our money. There is a ratio between risk and reward, and privately insured thrifts offer a higher and better rate of return for taking a greater degree of risk."

What to Look for in Picking a Bank

Even as you read this book, scores of privately insured or uninsured financial institutions will continue to leave frightened depositors or investors empty-handed. Here are some tips to help you keep your money safe and productive:

• *Federal insurance.* All but about 1,200 of the nation's almost 19,000 banks and savings and loans carry federal insurance. Federal insurance does not mean that your bank or S&L won't go under. It does mean that if the institution fails, you will get your money back without major delays.

• *Savings yields.* If a bank or thrift offers you considerably higher yields on your savings than its competitors, find out why. Compare terms, minimum deposits, and insurance coverage before you grab the higher yield. The easiest way today for financial institutions to offer high yields is to lend large amounts of money on unusually risky ventures.

• *Fees.* Be sure to check the charges and rules for keeping your money in the bank or S&L. Some banks attract you with the promise of low fees, but when your balance drops below a monthly minimum the fees they charge can be steep and you can actually lose interest.

• *Holds.* Find out how long the bank or S&L will hold your deposits before you can draw against them. The t' e can range from 3 to 13 business days, depending on where the check is drawn. Some banks, for better customers, will credit money the next day.

• *Interest compounding.* As I've already said, this is one of the biggest items to consider in building up your savings or investments. Simply stated, compound interest is "interest on interest." Interest earned after a given period is added to the principal amount and included in the next period's interest calculation.

For example: Say you invest $10,000 at an annual interest of 8 percent. After a year, you'll have $10,800 (1.08 × $10,000). After the second year, your investment is worth $11,664 (1.08 × $10,800). At the end of five years, $14,693. But the value of your investment jumps when interest is compounded more frequently. For instance, if interest is compounded quarterly, the $10,000 investment grows to $14,855 at the end of five years. With monthly compounding, the total is $14,898; with weekly compounding, $14,914. With daily compounding, the total is almost $15,000. With simple interest, on the other hand, your original investment of $10,000 earns interest each year of $800. At the end of five years you'd have a total of only $14,000. Because of the effects of compounding interest, a bank or savings and loan with a higher nominal interest rate but a lower effective annual yield can appear to offer more yet deliver less. It simply compounds less frequently. Before you open a savings account, ask the bank how much your money—the original deposit and earned interest, less any charges and fees—will amount to at the end of the savings period. It's an easy way to compare, and you'll be amazed at the difference among several banks even when they seem to offer the same deal for your money.

The Future: Confronting the Challenge of Saving and Investing

Financial regulations and the old system of banking are crumbling all across America, but our society is not falling apart. Far from it. More and more, people are discovering that they can save and invest with or without federal deposit insurance, and the smart money is going where the profits are. Financial deregulation is building our financial institutions anew, offering us more opportunities, and higher returns compared to inflation, than at any time in our nation's history. The decentralization of money has transformed our ability to save and invest, the way we do business, even our lifestyles.

We have also become a nation of shrinking services. It's become something of a ritual in recent years to watch gas stations disappear, their numbers cut to a few super stations in each town. Union 76 runs television commercials with good old Murph as its spokesman. He represents real America, a Boy Scout troop leader who's trustworthy, helpful, loyal. No matter how rough the car engine sounds, you always have the feeling that good old Murph can figure out the problem in no time. But let's face it, there aren't very many Murphs out there anymore. Nationwide, service stations have plunged to 130,000 from almost 200,000 in 1974 when Murph started telling us how full-service gas stations should be run. Our factories continue to shrink. Our farms have followed the gas stations, with less than 3 percent of our population growing food. And now our banks and savings and loans are disappearing. The hard truth is, society no longer needs all the factories, gas stations, farms, and banks. Technology and the free market have collapsed our global economy to a point where the few can do more than the many, and they can do it better.

The moneyshock is that banks and S&Ls are headed the way of gas stations. The savings and loan system is failing and the commercial banks as a whole are stuffed with questionable loans, both domestic and foreign. Deregulation may appear chaotic, but it really is a cleansing tonic, with its own rhythm and sense. We are not facing another 1930s-type banking panic. The Treasury still stands behind the banking system. What we do have is an outdated banking system that finds itself unable to cope in a world where money is no longer money but simply a blip on a computer screen.

Make no mistake, the U.S. banking system is under a severe strain. Bold new steps will be needed to merge banks and thrifts into the mainstream of the financial supermarkets of the future. Last-minute rescue operations or patched-together bailouts that regulatory agencies have used in the past to keep the system from unravelling will no longer be enough. Congress, which has sat on its hands, preferring to let the marketplace solve the problems, must now meet its responsibilities with an overall plan that will allow a streamlined financial industry of fewer but stronger players to emerge. If we are to save our banks, we have to allow them to enter the money game full force, compete on a level field, and generate the profits they need to build new security into the financial system. Most importantly, banks and thrifts must be allowed to meet the new competition.

We need a system of interstate banking in which strong banks and thrifts can merge and acquire the weak ones, so that, after the shakeout, a banking system will be built that is able to meet the challenges of the future. And the system must be able to do this without regulatory constraints (other than antitrust laws). We can no longer hold our banking system captive to the laws of the 1930s, when the technology and deregulation of the 1980s are breaking down barriers and allowing disparate financial firms to invade each other's turf.

The business of buying-and-selling money has become an irresistible attraction for some of America's largest corporations. In Hawaii, General Electric Credit Corporation (GECC) has opened branch "banks" all over the islands, offering hefty rates for money market passbook accounts, CDs, and jumbo passbook accounts. The headline of their newspaper ad sums up the new challenge best: "You can get excellent interest rates from GECC Financial while your money is fully insured to $100,000 by the Federal Deposit Insurance Corporation. *That's the same protection banks offer.*" For the individual, GECC offers *Super Credit*, a personal line of credit as high as $250,000.

Ford Motor Company, in the largest purchase ever of an S&L, bought San Francisco–based First Nationwide Savings. Overnight, Ford has a national financial network. First Nationwide has 180 branches scattered across New York, Florida, California, and Hawaii, a consumer thrift and loan with 144 branches in seven southeastern states, and a nationwide savings and loan franchising operation, First Nationwide Network. More impressive is the fact that First Nationwide Savings has made a deal with K mart to open in-store financial centers in southern California. With Ford's muscle in the financial marketplace, you'll be able to get a mortgage, buy Ford Motor Company insurance products, get a car loan, and do all of your banking with the nation's second largest car maker.

Moving from the Myth of a Rock-Solid Bank to a Celebration of Financial Diversity

We've come a long way from the way Americans handled their money in the past. The most formidable challenge ahead is to realize that, given acceptable levels of safety and risk, it doesn't matter where you borrow or save your money. Banking that is exclusively in the hands of banks and thrifts no longer exists. Today's confusion has not been caused entirely by deregulation (which has also affected the airline, trucking, and telephone industries), but also by the way our banking system operates, as if deregulation did not exist. Savers also contribute to the problem by expecting the highest possible interest rates with perfect safety of their principal; banks and S&Ls aren't supposed to fail. That's impossible. With deregulation, some firms will die, others will prosper. Before airline deregulation, no major airline had gone broke. Now airlines drop out of the sky on a regular basis. But banks and S&Ls are not airlines. Of all the industries affected by deregulation, these, we believe, must not be allowed to fail. They are the economic underpinning of our financial system and they are often as closely related to each other as the links in a chain-link fence. We found that out with Continental Illinois National Bank, whose failure could have damaged the entire banking system and raised new fears about a potential national banking crisis.

Under the current system of keeping the canaries flying, we have seen three of the nation's 25 largest banks—Crocker, Continental Illinois, and Seattle-First National—get federal bailouts. And the biggest S&L in the country, Financial Corporation of America (American Savings), was put on a federal financial heart-lung machine to survive.

So, what's to be done? We could strap on the regulatory straitjacket again, but that's like turning back the clock. Savers would not allow it. After all, why should they go back to subsidizing the borrowers again? The other choice is to give the banks and S&Ls the freedom they want, yet make them, and all the other financial institutions, assume some responsibility for the safety of their money. We could boost their capital requirements, in stages, up to, say, 10 percent of assets (rather than maintaining it near zero percent, as it is now). We could make sure that if a bank fails, the stockholders are the first to lose their investment, not the depositors. And we could ask the financial institutions or their depositors, the ones who benefit from deposit insurance, to pay the hefty rise in premiums that are needed to pay the bills.

The moneyshock of all of this: No matter what is done, by the end of this decade, more than half of today's banks and S&Ls will no longer be open for business. They will be victims of a surging world of financial superbanks and giant money centers. The natural cure for one-sided deregulation will turn out to be complete deregulation.

4

From Main Street to Nationwide Banking

How to Invest in Today's Deregulated World

Let's face it. The whole world of money is changing. If you're like me, you are amazed when you look back and compare the banks, brokers, mutual funds, and insurance companies of 1976 with those of 1986. And when it comes to 1966 . . . why it's like comparing night with day. In the year it took me to write this book, the way we saved and invested our money changed faster than it had in the previous decade! However, by understanding the larger patterns, the way other industries are changing, we can begin to make sense of the individual events occurring in the financial industry.

Putting It in Perspective

When I speak publicly about financial deregulation, I frequently trace the changes taking place throughout our society and draw parallels with the way we save and invest our money. The automobile industry is a good example. Like banks, auto dealers have until now been protected by a form of regulated monopoly controlled by the giant auto companies. Today, however, car buyers are caught in the middle of a scrap between a rash of new discount dealers on one side and GM or Ford and their conventional dealers on the other. Buyers are intrigued when a Chevrolet discount dealer offers to sell a 1986 Chevy Blazer for $15,000, when full-service Chevrolet dealers all over town quote prices between $18,000 and $19,000. Full-service dealers, like many bankers, become livid when customers flock to discounters who advertise a "$49-over-invoice" price. Discount dealers can offer such bargains because they order cars only as they sell them. Computers, rather than people, run their operation, and that holds down financing costs and prices. Conventional dealers, with substantial investments in product inventory, showroom space, and a large sales staff, must now operate in a deregulated world. It's difficult to persuade potential buyers to pay the price for all that overhead.

Franchise discount car dealers, like money centers and non-banks, are creatures of the change deregulation has brought about. Throwing off the old way of doing business, they have become the K marts of the station-wagon set. This has led to the same cries of alarm sounded during the current battle to control the money centers: If discount auto dealers remain unchecked, they'll eventually squeeze out many full-service, non-discount retailers—to the dismay of the manufacturer and those customers who want to pay the high prices to get the full service a conventional dealer provides.

"In the short run," an antitrust lawyer says, "it looks like discount car dealers are good for consumers because they get a low-ball price. But in the long run, both the national economy and the consumer may be better off by having more competitors survive. It's not an easy balance to strike."

I am not denying that in the normal course of business, this makes sense, but with the trends already under way in America, turning back the clock to save smokestack-like businesses is an idea whose time has gone. Changes in the way we buy cars, like changes in the way we save money, will occur with increasing speed. The information society is taking over the industrial society.

Take A Look At What's Happening *Right Now*

We are in the midst of moving away from traditional passbook savings accounts in banks and S&Ls in favor of more sophisticated accounts offered by the money centers of the 1980s. Believing that "it's always worked before" will get you nowhere in the new money game. Accordingly, successful savers and investors must understand the forces that are shaping the new marketplace—and use them to their best advantage.

One of the first signs of the shift from financial regulation to deregulation, and from a mechanical to an electronic society, is the absence of a reliable benchmark to measure our progress. Changes occur so rapidly that we have no time to react before the next change sweeps over us. The foreshortening of the information time float has so accelerated our lives and businesses that a letter that took three days to travel across country a decade ago can take seconds to make the trip by electronic mail. The past is no longer a guide. We must anticipate the future from the present. Even our sense of time itself—our time orientation—has changed. Farmers and factory workers learned from past experience how and when to plant and when to make or retool the machines that made our goods. Those of us who saved and invested our money also knew the rules; we knew in advance what would happen to our cash. But the time orientation in America today is *now*. What happened this morning tells us more about the future than what went on yesterday does. As you read this book, I hope you'll keep this in mind and understand that the financial ideas I've outlined—which represent only a small part of today's new money market—may be old when you discover them. Even so, they can form the basis for new savings and investing ideas for your future.

If I write about a high-tech information economy, I should be able to measure it in specific terms. I can't. Our past experience was with an industrial era, when we made hard goods you could see and touch. But we can't dismiss the high-tech information economy as some paper-shuffling adjunct to the physical business of producing "real" goods. It's much bigger than our hard-goods economy and it is now the driving force in new employment and business operations.

Similarly, high technology is driving the emerging money machine. The big winners will be the financial giants that can spend the millions it will take to develop sophisticated consumer banking and financial services hardware and software. In a deregulated society, the strategic resource will be high technology that can deliver a high-touch product offering the consumer a better deal, while at the same time cutting the delivery cost to the producer of the service—the non-bank money center. High-tech banks and money centers spell trouble for their competition in an increasingly fee-oriented business. "An awful lot of bankers think they're going to stay in business on their existing fee revenues," a financial consultant told me, "but what they fail to realize is that the low-cost producer is going to set the price."

In a broad sense, we're seeing a shift to high-tech merchandising of money. Citicorp's consumer banking division, for instance, is loaded with managers who transferred from the likes of Lever Brothers, General Mills, General Foods, and Pepsi Cola. Watching Citicorp use high technology to merchandise money, we can see the major trends of saving and investing becoming somewhat clearer. It helps to explain, for example, something that we know in a hazy way, but can't put our finger on: why smaller customers get less service at banks and brokers, yet pay more charges.

Banks Are Smashing Low-Cost, Low-Deposit Banking

For as long as any of us can remember, banks have handled America's money. We put our money in the bank to save and we got our money from the bank in the form of a check. As a kid we could open a bank account with anything short of a bag of marbles. A bank was like the Post Office: Everyone used it and everyone was welcome.

In the decade of the eighties, however, rich Americans have begun to disengage from banks as more and more competitors have emerged in the deregulated marketplace. The up-scale depositors have gone to the likes of Merrill Lynch's cash management account or to mutual funds. People in the middle class are paying more bank charges, but they can afford them. The poor have been left behind. In a sense, we seem to be coming full circle, back to the eighteenth century, where only the rich could afford to use a bank.

Deregulation of the securities industry brought discount brokers, trucking deregulation created cut-rate carriers, and air deregulation blew old, well-established carriers right out of the sky. Now it's the banking industry's turn. To survive, banks and S&Ls will have to cut costs, boost fees and charges, and red-line the blue-collar and the poor. The changes will infuriate some customers. When a bank begins charging a service fee of $5 a month on savings accounts with a balance of less than $500, where will that leave a depositor who opened three $20 accounts for her grandchildren? Like it or not, we will have to wean ourselves from our collective reliance on banks, learn to embrace the emerging money centers, and rely only on ourselves.

As far as your friendly banker or broker is concerned, if you ain't up-scale you're way down on the list of preferred potential customers. Financial firms no longer seek to attract the kids with their piggy banks who someday might become millionaires. The name of the game in attracting money is "Upwardly Mobile." Banks, brokers, S&Ls, and mutual funds of all sizes are fighting fiercely for this lucrative up-scale market. Banks' hard-driving marketing people, for example, are closing more and more branches, not because there aren't enough customers, but because there aren't enough up-sclae customers in those neighborhoods. Ten years ago, the shift was in the other direction: Banks rushed to open branches within walking distance of their depositors. They bragged about the number of branches they had. Not now. The banks are collapsing their branch system and discouraging small-time customers by tacking on hefty service charges in the hope they can unload the poor.

For those with at least a six-figure annual income, however, there is Rolls-Royce banking with personal attention and a host of free, gold-plated services. Just as airlines created frequent flyer clubs, banks like Citibank offer semi-rich up-scale customers with more than $25,000 on deposit "priority" service, including separate teller lines and a personal account officer to hold their hand. In three of Detroit's largest banks, personal tellers and even house calls are among the posh private services that await affluent up-scale customers. Typical of the new banks is The Financial Center Bank, a three-office bank headquartered in San Francisco. The median net worth of each of its 900 customers is just under $1 million. "These are the kind of people who want to do business when they want to do it," says a banker of an up-scale bank. "They want a banker available beyond the normal 9-to-5 hours of business, and that's what we give them . . . . beepers and bankers 24 hours a day."

For the middle class there is Chevrolet banking with sizable fees, high deposit requirements to make the fee system work, and long lines for service. The plain old wage earner is living in a banking no-man's land, and for the poor, it's mostly used-car banking, with little service and huge fees on just about everything the bank provides. In a way, it's reverse deregulation. As the banks and S&Ls cater to up-scale customers and charge low-balance depositors more service fees, they will ultimately discourage most middle-class, blue-collar, and service workers who are struggling to meet their current financial needs. By the end of this decade, many of the full-service, brick-and-mortar branch banking offices will become relics, replaced by a new breed of boutique banks for the affluent and the counters of Sears and K mart for the rest of us.

We are in the midst of a major shift from public banking to private banking. Constantly escalating service charges and fees and the banks' shift toward up-scale depositors threaten to cut off an entire segment of society from banking services. Bankers say that today's bank must be more like a retailer or wholesaler of financial services, and as such the bank should have the right to make voluntary choices in a competitive marketplace. One shift in the years ahead will be to some form of discount banking. Banks and money centers are already experimenting with low-cost banking, where a $100 monthly balance is maintained, ten or fewer checks a month are written, and routine business is done through ATMs. In some cases of "self-service" discount banking, you're allowed only two transactions a month with a teller before you are charged for trips to the window. Other banks boost their fee from $2 a month to $5 a month with the first visit to a human. For depositors who fall below the minimums—and most will at one time or another—the bank, savings and loan, or even the money center stands ready to clip the account with hefty charges and fees.

With this fundamental shift to income-related banking, financial services for the bottom end of the economic scale are fast becoming a socioeconomic problem. Although bankers do extensive secret studies on their customers, the public seldom finds out about them. But from the research that is publicly available, and from what I can glean from discussions with financial executives, each group—the rich, the middle class, and the poor—is slowly being herded into a segregated world of banking. "When you look at the future," a bank marketing executive told me, "you can clearly see the separation walls growing higher, not only to protect our up-scale customers, but to offer our services where we can make the most money."

Unfortunately, some form of banking is indispensable. Salaries and pensions come by check and consumer bills are safely paid that way. "The practical complications are enormous if people don't have access to banking services," says Lois Salisbury, a public advocate and attorney. "And if they have to pay for bank services, or if they carry cash and lose their money, it only exacerbates their poverty."[1]

Who Has the Best Deal?
Sometimes the Answer is Surprising

Whether we endorse segregated banking or not, we are forced to accept it as a consequence of deregulation. All financial institutions have been forced to raise the cost of financial services in order to pay the high returns that free competition has brought. Those who do have money to save or invest will find that brokers, mutual funds, banks, savings and loans, and the new money centers all now offer insured CDs. What's different—and many long-time savers may be horrified to learn this—is that you can often get a better deal on a bank's or S&L's own insured CD if you buy it from a stockbroker. What's new is that source of profits in the 1980s will not be money in the hands of many, but information in the hands of few. The strategic resource will be information.

Before a House banking subcommittee, William Isaac, then chairman of the FDIC, reported that the top five brokerage houses sold over $1.5 billion of brokered insured CDs during 1984. When the savings business falls off, as it does when interest rates slide, the volume of brokered CDs rises. "In a period of starvation, the financial firm that is best fed gets relatively stronger," laments an executive of an S&L.

Take the case of America's largest S&L, American Savings. Hungry for fast deposits, American Savings went to the brokers for $1 billion of purchased CD money. Their insured CDs were sold in multiples of $1,000, with maturities ranging from six months to seven years. With Prudential-Bache as the lead broker, the money began to pour into American Savings. And why not? American Savings, through its brokers, was offering as much as 1.5 percent above prevailing rates. Brokered CDs, however, are short-term bonds, and the value of your investment can rise or fall if you sell them in the secondary market before maturity. But investors snapped them up anyway. Outraged bankers and the FDIC went to court to prevent brokers from using federal insurance to sell CDs. But a federal court in 1984 overturned a proposed ruling by the FDIC that would have denied federal insurance for all but the first $100,000 that brokers funnelled into a bank or S&L. The securities industry association called the judge's decision "a victory for savers."

Or consider Allstate Savings and Loan, a big S&L in California that is, in reality, Allstate Savings and Loan Association, a wholly owned subsidiary of Allstate Enterprises, Inc., which in turn is a wholly owned subsidiary of Sears, Roebuck and Co. The Association is a part of the Sears Financial Services Group, which also includes Dean Witter Reynolds. With all that muscle, they were primed to fight back when the brokers began to grab a hefty share of the insured CD market. Allstate began selling the same type of no-load five-year insured CDs that brokers were selling their clients. They are federally insured short-term notes paying semiannual interest. Allstate says it will maintain a secondary market so you can sell the notes before the maturity date. And secondary market transactions, unlike those for regular insured CDs, are not subject to an early withdrawal penalty—but they are subject to the bond-basis risk. To sell these five-year insured notes, Allstate sweetened the pot by offering an annual yield of 11.7 percent, well above the normal interest rate offered savers on a regular five-year insured CD.

Smaller financial firms like Malibu Savings and Far West Savings in California, First Federal in North Carolina, and Murray Savings in Texas, countered by dangling a new lure for savers: an earnings-based federally insured CD invested in real estate. This is a hybrid investment that combines the insured CD's safety with profit sharing. "It's an investment rather than a limited partnership," a broker told me, "and unlike limited partnerships and real estate investment trusts, the CD's earnings aren't sheltered from income taxes." Sold by brokers, the CDs are for seven or eight years, or until all the mortgages on shopping centers, apartments, and office buildings are paid off. The minimum amount is $5,000 ($2,000 for IRAs or Keogh plans) with additional multiples of $1,000 up to the maximum federal insurance limit of $100,000.

The initial earnings-based CDs, offered in early 1985, came with a guaranteed rate of 10 percent. After two years, the bank or S&L pays 85 percent of the spread (the 10 percent cost of money and what the real estate mortgages earn) to the investor, boosting the accrued interest to as much as 13 or 14 percent. Thereafter, the CDs pay 75 percent of the profits until you reach an 18 percent accrued rate. After that, the profits are split 50/50 between the financial firm and the investor.

Prudential Bank, a federal savings bank in Seattle, Washington, offered $20 million in earnings-based insured CDs in late 1985, locking in a fixed interest rate of 8.5 percent. Additional interest, equal to 85 percent of the bank's equity return, will be paid to the investor and the bank estimates at least a 13.5 percent overall yield on the CDs.

Earnings-based CDs allow a financial firm to make mortgage loans with a known cost of money. In exchange, they cut out the middleman and allow the investor to share directly in the earnings of real estate mortgages. I call them a heads-you-win, tails-you-can't-lose investment. In the best case you make a lot more money than you would with a regular insured CD. In the worst case—a series of bad loans pushing a lender into insolvency—you get your original investment back through federal insurance.

Another new wrinkle is the tax-deferred insured CD. Since interest income on a one-year CD is not taxed until the certificate "matures," banks and S&Ls dug deep into their bag of tricks for a way to delay taxes. If this is an angle you may have missed, here's how it works: Say you invest in a ten-month CD in May of 1986. Your interest income will be reported as earned in March 1987. You'll then have until April 15, 1988 to pay your taxes. The variations are endless and the advertisments for this basic product are mind-numbing.

How would you like to earn tax-free interest with safety? Banks, S&Ls, brokers, and mutual funds all want to offer you single and double tax-free income—that's interest that is exempt from both federal and state taxes. With one-year insured CDs paying a fully taxable 8 percent, banks and S&Ls, for example, splash big ads in the papers offering highly rated, long-term tax-exempt bonds of excellent quality that also pay 8 percent. I'm often asked about this by callers on my radio show, who wonder if they have missed something in this puzzle. After all, both the insured CDs and highly rated municipal bonds are among the safest investments on record, and they are both instantly liquid with a trip to the local bank.

The answer to the puzzle is that power has been shifting from Washington, D.C., back to the cities and states. With federal revenue sharing and with local tax revenues lagging, local governments in increasing numbers have gone to the bond market in the face of high interest rates, and they have found hungry buyers for their paper. Simultaneously, the tax-free investments, paying interest rates competitive with savings accounts, have become an embarrassment to the banks and S&Ls that sell them.

"How in heaven's name," a bank executive asked me, "can we sell fully-taxable CDs paying the same rate as fully tax-free investments? Sure, for some people who have their money in a passbook savings account, it's ok, but for anyone with even a working knowledge of the money system, it doesn't make any sense." I am constantly surprised at people who grouse about the low rates their bank pays for an insured CD, as if that was the only game in town. Granted, investing in tax-free bonds carries a little more risk and takes a little more care and study than allowing the bank or S&L to suck up your money into an insured CD, but the payoffs can be handsome indeed. And private insurance is available for nervous investors from a group of America's biggest insurance companies: the American Municipal Bond Assurance Corp. (AMBAC), a private corporation, and Municipal Bond Insurance Association (MBIA), a pool of private insurers.

In today's fast-moving money world, it makes no sense at all for people who are in a 57 percent tax bracket (for federal and state income tax) to invest in insured CDs. Their net earnings before taxes are 9 percent, but with a double tax-free investment, their earnings before taxes are about 19 percent. With a triple tax-free investment, well over 20 percent.

But up-scale Bloomingdales and Brooks Brothers shoppers aren't the only ones for whom new savings plans are gushing forth. Now the blue-collar worker and the hard-pressed middle class can get a far better deal on saving money and taxes. The newest player in the lower-scale money game is not the banks, however. It's the U.S. government.

The new Series EE savings bonds offer a brighter outlook for savers than the savings plans of many banks and S&Ls. They have a face value of from $50 to $10,000, and they sell for half their face value. They are instantly liquid at virtually any bank, and of course they are safe.

Interest rates fluctuate for these new savings bonds, and they are adjusted every six months, but Congress put a floor under them, a minimum rate of 7.5 percent, provided holders keep them five years. The average return on Series EE bonds since the new rate system went into effect in 1982 has been a helfty 9.92 percent. The rate for the period May 1 to November 1, 1985, was 9.5 percent, down from 10.94 percent for the previous six months. The glamour of EE savings bonds is that six-month rate adjustment. If interest rates go through the roof again, yields on EE bonds will automatically ratchet upward. Holding conventional bonds, notes, or insured CDs, you can find yourself skidding from boom to bust.

Finally, the interest earned on U.S. savings bonds is tax deferred until the bond is cashed in, which makes them attractive even to high-bracket taxpayers, who can use them to defer interest income until retirement, when tax brackets are usually lower. Add to this bonanza the fact that there are no state or city income taxes, no sales or redemption fees, and no management charges to reduce your earnings, and you can understand why banks, brokers, and S&Ls are wringing their hands at the special deal Congress gave its bonds—and the hard-pressed middle class.

It really doesn't matter anymore why the government entered the money game in competition with private financial services. This new entry of the Treasury into the individual savings business, with its upbeat message of adjustable high interest and special taxation deals, could demolish the already crumbling walls that separate our financial firms. As one banker said about competing with the government, "The only guys in the money business who'll survive if the Feds make the rules in their favor are those of us who eat raw meat. Right now, we're muscling each other for every depositor and every scrap of turf."

To an extent, the bankers' fears are justified. Both high-braket sharpies and middle-class savers are elbowing their way into EE bonds, but it is the hard-working wage earners who should consider them a godsend when they can safely put away savings locked into the market interest rate for at least five years.

The deregulation of money has transformed politics, business, and our own savings habits in a way no one could have envisioned at the start of this decade. Elbowing its way into the savings market, the government is offering a terrific annual yield on its own bonds. The fundamental change, however, is so subtle that it can easily be overlooked. EE bonds and the federally insured earnings-based CDs are the forerunners of a new breed of financial investments that automatically adjust to allow future interest income to rise but not fall. Furthermore, the expansion of federal insurance to permit brokers, on behalf of banks and S&Ls, to sell insured CDs with the backing of real estate loans, opens a new set of questions. I would argue that federal insurance can become a tool of the government by channelling savings dollars to those places where money is protected. With Congress clearly unable to control spreading deregulation, Washington may decide to jump on the train and direct the investments "for the public good." Yet the country's sheer size is one factor against centralization from Washington. But, more importantly, with everyone entering the money game, and with consumers snapping up the higher rates, it may be too late even for Congress to direct the future of individual saving and investing. In short, we are a nation in the process of reinventing the savings account.

Another thing to think about: While you are stuck between an uncertain Congress and a wide-open free market, Shell Oil and Mobil Oil, whose names have been synonymous with the local gas station, may provide another place to take your savings. The big oil companies already know us as credit card customers; they could bypass the banks by going directly to the savers with CDs and money market accounts. Let's say you owe Shell $50 when your monthly statement arrives and you send the company $100. You could get credit for the extra $50 and earn interest from the day of receipt. The Shell and Mobil brainstormers think you'll like doing your banking with an oil company; after all, these two giants already manage more money than most banks in the country. Why not let them manage your spare cash as well? You could drive into one of their gas stations—and they have a lot more gas stations than banks have branches—and make deposits and withdrawals at an ATM.

The myth has been that only a bank can function as a bank. The fact is that there will be abundant banking services available from many kinds of institutions. When I talk about the shift from banks to non-banks, I use examples of department stores, supermarkets, and oil companies because the relatively swift and harsh judgments of the marketplace let us discover what is happening more clearly. In the case of Mobil and Shell Oil, they will have to reexamine what business they are in. For us, the shift from traditional banks to non-banks will require an almost universal reconceptualization about saving and borrowing money.

Another way to bypass the banking business is for a financial firm to keep your money, to not give it back. That's Mother Met's new idea.

If you are a beneficiary of one of Metropolitan Life's policies and your claim is for $10,000 or more, you can let the insurance company manage your money. Met calls its new savings and investment plan "Total Control Account." Instead of taking cash, a beneficiary can put all or part of it in a checking account, a CD, or a money market fund. Since Metropolitan doesn't need additional offices and employees to gather these deposits, its cost of acquisition is almost zero, and, by passing on these savings to the consumer, the life insurance company can offer a very attractive way to save and manage money.

The moneyshock is that if you are confused now about where to save—well, it's only the beginning. Almost any company, in and out of the financial services industry, can enter the market and change the pecking order among the money grabbers. Banks, brokers, and mutual funds, of course, still rank first, but corporations like Shell, Mobil, General Electric, and General Motors, which are newcomers to the free-for-all savings market, are jumping in. What's going on is that no one really knows what's going on.

When We Won't Come to the Bank, the Bank Wants to Come to Us

Instead of hiding your cash under the mattress, why not put a bank in your bedroom? You've seen the ads showing a guy in his pajamas doing his banking on one of the nation's major computerized home banking systems. New York's Chemical Bank was the first in this high-tech door in 1983 with it's "Pronto" home banking program. Since then, Citibank, Chase Manhattan Bank, Bank of America, and Manufacturers Hanover Trust have joined the scramble to convince depositors to bank at home.

The outlook for home banking and investing is not bullish, however. It was supposed to mean goodbye to long lines at the bank, but it turned out to be nothing like the ads suggested, for a number of reasons. First, many monthly bills aren't accommodated by the home banking program. Then, of course, in order to make home banking work, you have to have a personal computer, special software, a telephone modem (a computer gadget that links your telephone to the bank). It also helps if you're a whiz when it comes to high-tech data processing. Banks told us that home banking was for someone ready to embrace new technology; someone who balances home, career, family, and social life. I don't know about you, but I doubt if I can balance all that and fight a system full of floppy disks at the same time. To make matters worse, along with all this aggravation, you get a monthly bill for something like $12, to say nothing of the phone bill. And what a phone bill! The average computer-to-computer call lasts half an hour, ten times longer than an average human conversation. I'd probably have to rent a second phone line just to accommodate home banking. Security is another concern. Home banking systems are not that difficult for unscrupulous computer hackers to burglarize.

Finally, high-tech home banking has come without high-touch tradeoffs. The public has rejected it. Bankers have discovered what supermarkets discovered in the 1970s: that people like to be with people, in control of their affairs, taking part in a self-fulfilling social ritual of shopping and banking, rubbing elbows with others.

Back in the 1970s, grocers believed they could cut the cost of food if they put in fully automatic stores. Shoppers would simply fill out a punch card with their intended purchases and present it at the check-out counter. Their groceries would magically appear in front of the store, ready for the station wagon and the ride home. But shoppers wanted to touch, feel, and examine their purchases: They didn't want a stale sample staring back at them from the shelf. Grocers found out quickly that they could lure customers from their competitors and charge more money for their meat when they had real live butchers behind the counter who'd cut to order and tell the shopper how to cook a roast. Grocers found out—and bankers have yet to learn—that doing the grocery shopping or the banking is an important part of people's lives. And the importance is centered on the human contact. With home banking, people were being asked to reject their highly personal lifestyle for the impersonal and complicated nature of high technology. High-tech, if it is to succeed, has to balance with high-touch. If it doesn't, it's seen as illogical and we'll reject it. The high-touch tradeoff of traditional shopping and saving is simply too well ingrained for us to want to change without a high-touch advantage that leaves us in control.

If you're not ready for high-tech banking in your bedroom, you're not alone. A survey by the American Bankers Association in 1984 found that only 10 percent of retail banking customers will use home banking by 1990. A bank typically needs 15 percent of its customers on-line for a home service just to break even; under current trends that won't happen until well into the 1990s. But banks, once they latch on to a great "self-help" idea, are not easily discouraged. Like debit cards, they want home banking to succeed in spite of the customer's rejection, to keep people out of their rapidly shrinking branch system. To do this, the four heavyweights in the home banking and communications industries—Chemical Bank, Bank of America, Time, Inc., and American Telephone & Telegraph, have formed a joint venture to market electronic services to consumers and small businesses. Once on line, this venture will have the two largest home banking services in the nation. In 1984, Bank of America was reported to have 8,000 subscribers signed up, and Chemical Bank, in the New York City area, another 5,000, far short of the 100,000 customers everyone in the banking industry predicted just a few years earlier, when home banking sounded like a fine idea.

Commenting on this joint circling of the wagons, a B of A banker said, "We figured it would be faster and more efficient to find some major partners than to reinvent the wheel ourselves." The business of banking, more than other businesses, is product driven. In today's competitive financial marketplace, instead of selling products on the basis of how they can help the firm, bankers should be tailoring them to the customers' need. In fact, however, less than 10 percent of all American companies believe in customer focus; about 90 percent are product driven. When a company's identity is synonymous with its product line, it loses customer interest. Banks, for example, tell us how strong they are, how many loans they make; what I want to know is what they can do for me.

If home banking of any kind is to work it has to follow the pattern of Smart Cards, where the public can continue to do their banking in their own way, but let the Smart Card and the television or home computer simply keep track of the numbers. We don't have to own a high-powered computer system to talk to the bank or learn the art of computer programming. We can balance our bank account in our bedroom. We can climb on the financial fast track at our own speed. This way, home banking helps the consumer, and banks have a winner. It becomes a system that won't threaten our lifestyle, our banking habits, or our feeling of self-worth. It will be so user friendly that we'll gladly push keys and let the computer do the work. Yet today, home banking and debit cards remind me of two extinct dodo birds trying to mate.

We Are Shifting from Local to National Saving and Investing

One of the first signs of runaway financial deregulation is when depositors bypass the local banks and S&Ls. The banks and thrifts may not yet have the green light for nationwide banking, but the smart saver knows that it has already arrived. That's because the highest interest rate on your savings may no longer be offered by your local bank or savings and loan. "Out-of-town" savings are growing like gangbusters on a national level and a fierce rivalry is unfolding, much to the benefit of the consumer's pocketbook. The average saver can pick up as much as one or two percentage points on his or her money, and on $5,000, the difference a 2 percent increase makes comes to $100 over just one year. Take a $10,000, five-year CD from a bank or thrift paying 12 percent. Even without compounding, you'll end up with $16,000 in five years. The same $10,000 five-year CD from a bank paying 10 percent yields a return of only $15,000. The difference between the two: an extra $1,000.

The carpetbagger banks and thrifts pay different rates of interest depending on the competition in their own areas. The areas of high interest rates seem to be in Texas and parts of the South, in the Washington, D.C., area, and in California. To help you find the hot rates, several newsletters list the best places and many major newspapers run weekly tables of rates around the country.

The caveat about grabbing the highest rate in Omaha or Oshkosh is: Be sure that the institution outside your hometown or state carries federal deposit insurance and that you keep your savings and earned interest under the $100,000 insurance limit. That's what stockbrokers do when they sell high-interest CDs in distant banks and S&Ls.

The moneyshock of all of this: *The FDIC or FSLIC insurance guarantees your savings account, not the bank or S&L.* In other words, your federally insured CD is just as safe with a small S&L in Dallas offering one percent more on your savings as it is with a big bank in Chicago.

With interstate banking by mail legal in all states (although other interstate banking is not), here are a few tips on making out-of-town deposits:

- Telephone the bank (you can find out if it has a toll-free number by calling information at 1-800-555-1212) and ask to speak to an officer in charge of national consumer-deposit accounts. Before you send any money, find out (1) what current rates are, (2) how often they compound the earned interest, and (3) how long after opening the account you can withdraw your funds.
- Once you've decided on the amount you want to invest and for how long, ask the institution to preassign you an account number. Get their exact mailing address, since your interest will not start until the money is received and posted to your account.
- Checks should be made out to the institution, endorsed "for deposit only" to your preassigned account number.

Even as I write this book, we're in the midst of a major shift from local to nationwide banking. The latest wrinkle is to turn your touch-tone phone into an automatic teller machine at home. As investors adapt to obtaining information at any hour of the day or week by touch-tone phones, nationwide savings by mail will grow. Here's an example of how one such system now works:

Step 1: Using your touch-tone phone, call 1-800-USA-CASH to connect yourself to the system. Youll find out about the latest interest rates on savings.

Step 2: Holding the phone in your hand, touch 01234 to receive instructions for mailing or wiring money for deposit. Touch 0234 and you'll receive the information required to open an account.

Step 3: Touch 0335 and you can immediately start dictating the application information to open an account. Touch 8 and your information will be repeated back to you.

Step 4: Touch other codes and you automatically have mortgage and financial services.

Step 5: If you need help, simply touch 0 and you'll get someone who can put you back on track.

The Changes Are Being Felt on Wall Street

Small investors are saying goodbye to Wall Street. They are fed up with a market they find increasingly speculative. "It flies all over," a retired worker said. "You think it's hitting bottom, and it goes down more. To my mind, it's like crapshooting." Retail brokers across America find their small customers are asking a common question: "Why risk a 10 percent return in the stock market when you can get 10 percent in a government-insured security?"

The upshot is that the John and Jane Does of America have been deserting the market in droves. The numbers show it. Institutions, pension funds, and Wall Street brokers—a growing form of institutional participation—now account for about 90 percent of the volume on the Big Board. Individuals are doing only about 10 percent of all the trading on the New York Stock Exchange.

The retail brokerage business has traditionally made much of its money on the commissions paid by the small investor. Stockbrokers have opened hundreds of branch offices to accommodate the investing public. The number of branches will now begin to shrink as more and more trading is done by discount brokers and large institutions. "The bread-and-butter business that pays handsome brokerage fees from small investors is rapidly becoming a thing of the past," an executive from one of the giant firms told me. "The market has been like a floating crap game. If people lose at the game, they're going to walk away."

In the past, huge numbers of individual small investors gave the market extraordinary liquidity and both the individual and institutional players could buy and sell shares without any one of the trades causing a large leap or dip in stock prices. But without the millions of small investors, the stock market may not have the price stability to prevent wild swings in the price of stocks. With individual investors being overwhelmed by the big institutions, we are already seeing bigger moves in a day or week than used to occur in a month or year. When the market makes a big jump it tends to make small investors nervous, and they try to avoid situations they really can't understand. My own sense of the market tells me that if individuals continue to shun the market, this lost volume will make the stock market even more unstable and have enormous implications for the securities business.

From a practical standpoint, the large surge in institutional and pension traders has made it even more difficult for the small trader to make money. Many of the big traders on Wall Street, with direct telephone lines to brokerage firms, can be tipped off in minutes when a change is about to occur, long before the local broker or individual trader discovers the news. Then it can take hours or days to find the client, explain the new information, and get an order to buy and sell.

We are in the midst of a fundamental, yet little known, shift from the retail brokerage business in your hometown to a highly centralized, computer-driven institutional and pension business on Wall Street. The trend has already been established. From the late 1970s to 1984, the number of individuals active in the stock market has fallen from 33 percent to only 10 percent, and power has shifted away from the small investor in another, more graphic way. The institutional and pension traders have been elbowing out the little guy in trades. Buy and sell orders of 900 shares or less (the typical size of trades by individuals) have fallen from about 42 percent of the market in 1975 to only about 10.5 percent today. At the same time, trading of blocks of 10,000 shares or more (the size of institutional and Wall Street house trading for their own accounts) has risen to about 51 percent of the Big Board's volume, up from 17 percent in 1975.

What has saved the big brokerage house financially, however, could kill Wall Street as we know it today. This is the biggest lump of money in the world, a mind-boggling $1.4 trillion resting in the nation's pension funds. (The federal budget is less than $1 trillion and the total insured time and savings accounts in the nation's banks is close to that amount.) It already costs pension funds a whopping $100 billion a year just to trade their huge pile of securities, and on any given day they can control as much as 90 percent of the trades on Wall Street. Stocks are no longer bought and sold by pension funds, companies are. America's pension funds are clearly the OPEC of finance.

And the trend of pension funds dominating the stock market will continue. A decade ago, pension funds were thought to contain about $170 billion. Today, its almost $1.4 trillion. It's forecast that in a decade pension funds will be worth about $3.5 trillion. With corporate take-overs in full swing, the size of the pension funds is even more alarming. A corporate raider with a war chest of $2.5 billion in institutional backing could go after all but a few of the largest companies. There is no greater power in this country than the control over money.

The shift from the small investor to the giant trader is fundamental in an overall trend that is placing financial markets in the hands of a few. In the next few years we will witness the beginning of the transformation of the U.S. stock market. One of the first signs will be the increased closing of retail branch offices. The shift will be to discount brokers. From talking with executives in the market, I have watched the general outlines of a new Wall Street slowly emerge. Much of the trading will not take place on the floor of the Exchange. Individual investors that remain in the equity market will buy unit trusts and mutual funds. And much of the market information will be sped to jumbo traders, working from computers, who can make their buying decisions instantaneously.

For those individual investors who remain in the stock market, on-line investing by computer will be the way to play the market. Today, only about 4,000 private investors use personal computers to trade securities, but discount brokers and bankers believe it is the vanguard of a massive market. Currently there are seven computerized investment services to choose from and more are being added each year. Wired-up investors, too busy with their jobs during the day, transmit as much as 70 percent of their trading orders during evenings and week-ends.

The trend is toward totally automated securities trading where a customer, from home or office, can trade stocks and bonds without a broker's help. The leaders in this deregulated world are Fidelity Invest-ments Group (part of the big Fidelity Mutual Fund Group), the coun-try's second-largest discount broker, and Charles Schwab, Bank of

America's discount broker and the nation's largest. The full-service brokers, like E. F. Hutton, Dean Witter Reynolds, and Goldman Sachs, send customers up-to-date research on securities through their home computers, but to place an order customers must telephone a broker. Dow Jones News Retrieval is a data base for investors that research companies at home.

Like home banking, stock trading by home computer is off to a slow start. It will never grow large because the number of investors who will play the market in the years to come will decline, not grow. My sense is that its growth will be slowed even more as the new money centers make the same type of investments available, provide experts to manage them, and make them easier to buy and sell. The trend will be toward a merger with other financial services in the hope of attracting a wider range of investors. The systems will allow users to trade mutual funds and pay bills through a personal assets management account. Accordingly, home banking and home stock trading will merge. Chemical Bank in New York is expanding its ailing Pronto home banking system to include stock trading. Customers will automatically be able to transfer funds from a checking account to a discount broker at the time an order is placed.

The Big Players Will Get Bigger

It takes no great leap of imagination to envision a time when all computers will be connected to each other, when business can be done over the phone, by using a video screen or computer. We are headed toward a worldwide data communications network where on-line communications will be the critical link. We are already moving toward 24-hour securities trading on a global scale. In short, we are collapsing the time frame in business from hours and days to seconds, and, in a deregulated marketplace, hundreds of companies are rushing in to offer us high-tech products and services that most of us can't, as yet, fully understand.

The changes will come quickly. While the shift from hand ledgers to computer statements took several decades, the present restructuring of our business and financial markets is occurring so rapidly that not only have we been unable to react, we have been unable to conceptualize how these changes will affect our lives. We have rejected ATMs, debit cards, and home banking; yet those who are born in the decade of the eighties and who grow up in an information society will accept them as a matter of course. They will know automatically what we must learn: The strategic resource in managing our money is information.

Today we are faced with an America giving birth to a new kind of society, where, for the first time in our history, computers and deregulation will produce almost unlimited choices of financial plans. But with unlimited choice, only those firms that can provide massive marketing and computer skills on a nationwide basis will survive. The moneyshock is that we will no longer have individual insurance agents, brokers, and bankers. High-tech marketing will bring most of us together in a mass-marketing mode, in one place. The good news is that the human side of high technology will survive. Automated financial products and services have failed; high-touch has to take their place. We will be doing more for ourselves, expanding our knowledge, and we will find the world of money more exciting when our choices are unlimited.

5

The New Financial Bazaars

From Citibank to K mart

Thirty-seven years after the death of A.P. Giannini who founded the giant Bank of America (and who is usually portrayed as a folk hero), bank deregulation is in full swing. But even though he operated in days of structured banking, A.P. was a fiercely competitive entrepreneur who probably would thrive in today's freewheeling banking environment. He once attempted to buy the predecessor of Citibank. Failing that, he bought a small New York bank named Bank of America and promptly changed the name of his California bank from Bank of Italy to Bank of America. Until federal regulators put the clamps on Giannini in the 1930s and 1940s, he had assembled a financial services network that spanned a banking empire in five states. His bank offered investment banking, sold securities, owned a life insurance company, and was even then on its way to becoming a money center. When A.P.'s continued focus on the New York market made Northeast bankers jittery, J. P. Morgan met with him in a historic conference, during which the two financiers reached an agreement that "New York was for J.P., the West for A.P."

Merchandising Money Is More Important Than Banking

Today, financial supermarkets are operating across America. Edward R. Telling, chairman and chief executive officer of Sears, Roebuck, puts it this way: "The plain truth is, the American banking industry has arrived at a crossroads and there's nobody out there directing traffic. Instead of blowing the whistle on the broken-down policies of the past, our regulatory policemen are busy sitting on their hands."[1] To many Americans, that's especially baffling in light of what's occurring in a financial marketplace uprooted by deregulation. Spurred by the demands of increasingly sophisticated consumers, new financial services firms are offering a bewildering number of increasingly innovative products—and new ways to run banks—that are high-touch in contrast to high-tech. In most cases these new products have been introduced without the blessing of the federal governments. This lack of direction from the regulators has enticed some of America's largest non-bank corporations to invade the bankers' territory. That's the essence of the shift from regulated local and statewide banking to unregulated nationwide money center banking.

The next ten years will see non-banking giants, major corporations in the retail and services industries, rushing to put their huge retail muscle to work in a wild scramble for the financial services customers. This all leads me to believe that today's business of banking and financial services is greatly misunderstood: Banking per se is no longer as important as merchandising. Almost any major corporation can buy a bank on the cheap and attract deposits. In the past, with tight controls, with products and services spelled out by law, the marketing of financial products drew frowns from the protected banks and thrifts. Their lack of aggressiveness was largely attributable to the fact that when all banks and thrifts were offering the same financial products, advertising made little difference. Even today, with wide-open cut-throat competition, banks and thrifts, by and large, have not yet made the crucial psychological shift to a merchandising environment.

When banking moves into department and grocery stores, what do the consumers tell us? Simply that, on the whole, the invasion of the money game by companies like General Electric, Sears, American Express, Kroger, Stop & Shop, and K mart is a welcome relief. Surveys tell us that investors believe these merchandising companies are more innovative and do a better job of meeting consumer needs than traditional banks or thrifts. Former U.S. Comptroller of the Currency C. Todd Conover observed, "The public wants financial services, but it could care less whether it get them from banks."[2]

This is another example of the stress any system goes through in the transition from tight regulation to a free market. Rapid changes will continue to permeate the world of money; current methods of saving and investing will become obsolete. Faced with a blizzard of new products, you will be forced to seek new information again and again. Accordingly, financial firms will grow larger and offer more services. They will split up into separate businesses: either commerical financial centers or consumer money centers. This major shift, with the big players holding all the cards, will occur before the end of this decade.

All this may sound like an improbable scenario, but it stems from a very simple premise: Big banks and brokers are best equipped to raise the huge sums of money needed to finance our global economy. Money centers and consumer banks can best serve the investing public. Instead of trying to put deregulation back in the bottle, instead of assailing the banking system with a regulatory meat cleaver, we should devise a structure where both the commercial markets and the consumer can best be served. For the consumer there are only really two areas of concern: safety and choice. Financial deregulation means change, of course, but it also must mean equal access to financial services, the widest possible range of investment options, and guarantees of safety when that is required. If we have learned anything from years of tight financial control it must be this: A system in which the consumer's interest is paramount over any company's desire for built-in profits will be better for consumers and companies alike.

Non-Banks Find the Loopholes

A fundamental change occurring in the banking business today concerns the difference between a regular full-service bank and a non-bank like Sears or General Electric. The latter should more appropriately be called a consumer bank or a family bank. The most important difference between the two types of institutions is that under federal law a full-service bank offers regular checking accounts (takes deposits and makes withdrawals on demand) and also makes commercial loans. A non-bank can't do both. By sacrificing one of these services—usually the power to make commercial loans—non-banks escape the 1927 McFadden Act, which bars banks that make commercial loans from jumping state lines unless state law otherwise permits. Similarly, these non-banks also elude federal rules that prevent securities firms, insurance companies, finance companies, and other financial firms from owning banks. In reality, until recently, savings and loans were non-banks since they took deposits and made consumer loans in the form of mortgages rather than commercial loans. In fact, almost half the traditional full-service banks are really non-banks, since less than 10 percent of their assets are in the form of commercial loans. So the idea of a non-bank is not new. What is new is the variety of ways firms in and out of the banking business have exploited the legal loopholes to open non-banks. The prevailing logic from the Depression era was that commercial loans were the most important part of banking and no one would start a bank just to lend to consumers, but in the deregulated era of the 1980s, with its intense competition reminiscent of the pre-OPEC gasoline station wars, consumer banking seems the natural thing to do.

The first non-bank was established in 1980 by Gulf & Western, a conglomerate based in New York. That was followed by Parker Pen, when the pen and pencil maker found it could also make money in banking. But the one I refer to in my talks around the country is the Western Family Bank, the brainchild of McMahan Furniture Company, a California-based, family-owned retail furniture chain that now dabbles in banking. You may have to walk past the love seats and mattresses to get to some branches of the Western Family Bank, but the walk may be worth the effort. With a small fraction of the overhead of a major bank, Western Family Bank can offer some incredible opportunities to save and borrow money. "A bank in a furniture store? Why it's illogical, and it evades the real meaning of a bank," a banking executive told me. "Besides, how in the hell can a full-service bank compete with a furniture-store bank that practically gives its product away?" Translated, the message is this: The banking business is becoming less a gentlemanly pursuit based on long-standing relationships and more a cutthroat scramble for business.

By 1984, responding to howls of protest from small banks and thrifts about non-banks setting up shop and stealing their customers, Congress once again tried to close the non-bank loophole. To give the lawmakers a chance, then Comptroller of the Currency C. Todd Conover—chief regulator of national banks—called a moratorium on processing applications for new non-banks. But Congress was unable to plug the loophole when the House and Senate banking committees couldn't agree on what new powers banks should be given to offer additional financial products. Mr. Conover then began processing applications from non-banks and issued more than 100 new bank charters. Some 60 companies, including J.C. Penney, Prudential Insurance, and Sears, Roebuck, seized the opportunity and began planning their own chains of consumer non-banks.

Sidestepping its way through the tangle of banking laws and

regulations, U.S. Trust Company of New York became the first national bank to win approval to operate a non-bank, and the means of escape from full-service banking became clearer. The New York bank, prohibited from opening a branch in another state, saw the non-bank principle as a golden opportunity and opened a "consumer bank" in Palm Beach, Florida, where many of its wealthy customers flee for the winter. Other banks and financial firms realized that U.S. Trust's end run on the interstate barrier was also a way to jump state lines for themselves, and the race to open non-banks picked up speed. More than 50 firms promptly filed applications for over 300 non-banks in 38 states and the District of Columbia. To be sure, Congress had not yet legitimized nationwide banking, but the new money players were confident that consumers would approve of the new banks. And if they did, much of what was left of the nationwide banking barrier would soon collapse.

Picking through this tangle became a difficult and frustrating process for a Congress split over just what powers banks should be given. In 1984, the Senate Banking Committee passed legislation that would authorize bank holding companies to underwrite mortgage-backed securities and municipal revenue bonds and to conduct limited interstate banking. The committee also voted to allow banks to cross state lines on a regional basis. But the Senate panel found itself on a collision course with the House, which wanted to restrict the powers of banks. By 1985, with the issue of nationwide banking still in doubt, Federal Reserve Board Chairman Paul Volcker urged Congress to approve limited interstate banking. The technological advances, he said, have already blurred the state lines that once sharply divided the industry. "Looking ahead," Volcker warned, "banking through home computers would be difficult to confine within a state's boundary."

Chairman Volcker was not to prevail immediately, however, and what Congress was unable to do for itself, the Federal Appeals Court did for it. In a May 1985 ruling, the court declared that the new chartering of so-called non-banks across state boundaries was illegal because it violated the intent of Congress when it wrote the Bank Holding Company Act. In a case involving the enterprising U.S. Trust Company of New York, the court held that the Federal Reserve Board's decision was illegal when it granted the bank's application to change the function of its Palm Beach, Florida, representative office from offering investment advisory services to taking "non-bank" deposits.

The U.S. Trust case provides, I think, a great lesson in the workings of financial deregulation. In 1970 U.S. Trust Company opened its representative office on the second floor of an office building in Palm Beach to provide its banking customers with investment services. In

1980 the representative office became a state-chartered non-deposit trust. In 1983 the Comptroller of the Currency approved its metamorphosis into a federally insured consumer bank (non-bank), which could not make commercial loans. And in May 1984 the Federal Reserve Board's approval allowed U.S. Trust to open the doors of its "bank." Horrified Florida bankers feared that other giant New York banks would invade their state, not only grabbing their winter customers, but their traditional year-round customers as well. They immediately put the wheels in motion to overturn the Federal Reserve Board's approval, and one year later the Florida banks won. Well, almost. U.S. Trust's non-bank remained open, but for the time being the state's borders were sealed to other outside banks. "Building legal barriers that start at the state line," a bank executive told me, "is like trying to stop a raging river after the dam has broken. You can close off a deal like U.S. Trust in Florida, but another will pop up somewhere else. Deregulation can't be put back in the bottle and everyone knows it, but for many smaller banks it's a last-ditch battle to stay in business."

Then, to the amazement of Congress, the Supreme Court unanimously approved interstate banking on a regional basis. The Court's decision strengthened a regional compact established by Massachusetts in 1982, when that state passed a law permitting the purchase of its banks by a bank from another New England state with a similar law. Connecticut and Rhode Island have since joined the New England regional group. Seventeen other states have passed reciprocal regional banking laws.

Today, U.S. Trust's problems establishing a bank in Florida are old hat. In 1986, Chase Manhattan became the first money center bank to gain a foothold in Florida when it outbid rival banks. Chase paid over $62 million for the failed Park Bank of Florida in St. Petersburg. Chase officials acknowledged they paid a hefty price for a bank with a negative net worth, but the right to operate a full-service bank in one of the fastest growing counties in Florida was too good to pass up.

Chase will rename its acquisition the Chase Bank of Florida and add consumer lending offices and a mortgage company to its already established multi-branch trust company. Chase's interstate strategy, like that of other big banks, is based not on federal laws that allow interstate banking, but on the loopholes of the 1980s that allow it to buy troubled state-chartered banks and thrifts.

The danger in shifting from intrastate to regional banking is that it could, in the words of Fed Chairman Paul Volcker, "Balkanize banking." If Congress does not take the final steps to allow fully nationwide banking, we could end up with a patchwork of restrictive regional banking markets in which a few big banks could control the market and reduce competition.

Politics Doesn't Really Affect Banking Any More

In the United States, the banking system is subject to two types of regulation: Federal regulators make the rules for federally chartered financial institutions, and individual states regulate state-chartered institutions. In the past, state governments introduced most of the innovations, particularly when they allowed banks and S&Ls to offer interest-bearing NOW checking accounts. And recently several states have accelerated the move to deregulation by allowing state-chartered financial institutions to engage in business activities that aren't allowed under federal law. As a result, the number of state-chartered banks insured by the FDIC has soared to well over half of the 14,700 federally insured banks.

South Dakota invited out-of-state banks that wanted to get into the insurance business to establish a bank in that state and sell insurance in every other state. Alaska, Arizona, California, Iowa, Indiana, Minnesota, Nebraska, North Carolina, Wisconsin, and Wyoming now permit banks to sell insurance.

State-chartered banks can now sell real estate in Alaska, Arizona, California, Florida, Iowa, Maine, Massachusetts, New Hampshire, New York, North Carolina, Ohio, Rhode Island, and South Dakota. They can sell securities in Alaska, California, Georgia, and North Carolina. They can open a travel agency in Alaska, California, Indiana, Iowa, Nebraska, New Jersey, New York, North Carolina, Ohio, Pennsylvania, South Carolina, and South Dakota.

"States are giving banks a hell of a lot more powers than the Fed is," says Kenneth Guenther, executive vice president of the Independent Bankers Association of America. "States use expanded powers to attract financial institutions to their area." Some of these new powers allow state-chartered financial institutions to invest in fast-food franchises, junk bonds, wind farms, Arabian racehorses, and even oil and gas drilling ventures. "As Congress moves toward interstate banking, it can't allow individual states to regulate entities that cross state lines," Mr. Guenther believes. "This trend is a premonition of doom for the dual banking system."[3]

In the meantime, with Congress unable to authorize interstate banking, the big bank holding companies have been forced to become defenders of the dual banking system because they have already taken advantage of many of the new authorities given them by the states. "We have invested millions of dollars in assets to exercise these powers, and we don't want to divest them," says an executive with a bank holding company. But Federal Reserve Board Chairman Paul Volcker told a congressional panel that the expanded powers given by some states "raise serious safety and soundness considerations, particularly when the primary motivation for the adoption of these powers is parochial consideration for jobs and revenues."[4]

At the same time, we are caught up in an irreversible shift from small to medium-size financial firms on a state-wide basis, to major firms on an interstate and global basis. These new financial networks will require new technology, with huge computer systems and marketing skills that only a large corporation can support. That's one reason why big banks like Citibank and giant corporations like General Electric and Sears will be the big winners. Citibank, for example, has already spent more than $700 million since the mid-1970s on product development and sophisticated consumer-banking computer systems. In the battle shaping up to attract your money, the low-fee competitors in the mass market of the future will be the winners. Everyone else will merge or die.

Regional banking will give way to interstate banking before the end of this decade. The barriers will crumble from three sides: The money centers will continue to exploit every loophole they can find. The big banks, their traditional corporate lending business eroded by the growth of commercial paper, will push harder for consumer banking that benefits from nationwide business. (Some states' regional laws already contain "triggers" to allow full interstate banking within a few years. Big states like California, New York, and Texas, that want to welcome all comers, could be set adrift by the restrictions of regional banking, and these states contain 18 of the 25 largest bank holding companies within the country.) Finally, the new regional superbanks will again seek to jump state lines and pressure their state legislators to allow nationwide banking. For Congress, holding back nationwide banking will be like trying to tame a raging river after the dam has broken.

The Big Players Gamble On Congress Making It Legal

Under the umbrella of deregulation, dramatic change is occurring all around us every day. Each financial firm is deciding for itself how best to serve the consumer, and the variations have baffled and surprised most Americans. Behind all this activity, bankers are gambling that Congress will make interstate banking legal. When that happens they will close more of their costly branches and open low-cost money centers in head-to-head competition with K mart and Sears.

Actually, many giant banks are already doing that. In the money centers of New York and California, banks have bought up thrifts and loans with hundreds of offices nationwide, just waiting to turn them into non-bank money stores. Chase Manhattan and Manufacturers Hanover Bank of New York have purchased thrift and loan companies to establish nationwide chains of consumer-oriented banking offices. Citicorp operates Nationwide Financial Services Corporation with almost 200 offices in 27 states (not to be confused with First Nationwide Savings, an S&L that owns TranSouth Financial Corporation, a consumer thrift and loan headquartered in South Carolina that operates 144 branches in seven southeastern states.)

Defining the differences among a bank, a savings and loan, and a thrift and loan has led to confusing banking regulations. Generally speaking, thrift and loans today don't have federal deposit insurance and, therefore, don't come under federal regulations. Although thrift and loans aren't "complete" banks, they accept cash deposits (and the same day take them to a bank with a vault) and make withdrawals from your account by check. To the typical consumer, their advertisements look like those of a federally insured bank or savings and loan. They offer passbook accounts with rates at least two points over bank rates and well above money market rates. Their CDs, which run from three months to five years, carry hefty rates above the competition. They make personal and car loans as well as real estate mortgages. But these are only functional similarities to "real" banks.

The fundamental difference, from the consumer's point of view, among full-service banks, S&Ls, and thrift and loans, is the presence or absence of the safety net of federal deposit insurance. Many thrift and loans don't have it. For many savers this lack of federal insurance calls up the visions of a failing thrift and loan's anxious depositors camped out on folding chairs, victims of a spreading panic caused by inadequate state insurance. But when some of the nation's largest banks buy thrift and loans we get the unlikely scenario in which a substitute for federal deposit insurance can be the bank's own full faith and credit. After all, we've already learned that the nation's major banks won't go broke, because the Treasury will pump in as much money as it has to to keep them financially afloat.

A vivid example is when a major bank buys a state-insured thrift. The bank's name is plastered across the storefronts of the thrift's branches. Inside, the bank's name leaps off the pages of every form and savings booklet. Most Americans knew little about state or private deposit insurance before the thrift crises in Ohio and Maryland; they won't learn anything more inside a big bank's thrift and loan branch.

There is no point in rehashing the difference between the two institutions, because for all practical purposes they are the same. While the big bank's thrift is technically state insured and the bank itself is federally insured, the real question is: Can the big bank allow its subsidiary to fail? Most banking experts I've talked with think not. It would be a public relations nightmare. So you ask, how can the parent company offer substantially higher rates on savings and better rates on loans from its thrift than from its bank? It's taking a chance. In the absence of a clear national banking system, major banks want to be ready to change the name on the front of their money stores when full-service nationwide banking is approved. Caught up in the uncertainty of the regulators, the bank hopes its regular customers, who earn low interest and pay high fees, won't notice that a few are getting a much better deal than the rest when they save or borrow money.

To add to the confusion, many savings and loans are changing their names to include the word "bank." When United Bank in San Francisco had a run on its money in 1985 and the news media said that its deposits were protected by FDIC insurance, the "bank" was actually an S&L and its deposits were protected by the FSLIC. Sears' Allstate Savings & Loan in California changed its name to Sears Savings Bank. "People want to go to a bank," a savings and loan executive told me, "so we're going to change our name to a bank. With all these S&Ls failing around the country, the word 'bank' seems to have a safer ring to it."

Banks Find Ways to Skirt the Law

Current banking laws prevent banks and thrifts from buying an insurance company or mutual fund, but no one ever thought of barring them from renting space to sell these financial products in their lobbies. Accordingly, banks are discovering that, as landlords, they can hang out the "for rent" sign and skirt federal and state laws that forbid them from selling many financial services. As with money centers, consumers will be able to buy insurance, securities, and real estate, see a travel agent, deposit checks, and borrow money from the expanding banking centers.

After decades of sitting on their hands, growing numbers of banks and S&Ls are becoming less stodgy and more innovative. Outwardly the banks and S&Ls may look unchanged, but inside the front door their lobbies have become beehives of activity. Banks already own discount brokers and through them they now offer mutual funds and other securities for IRAs. S&Ls offer discount brokerage services and they are aggressively selling tax-deferred annuities, mutual funds, and tax-free bonds in direct competition with the big Wall Street brokers.

Taking in boarders gives banks and S&Ls another new dimension in financial planning as well. Prudential-Bache Securities, for example, wants to put full-service stockbrokers in high-traffic branches. This is in direct response to the presence of Dean Witter brokers sitting at Sears Financial Network shops inside Sears department stores. Prudential Insurance, the parent of Bache Securities, will provide, in addition to full-service stockbrokers, an insurance counter. Equitable Life Assurance Society wants to sell policies inside bank branches. However, when banks and S&Ls move into the fast lane with outside financial firms, they attract new customers, but earn only rental income, not the hefty commissions and fees from selling the products. My own sense of it is that as banking rules change, banks and S&Ls, will push out the tenants and sell the financial products directly.

To the bewilderment of almost everyone, some of the nation's largest retailers and industrial corporations have used back-door interstate banking to position themselves for the shift to unregulated nationwide banking. According to a survey by *American Banker*, non-bank companies now operate at least 65 banks in this country, and plans are in the works for these non-bank giants to open substantially more banking offices. The feeling everywhere is that if large numbers of consumer banks are set up before Congress acts, there would be reluctance to close these money centers in the face of strong public protest. Never in the nation's history have we seen such a whirlpool of money waiting for the dam of banking regulations to break up.

Every day the pressure builds to give consumers fatter yields on savings, cheaper loan rates, and a raft of new services in one convenient place. When the legal barriers finally erode away and competition is on a nationwide basis, high technology will bring nationwide banking almost instantly.

We are in the midst of the transition now. I can't begin to cover all the new players and how they are establishing a toehold in financial services, but here are some examples of the breadth and scope of the changing marketplace.

K mart, whose name is synonymous with discount shopping, has now opened in-store financial centers. "Attention K mart shoppers: We now offer checking accounts, insured CDs and money-market funds (called K mart Certificates and K mart funds), IRAs, insurance, and other financial services in the back of the store." K mart will enter the

money game on the cheap by "renting" banks and insurance companies
to outflank the banking regulations. They can then duplicate financial
services without incurring the cost of setting up a brick-and-mortar
building, passing the savings along to the consumer. As a K mart
spokesman says, "We will provide a good value for K mart customers."
And with K mart's 2,000 stores, visited by up to 15 million people a
week, nationwide branch banking takes on a new meaning.

Kroger Food Stores in the Midwest and Stop & Shop markets in the
Boston area now operate in-store financial centers. You can pick up a
quart of milk and a hundred shares of AT&T, buy life insurance, invest
in mutual funds, and open an IRA. That's as close to one-stop money
supermarket as the supermarket can make it. The supermarkets are
after the 25- to 35-year-olds who have not yet begun a systematic
savings program, who need more insurance than older Americans, and
who have not yet begun to plan for retirement. Most people in this age
group are in the habit of making financial decisions after talking with
someone they know: their spouse, relative, a neighbor, or a fishing
buddy. To try to understand the secret of the financial supermarkets'
success, consider this: Most people who use financial services in places
like K mart and Krogers do so because they find conventional bankers
and stockbrokers too intimidating.

Bankers have become downright unfriendly to small and medium-
size savers, and stockbrokers, with plush offices, computers on every
desk, and green-lighted numbers flashing along big signs, present a
hostile appearance to many people. If you stop to talk with one of these
brokers, you'll swear he's having trouble with the English language. He
wants to grab your hard-earned cash, touting a "money multiplier
trust" (don't you just love that phrase?). Or else he wants to help you
make big bucks by investing in almond groves because you've suddenly
realized that the inflated value of your home is money in the bank. No
wonder millions of Americans are flocking to the money centers.

Instead of getting into the business by *renting* a bank and insurance
company, Sears, Roebuck and Co. went out and *bought* them. They
acquired Dean Witter Reynolds (a stockbroker) and Coldwell Banker (a
nationwide chain of real estate offices) and put them together with
Allstate Insurance Company (the nation's second-largest property and
casualty insurer) and Sears Savings Bank. Then, to make their money
center package complete, they began buying savings and loans and
banks. They acquired a Delaware bank, and to sidestep the Bank Board,
plan to sell the bank's commercial loan portfolio to turn the bank into a
non-bank.

Sears, in other words, is assembling a nationwide banking system.
Called Sears Financial Network, the system has expanded to over 300

offices nationwide, and that's just the tip of the iceberg. There are 851 retail Sears stores, 4,110 Allstate insurance offices outside their stores, more than 900 real estate offices and branches of Coldwell Banker, nearly 500 Dean Witter offices, and 110 savings and loan branches. Sears' strategic planners figure that you will shop for financial services at Sears for the same reason you buy rototillers and clothing there: Because you believe that you get good value for your money. And Sears has deep pockets in case something goes wrong. How can you doubt that when actor Hal Holbrook tells you in fancy commercials, "Trust us to make it work for you."

Merrill Lynch, whose name has been synonymous with stocks and bonds, is also establishing a financial network. It already has banks, brokers, and financial services, but most Americans may be unaware that Merrill Lynch Realty is the nation's second largest. Its real estate network includes 43 major markets in the United States, more than 12,000 agents and 400 residential sales offices. Although Merrill Lynch sells homes in all price ranges, it aggressively pursues upscale buyers who can become customers for its other financial services, including stock brokerage, real estate loans and insurance. Not surprisingly, Merrill Lynch will emerge as a major player in the money game by setting up its own financial network.

These one-stop financial supermarkets—a real estate broker next to a stockbroker next to an insurance agent next to a bank—can sell you a home, get the mortgage, and insure it; or, if you're not ready to buy a home, it can help you save for one.

Executives at banks and savings and loans are worried. Financial networks like Sears' and Merrill Lynch's may work too well. In a recent sales pitch, Coldwell Banker made a tantalizing offer to new-home buyers: Buy a home from Sears and you'll get a booklet of deep discounts on home furniture and appliances. Sears has taken advantage of deregulation to open new doors. I believe that this kind of merchandising will eventually extend to other financial services.

Not yet in the same league with Sears, J.C. Penney has joined the crowd rushing toward the money center business by opening limited-service financial centers in its stores. And, to be on the safe side, Penney's has also bought a bank in Delaware.

Everyone Wants to Play

The way to enter the money game is no longer very complicated: A company simply buys a bank. General Electric, through its subsidiary, General Electric Credit Corporation (GECC), bought a small bank in

Hawaii. I talked with bankers and thrift executives about this new deep-pocket money player. For the most part, they were filled with amazement and frustration by the way giant corporations can descend on them and buy their way into a major share of the banking and financial services business. With seven offices around the state, GE has big newspaper ads that come right to the point: "GECC & FDIC are a super team for your investments." And they are. With money market passbooks, seven-day and two-month money-market accounts and jumbo savings accounts, the consumer has high rates and federally insured safety. For borrowing money, GCEE offers a personal line of credit as high as $250,000 called "superCredit," with no points, no prepayment penalties, and optional interest-only payments.

How GE got into the banking business makes no difference. What regulatory walls they scaled and what loopholes they found are irrelevant to the fact that today this giant manufacturer of washing machines and atomic power plants controls one of the major consumer banks in Hawaii. The result is that smaller banks and thrifts will die or merge because GE can spend big bucks to advertise and can suck up money on a grand scale.

General Motors is also zeroing in on financial services. You'd be able to open a money market account or buy a CD from GM, carry a GM credit card, mortgage a house, borrow money for your car or business, and do your financial planning in one place. You wouldn't be doing business directly with GM but with its subsidiary, General Motors Acceptance Corporation. GM, however, is already in the banking business in a big way. With $57 billion out on loans here and abroad, it's a giant among banks. Chrysler Financial Corporation, continuing its expansion into financial services, and General Electric Credit Corporation will team up to form a joint venture to finance equipment and real estate, further blurring the boundaries between one corporation and another, one kind of business and another.

We are in the midst of a major shift in consumer lending, one that has gone almost unnoticed by the public. The nation's largest consumer lending company in 1984 in terms of net income was not a bank, it was General Motors Acceptance Corporation. The next four are General Electric Credit Corporation, Ford Motor Credit Company, Household Finance Corporation, and American Express Credit Corporation.

When companies like General Electric and General Motors transfer their nationwide marketing skills to selling money, they can become a major competitor to the money supermarkets operated by K mart, Sears, and American Express—and to the banks and savings and loans. Despite (or, perhaps, thanks to) congressional inaction, nationwide banking is fast becoming a reality with the entry of the giant corporations. In fact, there is virtually no limit to the number of new players that can join the game. As an executive of one of the major corporations planning the jump into banking told me, "It's a market that's about to explode. Now that the barriers are down anyone can come in and we intend to get in early and establish ourselves as the best place for consumers to do their money business. We're taking our best people and putting them on the front lines."

When organizations like K mart, Sears, and General Motors, with their financial clout, jump into nationwide banking and financial services, it also triggers an outbreak of bank and thrift buying. The big brokers and mutual funds, worried that they will be left behind, have bought banks. Whether we endorse these new directions or not, we must accept them. In a sense, we have come full circle and are back where we were in the 1920s. Once again small banks or thrifts are terrified that the Citibanks and K marts of the country will elbow them out of business by offering better rates and more complete financial services. The difference between the 1920s and today, however, is that the nation is in a decline in regulations, and with this decline, the big corporations, bounding across the country like foxhounds on the chase, will sweep everything before them.

Are We Ready for the McDonald's of Money?

We franchise pizza parlors, computer stores, and fast food outlets, so why not financial services? The idea seems like a natural to attract the Pepsi Generation and the well-established middle class. Franchising can create nationwide banking without individual banks or thrifts crossing state lines. By joining forces, smaller firms will be able to compete with the monster companies in the financial arena. For the thrifts, San Francisco-based Nationwide Savings, with 180 offices in California, New York, Hawaii, and Florida, already offers First Nation-wide Network. With a score of S&Ls signed up across the country, the franchise network expects to have combined assets exceeding those of any single savings and loan in the country.

The leading franchise bank is First Interstate Bank, also based in California. Some 60 years ago, before Congress prohibited bank holding companies from interstate banking, First Interstate inherited a holding company with 21 banks in 11 Western states. The bank's geographic territory makes it a natural for franchising, because banks can join other nearby banks, retain their hometown ownership, yet hoist the First Interstate banner.

Another example of franchising waiting to happen is a bank

without cash. The Lone Star National Bank in Dallas became the nation's first cashless bank. With only 700 square feet of space, the bank cut costs dramatically by doing away with expensive armored cars, vaults, and security guards, insurance, and burglar alarms. Customers can make cash withdrawals from the automatic teller machines and can make deposits at the bank or by mail. They can conduct banking business by phone or with the tellers in the bank. The payoff is higher interest rates on savings and lower costs on banking services. The bank's chairman says, "The idea is natural in an age of electronic transfers and deregulation. Our society is dealing less and less in cash. I think the idea will catch on."

Some people in Omaha, Nebraska, might think they are in a bank when they visit a Citicorp subsidiary in a local shopping center, but they're not. What appears to be a branch bank is really a "sales office." Citicorp, of course, is not yet allowed to own a "branch" bank in Nebraska. The trickiest part of deregulation is finding the angles others may have missed, and Citicorp found one by calling the money center a sales office instead of a branch bank. Citicorp presumably can set up sales offices around the country themselves or franchise them as the centerpiece of shopping malls. Roger Beverage, Nebraska's state banking director, says the Citicorp Centers are "a slick operation." They sidestep the banking laws because, he notes, the sales officers don't physically take money, and machines, not people, dispense cash. Customers use pre-stamped envelopes to mail in their deposits and automatic teller machines for withdrawals.

With Citicorp muscling in, there is clearly going to be a scramble for deposits in Omaha, and frustration for Nebraska bankers as they see a strange-looking booth in a shopping center collecting deposits in their state. As one local banker put it, "They (the Citicorp Centers) look like banks, they offer all the bank services, they advertise like banks. The only conclusion we have is they are banks." Citicorp, using its high-powered merchandising mode, flooded the Omaha TV market with catchy spots offering depositors interest rates on certificates of deposit that were more than one percentage point higher than what local banks and savings and loans offer. The local banks simply can't compete against that kind of advertising power by standing alone. Bankers have to realize they are no longer in the banking business, but in the business of merchandising money. That realization can expand their opportunities enormously. Hiding behind state barriers can not.

Franchising banks—either full-service or cashless banks—or opening "sales offices" in shopping malls will turn retail banking into a mad scramble reminiscent of the fast-food franchising of the 1970s. Cashless banks and sales offices will be able to do nearly everything a full-service bank or S&L can do except make commercial loans. "Consumer loans are just a cover-up," says a small-town banker in Illinois. "How can anyone tell, when these 'banks' are making loans to the dentist or the doctor, whether or not they are making commercial loans?" Thus, the new breeds of non-banks will lure away the essential core of profitable customers from the smaller banks and thrifts by cutting overhead to the bone and offering the customer a much better deal on saving and borrowing money.

The emerging new era in banking is not only the result of Congress's inability to close a loophole, but also the result of a sudden realization that banking can be packaged and merchandised like fast foods and instant printing. Accordingly, big banks and non-bank companies that understand the forces shaping the new way of banking will gobble up much of the banking business as we know it today. Evidence is mounting that we will get the Citicorp equivalent of a McDonald's on every other corner. Again, a period of change that appears chaotic really has its own rhythm and sense.

When the financial environment changes, companies or organizations that seek to attract business must reformulate their purpose in light of the new situation. Strong, competitive banks, mutual funds, and savings and loans are already changing. Those that remain stationary will die. A financial consultant told me, "Companies can't prevent change. The market, and ultimately the public, sets the pace of change. They vote with their feet and any company can be bypassed unless it stays on top of changing markets and technology. And in some respects, technology is the biggest change of all, driving the marketing before it. The changes are so fundamental, yet so elusive, that many financial executives' thinking, their attitudes, and consequently their ability to reorient their businesses to just what they should do, have not caught up with reality of things."

For example, it makes no sense to allow non-banks, operated by non-financial firms, to offer a wide range of financial products on a nationwide basis, while traditional banks and thrifts sit with their hands tied up in regulatory knots. It also makes no sense to allow restricted de facto nationwide banking, which is happening now when healthy banks and S&Ls take over failed banks and savings and loans in other states.

This phenomenon started in 1982, when Fidelity Savings and Loan Association, a large northern California S&L, was forced by the Federal Home Loan Bank Board to close its doors. To keep Fidelity from collapsing and forcing payments of huge insurance claims, the FSLIC began to look for a white knight with deep pockets to cut their losses and rescue the sick S&L. Citicorp was ready, irresistibly drawn by the magnet of premature nationwide banking. Fidelity Savings and Loan became Citicorp Savings, and in three years has grown to a $3 billion institution with over 250,000 customers. Since then, Citicorp has also acquired troubled S&Ls in Illinois and Florida. Nationwide Savings has spread its branches nationwide by a bailout of Washington Savings and Loan in Florida and West Side Federal Savings in New York. California-based World Savings and Loan jumped to the Midwest and in 1985 acquired Bell Savings in Texas. World Savings, whose appetite for devouring sick financial institutions across the country is spurred on by the vision of nationwide banking, now has almost 200 branches in California, Colorado, Kansas, and Texas.

Bank of America, not to be left behind, set out in 1983 to acquire Seattle-First National Bank, the largest bank in the Pacific Northwest. "Seafirst" had been stung by the failure of the Penn Square Bank of Oklahoma City, which dropped $400 million of bad loans on its books. The state of Washington, eager to keep its biggest bank from collapse, quickly passed a new law allowing an out-of-state bank takeover and B of A moved in. Bank of America has since acquired a large bank in Oregon.

In spite of all these anomalies, Congress has been reluctant to step in and change the federal laws on interstate banking because of the political influence of the small banks, which make up most of the 14,500 commercial banks and are opposed to any change in existing laws. "Congress prefers to let it happen, to let the market make the changes," believes economics professor Edward Kane of Ohio State University. "If no one protests too loudly, then Congress will add its stamp of approval. The federal laws against interstate banking have looked silly for quite a while."[5] In fact, banks and S&Ls just step around the law, paying a hefty price above a failed firms' assets to set up offices outside their home states. Regulators, too, ignore the old restrictions on state lines because the high bids for the failed banks and thrifts help them overcome the losses the federal insurance fund incurs when it steps in and saves the day.

Turf wars between bankers reached a new high with the collapse of Ohio's and Maryland's private insurance funds. Eyeing the chance to once again jump state lines, big banks began a feeding frenzy on the corpses of the troubled state-insured savings and loans that closed their doors after a run on their deposits. The time-honored way to deal with a bank run is to throw money at it. The bank or S&L in question starts to liquidate assets, borrows to the hilt from the Feds to meet the withdrawal crisis, and then waits for the run to play itself out.

For many state-insured S&Ls in Ohio, time had run out. Chase Manhattan Bank planned to acquire Mentor Savings Bank, near Cleveland, and Federated Savings Bank, in Cincinnati, and establish a commercial-banking base in the state. Chemical Bank of New York was after the failed Home State Savings Bank in Cincinnati. Once these privately insured thrifts were acquired, they would be reopened as federally insured banks with full banking powers.

In Maryland, the same takeover of the privately insured savings and loans was underway. Chase Manhattan Bank was gaining a leg up on banking rivals in the race to begin commercial operations in the state by seeking to buy troubled thrifts, including Merritt Commercial Savings and Loan of Baltimore, Chesapeake Savings of Annapolis, and Friendship Savings and Loan of Bethesda.

Ironically, it was the state itself that now wanted carpetbagging big city banks to rush in and rescue its failed S&Ls. Maryland officials were eager for troubled thrifts to be purchased because the state had agreed, as part of its bailout plan, to guarantee their deposit accounts for as much as $100,000 each. In a power shift away from Washington, D.C., the Maryland state legislature passed landmark legislation that gives the nation's biggest bank, New York–based Citicorp, full banking powers in Maryland, the right to open 20 full-service branches, and direct access to the lucrative Baltimore-Washington market. But the buy-in cost won't be cheap. Citibank has promised to invest $25 million in the state and to offer at least 1,000 new jobs in its economically depressed area. Citicorp says it will meet this buy-in requirement by moving its East Coast headquarters for its Visa and MasterCard operations to Hagerstown.

What makes the new Maryland legislation unusual is not that it kills off the last vestiges of restriction against interstate banking but that it allows any out-of-state bank operating on a limited-service basis to convert to full-service banking if it promises to invest millions in the state and hire 1,000 employees. In politics, it doesn't really matter any more who is jumping state lines with banks and savings and loans, because everyone is doing it. What matters is to what extent the taxpayers will benefit from the states' gamble that Congress will make it legal anyway.

Meanwhile, as we tread water, banks and S&Ls, little and big, are reaching across the miles to complete takeovers. The little Bank of Oregon in Woodburn, Oregon, became a unit of the Alaska Pacific

Bancorp. of Anchorage, Alaska. On a larger scale, to cut its losses the Federal Home Loan Bank Board hung out the "for sale" sign on the two divisions of State Savings and Loan in Utah and Hawaii. The winners: in Utah, Sandia Federal Savings and Loan Association of Albuquerque, and, in Hawaii, First Nationwide Savings.

By the time Congress gets around to legalizing nationwide banking, it won't make any difference. Banks and S&Ls have already reached from border to border and over the ocean to Hawaii in their quest for acquisitions. Small, highly merchandised, consumer-oriented banking and money center offices are popping up in high-traffic areas such as shopping centers, large office buildings, and malls. These low-cost, low-overhead money centers will not compete with the long-established, high-overhead full-service banks and savings and loans, but with the money centers in K marts and Sears and with the high-powered bank boutiques of General Electric and General Motors.

They are all operating in an open environment where the low-cost, high-interest players often get the business. The resulting squeeze from the new money players will push the old full-service banks and S&Ls into either entering the new competition or generating higher fees and charges on their declining customer base. If they choose the latter course, their customers will slowly slip away, and most small and medium-size banks and thrifts will be snapped up by the money centers or they will vanish. All of which will leave many people wondering whatever happened to the gentlemanly bankers of the 1960s.

6

Working for Yourself

How Entrepreneurs Profit from Current Trends

In the 1800s, industrialization spawned mass production and in the 1920s, mobility and prosperity provided the setting for major corporations to flourish in. Today extraordinary factors are again at work in our society. The trends seem unrelated: the return to specialization among some of the nation's giant businesses; the diversification of other businesses—at blinding speeds; the use of the ubiquitous computer as a marketing tool; the decline of security in the workplace; the graying of a major segment of the population; and the increasing sophistication of the American consumer. Yet all of these trends are closely linked and are being driven by a force that is giving fuel to an emerging economic revolution. That revolution can be summed up in one word: *entrepreneurship.*

Finding New Opportunities

Many of today's opportunities lie with small businesses. The manufacturing and marketing of products for relatively small, select markets

presents one such opportunity. Another is found in the service industry, which can provide consumers with an unending expansion of
services that large firms no longer want to offer.

"There has never been a better time in U.S. history to realize an
ambition of getting rich," says Don Gevirtz, author of *The New Entrepreneurs: Innovation in American Business.* He's right, but today, more
than ever before, you need the guts to rely on your own instincts to
choose a field that's just catching fire. Opportunities resulting from the
dramatic changes taking place in all business operations have never
been better. And the new products and services are almost unlimited.
Some of these products will themselves create more products and
services in a high-tech world where many businesses will be based on
ideas and technology only now coming into focus. The age of the
entrepreneur has arrived. Yet the determination to achieve success is
not enough. Perhaps the most critical element in turning a business
into a fortune today is the ability to seek out those fields that are
expanding faster than the economy. The good news is that most of these
expanding fields require more savvy than capital, and by looking at the
trends beneath today's successes, you can identify the probable sites of
tomorrow's winners.

Take, for example, the drive-up photo-developing business. For
years the business depended on developing and selling film. Customers
wanted to see the latest snaps of their vacation, and they wanted to see
them quickly. One-day and even same-day service became a trademark
of the drive-up photo business. But in the 1980s, smart entrepreneurs
began to rethink what business photo drive-ups were in and to conceptualize other products or services that would be useful to the public.

By identifying consumer needs and behavior patterns and then
applying information about shopping habits, those entrepreneurs are
now on their way to coming up with the next Cabbage Patch doll. They
realized they were in a *service* business, not just the business of
developing film. First, they put in do-it-yourself photocopying machines and offered lower prices than the print shops. Business boomed.
New customers using the copy machines brought in their film for
processing. Next, with the advent of video rentals, they found they
could rent and sell VCR tapes below the prices of the video stores. And
when the Civil Aeronautics Board deregulated the travel business so
that anyone could be a travel agent, many photo drive-up stores became
airline ticket agents. You can order your tickets by phone, pay for them
with a credit card, and zip over to the photo drive-up on your way out
of town.

Moving from a Specialized
to General-Purpose Businesses

Look around you. One-product merchandising dinosaurs seem to be stuck in a quagmire. Big outfits like Sears, K mart, and J. C. Penney are moving into financial, real estate, insurance, and travel services. One-stop shopping thrives. Take gas stations. Once, full-service stations sold gasoline and fixed cars. Now they also house convenience stores, ATM banks, and food stores—and customers pump their own gas.

We are in the midst of a major shift from one-product or one-service stores to one-stop shopping, and those who can adapt to the changes will be the winners in the race to cash in on the coming fortunes. The rule of the 1980s applies to drive-up photo stores, gasoline stations, banks, brokers, and discount stores. Convenience and low prices win every time over single-product marketing at fixed prices.

Five years ago video rental shops were in an emerging field that was just beginning to take off. Those who got in on the ground floor profited from the market's explosive growth as video shops grew from 7,000 outlets in 1984 to over 80,000 by 1985. But then swarms of multiproduct competitors got in on the act and the one-product video shops are now on a fast track to oblivion. Record shops, book stores, photo drive-ups, grocery stores, and drug stores, renting movies for $1 a day, are squeezing out the video stores. For small video stores, it's tough to make money renting movies at $2 and $3 a day; but for stores that are expanding their products, videotapes are a tool to build business, cut their overhead, and expand their marketing clout. For one-product video rental shops, the shakeout will continue unless they adopt diversified one-stop shopping.

The concept of one-stop discount shopping is already apparent in the way we buy our cars. Long a one-product business, auto dealerships are now megadealers, some even taking over old discount department stores. In San Francisco, The Autocenter has a single showroom selling Toyotas, Nissans, Isuzus, Mazdas, Chrysler-Plymouths, Saabs, Alfa Romeos, and, for the big spender, Rolls Royces. In southern California, about ten so-called auto centers have 5 to 15 dealerships each. "The driving force behind these parks," says a dealer, "is the cost of real estate and the desire of customers to have selection and convenience. The razzle-dazzle style of selling cars is history; consumers have become smarter."

Full-service auto dealers are also taking a beating from another side: the franchise discount car dealer. Discounters, who buy cars only as they sell them, offer substantially lower prices than full-service dealers for the same makes and models. Like video stores, full-service, one-product auto dealers will find that other people can offer greater choice and lower prices.

Using Computers to Make the Sale

We are in the midst of a major shift in the way we buy things. A new term in computer language is *transactional terminals,* computer screens that help make a sale as opposed to those that simply present information. In the explosion of computerized selling that's sure to come, retailers will use this new technology to sell everything from shoes to cars.

Auto dealers will be able to show a customer a graphic of every model they sell, every new color and every option, and then compare those models with any other car on the market. The computer can even make it easy for the customer to decide if it's better to finance or pay cash. In some stores, clothing shoppers can stand in front of a full-length computer screen and "try on" as many as ten different outfits in just one minute. They see a reflection of their face, but from the neck down the computer takes over, shaping a figure that conforms to their own on which it projects any number of outfits they want to see. Cosmetics makers will use transaction terminals to create an image of the customer's face wearing the suggested makeup. Women can look at a split screen and compare four different suggested treatments at one time. Computers will be used to make up any paint color and match it exactly to the color in the customer's hand. Computers will help measure curtains. Transactional terminals will expand the retailer's inventory by letting him sell goods he doesn't have on the shelf. Customers can get a look at the product, in any color or style they want, and then have it delivered to their homes.

Saying Good-Bye to Job Security

The recent rise in part-time or full-time business entrepreneurs can be traced to two important changes in our economy. First, pink slips today can come at any time, at any age. The days of 30-year service pins are about over; companies can let thousands of employees go in one move. Teachers are fired. Middle managers, with years of service to their company, are cast adrift in a sea of mergers. Perhaps hundreds of thousands of managers over 40 now find themselves unable or unwilling to cope with the technological revolution sweeping their plants and offices. On the human side of the information society, there is no security in the workplace any more.

In the growing high-tech industry, 25-year-old rising stars are scrambling over middle-aged department managers with less training who will become obsolete has-beens if they can't come to grips with the computer. In fact, in the emerging information society, middle managers and supervisors are fast becoming the lost generation of American business. "Technology is scaring the hell out of these 35- to 45-year-old middle managers," says a management recruiter. "A lot of them either get shoved aside, with younger people getting their jobs, or they get fired. As unbelievable as it may sound, they are finished at 40."

The wide generation gap is evident everywhere, but especially in the service and financial industries, where the computer is taking over rapidly. The information society has taken people who have performed adequately for years and turned them into non-performing managers. Companies are putting more effort into retraining, but many employees can't manage the switch from first to second-generation computer operations. And once out in the cold, their lack of knowledge of computer systems put them at a big disadvantage in today's job market.

The loss of job security and high-tech obsolescence are not the only reasons for the swing to self-employment. Five years ago, when employment in auto companies and other smokestack industries was declining, everyone thought high-tech and computers were the way to go. But people are discovering every day that jobs in high technology are no more immune from shakeouts than jobs in heavy industry. Companies hire and fire on a massive scale as business expands and slows. Many workers in both heavy industry and high-tech fields have been laid off two or three times in the last few years.

Finally, the transition from an industrial to an information society has brought about a realization on the part of companies that they can do without a lot of middle managers. Between 1979 and 1984, about 5.1 million workers with at least three years seniority lost their jobs because of plant closings or employment cutbacks. Many of these workers were in middle management and they were let go not because they weren't doing a good job, but because firms were trying to adjust to intense foreign and domestic competition by "cutting out the fat." In every recession work forces have shrunk, expanding again as times got better; but today, with the economy on the rebound, scores of middle managers are sitting ducks. They are being pruned as if the country was in the midst of a deep recession. Big companies as diverse as American Telephone & Telegraph (where, of the 24,000 jobs eliminated, the lion's share, or 30 percent, were in management), Ford, Union Carbide, and CBS have all made massive cutbacks of middle managers through dismissals, early retirement, or voluntary separations. Since 1980, 89 of the 100 largest U.S. companies have reorganized to reduce the number of management layers. The information revolution now lets fewer people do the same job with more data in less time. "There is no turning back," says W. James Fish, Ford Motor Company's personnel manager. "We're looking at a total restructuring of American business."[1]

Another compelling reason for self-employment is the tax code. As an employee, you receive a salary from which every tax that Congress, the state, and your city government have levied is taken off the top before you get your hands on the cash. (Clipping off part of our pay goes back to the times of the Romans. Part of the soldiers' pay was a lump of salt, giving the word *salary*, from the Latin *salarium*—soldiers' salt money—to the English language.) Obviously, when you pay your own taxes, it's a pretty attractive thing to write off your business and personal expenses *first*. To make real money it's important for most people today to have their fingers in some kind of business operation. As a self-employed (part-time or full-time) person, you can write off your car, your health insurance, your travel, your entertainment. You can buy buildings and take depreciation. You can delay taxes on almost every dollar you save for the future. Contrast that with the Roman soldier of ancient times who was on a fixed salary, where every deduction for taxes, benefits, and of course salt, came right off the top of his pay check.

The New Captains of Industry

The first industrial revolution in the late eighteenth and early nineteenth centuries introduced the reign of mass production, division of labor, standardized products, and big corporations. Today a profound shift is occurring toward smaller-scale companies that rely on ideas to replace huge amounts of capital. The good news for potential entrepreneurs, therefore, is that one ingredient that was necessary for success in an industrialized society—access to capital—has now been replaced to a large extent by information, experience, know-how, and ideas.

That means you don't necessarily need much money to make

money today. Some money is necessary, of course, but brains count for more. What is necessary is your burning desire to become self-employed, and the ability to face insecurity with confidence so you can overcome the many setbacks that are sure to come. You must be able to harness a continuing stream of motivation so the peaks and valleys won't affect your business, your family, and your life. In other words, you need to guard against the many forms of depression that visit most entrepreneurs in their early years. True entrepreneurs will take such setbacks in stride; dreamers will be shattered. There are no typical entrepreneurs, just as there are no typical Americans; we come in all sizes and styles. What sets those who become self-employed apart from others is their tenacity in achieving their goal of becoming self-employed. It overrides all other goals. When lack of money is a problem, businesses can be built with a minimum of cash. Ideas, backed by very little money, have launched successful service industries where none existed a few years ago: in videotaping, computer software, specialized ice cream shops, earth stations for home television sets, new financial services, and hundreds more.

Today, the best way to get both security and tax breaks is to start your own business—either full time or on the side. Over 17 million people operate part-time businesses while they bring home a corporate paycheck. And almost 1 million full- and part-time small businesses are started each year. Of 11 million businesses in which the owner is employed full time, 10.8 million are small businesses, with 60 percent of all workers employed in these small firms. Approximately two-thirds of all new jobs now occur in firms employing less than 20 people. What's less well known is that women are starting more and more of the new companies. The National Association of Women Business Owners says that more than 25 percent of its members run businesses with annual sales of over $800,000. With women starting businesses at four to five times the rate of men, a lot more women will emerge as millionaires in the years to come.

More and more people are learning that entrepreneurship provides security of employment, a higher income, and a better lifestyle. People who have made the switch report greater job satisfaction, more freedom, and, in many cases, more income.

Getting into business for yourself is not as difficult as it once was. Ronald Reagan may have been elected to get the government off our backs, but it was Jimmy Carter's administration that first began the trend away from big business by deregulating the airlines and the trucking industry. Deregulation allowed smart entrepreneurs to cut into these businesses by establishing new carriers that could compete. Deregulation has since spread into the financial, travel, insurance, and telephone businesses, and the trend is clearly set for greater opportunities for the self-employed in the years to come.

The good news today, when you finally decide to chuck your regular pay check, is that you have a choice. In the service field, you can still start with a modest amount of cash. When you buy a business that uses real estate or makes a product, the entry-level cost can rise. Nevertheless, the most important ingredient is desire, the gut feeling that you can't be beat. You've got to find the new trends that are about to take off. You must have a clear vision of what you want to achieve, then organize every step toward that goal. In today's fast-moving business world, planning must be tied to vision so you know exactly where you are going with a clarity that remains in spite of the confusion of the market place.

The basic rule today: Products and services are not as important as staying on top of the trends. Think of some red-hot products that have taken America by storm: personal computers, Cabbage Patch dolls, designer jeans. In each case, entrepreneurs had the inspiration to create them. In classic marketing fashion, they found a void (not necessarily a need) and filled it.

Americans over 50 (the fastest growing market today) account for more than 42 percent of the consumer demand in the United States and over $800 billion in buying power. Households aged 50 to 65 years old have an income 20 percent higher than the national average, and those with an average age of between 65 and 75 have more income per person than those under 45. If you're in the high-priced end of business, older consumers could well be your market. Some 77 percent of all households' financial assets are controlled by Americans 50 and over. More important for the entrepreneur is the fact that over-50 households have half the nation's discretionary income—the money that's left over after paying for the necessities.

The ramifications of this rapidly expanding and well-to-do consumer group are just now being felt throughout society, and for the smart entrepreneur the shift will create tremendous opportunities in the 1980s. Unless you're counting on selling to the tail end of the baby boom, you'll need to figure out a way to make your consumer product or service attractive to this market—or create a new product or service for older Americans. With generally helfty incomes and decreasing needs, it's a promising market for many luxury goods and services and, as the graying of America picks up steam, it will be a growing market.

Finding Tomorrow's Fortunes Today

The irritating thing about sudden change in what we buy or use is not that the new is wrong, but that the cherished old is often abolished. Technology occasionally does bring genuine improvements. New drugs extend our lives, the VCR makes it possible to watch movies in our homes, and microwave ovens let us cook our food in a hurry. Along the way, however, we can lose some valued old friends—unless, as happens occasionally, public outcry brings them back.

Several years ago the experts that tell us what kind of car we want decided that we no longer wanted convertibles, so the car makers stopped making them. When convertibles were no longer available, a growing number of consumers wanted once again to ride with the top down. Small businesses began changing standard cars into convertibles and selling them. Eventually the big automobile companies caught up and starting producing convertibles again. Recently, Coca-Cola introduced a "new and improved" product: New Coke. When the public could not buy old Coke, everyone wanted it. It was not so much that the new Coke was bad, it was that the old Coke was somehow better. So the company bowed to public pressure; it now makes the old and the "new and improved" Coke.

As big corporations junk the old for new, tremendous new opportunities will spring up for thousands of new businesses to fill the void. There are many old products that people still want to buy. Small businesses can either import these products or have them crafted by hand in small shops. Many products have become (or will become) too expensive for big business, saddled as it is with high overhead and union wages, to make. In the midst of all these changes, smart entrepreneurs will figure a way to make and sell products to those of us who resist change for the sake of change. Because change threatens all kinds of cherished ways of life, for this group of consumers, quality and service will outweigh price. In the next decade, as changes continue to rumble across the country, the business of nostalgia will boom.

Instead of finding a product or service and then marketing it, find a market and then invent the product. Your objective will be to invent a product or service that's so good wallets will tumble open at the sight of it. Cookies, for example, have been in grocery stores for decades, yet the smell of fresh chocolate chip cookies wafting through a shopping center signals a new big business. It's not the cookies but the idea of cooking them right before the customer's eyes.

The rule of thumb for any would-be entrepreneur is that having a product or service won't do you any good unless you can create a need, or the impulse to buy. The Patent Bureau is filled with millions of patents that never earned a dime, frequently because the product was designed before the market was defined. Would-be entrepreneurs designed new-fangled gadgets ahead of the market only to realize that people would not accept technological advances simply for their own sake. The development of electronic funds transfer within the banking system is a good example. The new-fangled gadgets made it easier for banks to usher in the cashless society, but at the same time they deprived us of our right to write a check without giving us a corresponding replacement. And, by and large, the public has rejected them.

To understand where the best opportunities lie in the future, you have to examine closely the environment of the coming decade. We are a nation that is undergoing profound change—social, political, economic, and technological. We are no longer held together by a culture that assumes what is good for one is good for all. For small business, the tide of specialization is running counter to the tide of generalization for big business. Small business will supply the parts for big business. The chocolate chip cookies live off the department stores and shopping malls. Employee training firms and janitorial services live off the big corporations.

Zero-In On Your Market

If you know how to do something that gives you an edge, or offer a product that fills a need, you have completed the first step in becoming an entrepreneur. If you are still looking, here are some guidelines for ways to find a service or product:

1. Search first in your own sphere of interest for "market voids." When you see a service or product that's not doing the job it's supposed to do because it's too slow, too clumsy, or the turnaround time is too long, you have an open invitation to come up with a better idea. Because you have firsthand knowledge in the field, you know what the product must do to sell and who is likely to buy it.

2. Don't invent a new wheel, remodel an old one. Profitable businesses have been built by modifying existing products and services to fit a changing market. People are already using the product or service. Your job is to make it faster, more efficient, less costly, and, therefore, more attractive. If you don't have to

educate your customers on the basic concept, you'll have a significant head start in the race for profitability.

3. Identify where your market is. If you're offering a business product or service, you can identify your customers within that sphere of business. If you're shooting for the consumer, you need to consider income and lifestyle. Of the two, lifestyle is often the dominant factor in your success. You've got to determine which of these four major lifestyle categories represents your target market:

Need-driven buyers.	Need-driven consumers want good value for their money and are rarely given to impulse buying. A low price would attract this group.
Belongers.	These consumers are brand-name buyers who look to the company for product quality and service. They feel they can reduce their risk when they buy from a well-established firm. Image is important here.
Personal achievers.	These trend-setting consumers place fashion, innovation, and personal improvement ahead of value. They tend to spend lavishly for products and services that will keep them ahead of the crowd. Marketing would be your most important tool.
Socially aware consumers.	These consumers favor products and services that reinforce their strong health or environmental instincts. The integrity of your product will sell it to this group.

Let's see how these rules apply for a new product. Say you want to enter the fast-growing (and yet so old-fashioned) ice cream field. If you sell your product to groceries, you'll focus on need-driven consumers who want reasonable prices. Quality and value are your buzz words. On the other hand, if you want to sell your ice cream to fashion-conscious gourmet shops, you'll focus on the upscale personal achievers. Status and high prices will be your buzz words. You may have two different labels, but in the end only one type of ice cream. Again, marketing, not the product, is the key.

If you turn to services, you'll find a growing market. One entrepreneur videotapes vacant offices and makes it easier for companies who are looking for more space to shop the market. Another, cashing in on the break-up of American Telephone & Telegraph, provides a computer printout of phone service based on customers' needs, then counsels them on the types of phone service that will provide the lowest cost. Yet another has set up a nationwide life insurance agency that sells insurance by mail. With the recent drop in premium rates, his ads say, "You're probably paying two or three times as much as you have to for life insurance coverage." Using an 800 number, he provides a computer printout that compares 12 of America's top-ranked companies and their rates. You then decide which is best for you. "It's easy to compare and shop at home," this small-business owner says. "No salesperson will call."

Pay Attention to Trends

By looking at the trends underlying today's changing marketplace, you can get some idea of where the new business opportunities lie.

• *Deregulation.* The breakup of the telephone business is a good example of deregulation in action. With over 200 long distance carriers, there is an uncharted cosmos of opportunities for entrepreneurs who can figure out what new services or products the consumer will want—services like comparing costs of long distance companies, providing teleconference and equipment consulting, and making use of satellites to provide low-cost telecommunications.

Bypassing the phone company itself will create opportunities that only now are coming into focus. The federal regulators now let FM radio stations lease unused spectrum space to business customers looking for a way to beat the high cost of telephone lines. Radios can send one-way coded data across the nation over FM receivers at rates close to those of the post office. The customer, to whom the signals can be individually addressed, decodes the message and prints out a copy.

• *Unbundling business.* As big companies slim down, they will hand over an increasing bundle of their specialized duties to smaller, more efficient service companies. Already fortunes have been made in employee training, marketing and product design, site selection, market research, and sales promotion. As big companies continue to shrink, opportunities will abound for helping them stay in business.

• *Financial services.* As deregulation expands and complicates the marketplace, companies will seek people with financial expertise to help them stay abreast of new products and services. And the market will explode with new financial products. Trends will occur both at home and in international markets. Fortunes will be made designing new financial products, creating the services to make them work, and marketing them.

Fortunes will also be made by helping people understand the avalanche of new savings and investment products that are even now descending on the consumer, and by bringing financial products to the consumer in department stores, gas stations, and banks. For many creative entrepreneurs, the financial services industry will be power on a shoestring. Brains and service will be more important than huge amounts of capital.

Starting Up

There are two basic ways to go into business for yourself: Start your own business or buy a going business. True entrepreneurs, who want to satisfy their achievement instincts, will build a business from scratch. Others seeking self-employment will take the safer route. Here are some differences between the two approaches:

• When you buy a business, almost everything you need is already in place. You have a name, a purpose, established customers, and a track record of sales and profits. Your only problem is to determine if the profits are real, the customer base solid, the price right, and of course, whether you like the business. On the other hand, when you start a business, everything must be created. Chances are you'll need more cash than you think while you're waiting for the profits to build, and you'll have to make sure your product or service will find buyers in numbers large enough to keep you from going broke.

• It's usually cheaper to buy a going business than to start one from scratch. The person who started the business did a lot of things in the early years for which he or she was never fully paid, like building a reputation, establishing a market, and developing the product or service. When you start a business from scratch you must do all of those things for yourself.

• It's easier to find the financing for an established business than for a start-up one. Sellers often help in the financing and banks can look at the profit margins and past history of the business before making loans to the new owner. In some cases, parts of the business can be sold off to create cash to pay for part of the acquisition or expansion.

• It takes more skill and energy to start a business from scratch and, therefore, the risk of failure is much higher. The best figures I can come up with are that only two out of ten businesses built from scratch will last five years; for purchased businesses, eight of every ten will survive.

Another way to become self-employed is to buy a franchise. Franchises of all kinds now account for more than one-third of all U.S. retail sales, and it's estimated that by 1987 they will be closer to one-half. As sales grow, people are buying franchises at a record clip of about half a million each year. Franchisers, more than 1,300 of them, are eager to fill the need. Franchises come in all shapes and sizes. Almost every retail or service business you see has its counterpart in franchising today.

While buying a franchise can minimize the risk of a start-up business, the risk can be just as great as starting from scratch if the franchiser lets you down. Franchisers say the failure rate is only 4 percent, but it's closer to 20 or 25 percent. And, unlike buying an established business, you will be tied to the ups and downs of the franchiser and the industry for as long as you own the business. ComputerLand is a good example. The business exploded for several years, then the franchiser got into trouble when people began to lose interest in buying home computers. The fast food business, however, continues to boom; people have to eat. As with an investment in stocks, you have to know when to buy and when to sell a franchise as the public's mood changes.

A new franchiser may need to sell franchises to cover overhead; that could set you adrift. If the franchiser is well established, like a McDonald's or a new car dealer, the price may be too high. Your job is to find one that meets your cash requirements, suits your lifestyle, and will make you the kind of money you want. You have to take your time, analyze the profit claims in your area, get the names of investors and customers, demand detailed financial information, and find out the firm's litigation record. In short, do your homework. Then if you decide to operate a franchise, cut your expected earnings in half and double the time you think it will take to reach the big money. If it still looks good, go for it.

Taking Advantage of Tax Breaks and Write-Offs

Beginning in 1986, the self-employed—those who have a small business on the side and those who set out to make their fortune from business ownership—will find more tax savings than ever before in history. It's no accident. The government intends it. The enormous tax saving is the government's way of encouraging the entrepreneurial spirit as part of its bid to boost the economy. Part of the tax windfall comes from the fact that if you run a business today you can take advantage of the same tax breaks that IBM and General Motors can, and you can do it on a personal basis.

You can organize your small corporation in such a way that you can deduct all of your family's medical premiums and out-of-pocket costs for medical, vision, hearing, drugs, and dental costs, and most insurance protection. The nicest thing about a medical expense reimbursement plan (called MERP) is that it's tax free to you and tax deductible by the corporation. Contrast that with today's version of the Roman soldier who lives on a pay check. He can't deduct most medical expenses and President Reagan wants to tax him on the medical premiums his boss pays on his behalf.

Or consider the new flexible spending account (FSA) that lets you fill your plate with a choice of benefits and then pay the bills with tax-free dollars. These accounts—set up independently as part of a full-scale flexible benefits plan or cafeteria plan—allow workers to receive a portion of their pay on a pre-tax basis because it is considered a reimbursement of certain nontaxable expenses. The dollars used to finance these accounts can come from the company or from the worker or from both.

One way to use FSA money is to pay for out-of-pocket medical expenses, voluntary life insurance, dependent care assistance, legal expenses, financial planning, even adoption costs. The money in the fund must be spent each year, but with so many options for using tax-free dollars, it's not that hard to do.

Business-owner perks abound as big companies set the pace. For example, you can use your company car, purchase the used company car, upgrade your travel to first class, use personal computers at home, and, to keep track of your money, get financial consulting. Tax savings are available to the business owner in every area of business that is directly involved in producing both company profits and personal income. The biggest tax windfall of all, however, is in saving for the future.

When you are self-employed you can allocate your income into ordinary income and tax-deferred savings almost at will. It's always been that way, of course, and it doesn't matter whether you're a big corporation, a little corporation, in business for yourself, or in a large or small partnerhsip. That's because, as a business owner, you decide what type of retirement plan you want.

Here is a list of the possbile choices you have if you are incorporated: a pension plan, money-purchase pension plan, profit-sharing plan, 401(k) salary reduction plan, thrift plan, simplified pension plan, and IRA. If you are not incorporated, you can choose from a Keogh plan, defined-benefit Keogh plan, simplified pension, and IRA.

From this list, let's pick out a tax savings plan for a 55-year-old business owner. Business owners this age may hold winning tickets to the affluence of the 1990s, simply because they were born at the right time. At this stage in their life the business can be making more money than they can reinvest into it or use in daily life. This could be such a time for Jack Smith, who may be earning big bucks as a doctor, lawyer, architect, dentist, or as owner of Ajax Company. Smith may also have a job on the side where he'd like to shelter most of his part-time income. He has few, or in many cases no, lower-paid employees, and those he has are typically young and decades away from retirement age. Or Smith might lease employees instead of hiring them. Leasing employees like so many automobiles may sound a bit cold, but a growing number of small business owners are doing just that. Under leasing arrangements, employees get benefits they otherwise might not have and the owner is free to write a fat pension plan for himself. That's because, under current pension plan requirements, employers must offer the same benefits to all full-time employees even though they may prefer to offer lesser benefits to lower ranking workers. Once leased, however, the staffers are legally the employees of the leasing company, but they still work for and are paid by the employer. Leased employees, unlike temporary ones, are usually hired on a permanent, full-time basis and provided a variety of benefits. Job security and hefty benefits often keep leased employees from regarding themselves as the human equivalent of rented furniture.

If Jack Smith is incorporated, he might select a defined benefit pension plan, the favorite of the fat-wallet crowd. Let's say Jack Smith is a dentist earning $150,000 a year. It's likely that Smith will put a new shiny pension trust in his closely held corporation, pay himself a good salary, dump the rest of his income into his personal pension, and let the government pick up the tab. His annual contributions can be any amount he can scrape together that will buy him a $90,000-a-year pension when he retires. The fewer years to retirement age, the larger the annual contribution. Defined benefit plans are attractive to people nearing retirement because there is a short time to accumulate sufficient retirement sums and they can place 50 percent or more of their income into their pension trust. For a younger person starting out in business, in contrast, other retirement plans based on defined contributions do a better job, such as a simplified employee pension (SEP), in which the owner can put up to $30,000 in an IRA.

With only ten years to retirement, Smith may be contributing well over half his income to his retirement plan, but when he gets a little short of hard cash he can borrow big bucks from the pension trust, paying the going interest rate, which itself is tax deductible. And, incidentally, the interest he pays on the loan is tax-free income to his pension trust. Smith can also have an IRA to add to his growing retirement nest egg.

If Jack Smith is not incorporated, but is self-employed, he can use a defined-benefit Keogh plan and bankroll his retirement with over half his self-employment income. Defined-benefit Keogh plans are virtually equivalent to corporate pension plans, which are designed to pay a pre-established benefit—up to $7,500 a month—in retirement. A pension actuary calculates how much must be deposited each year to accumulate a sufficient sum to pay the benefits at retirement. That compares to a regular defined contribution Keogh plan, where Smith can contribute a maximum of 20 percent of his income or $30,000, whichever is less, with cost-of-living adjustments starting in 1986. For people who are 50 years or older, are at least partly self-employed (income from an unincorporated sideline business or from corporate directorships), and have substantial income they would like to shelter from taxes, Uncle Sam has an attractive variation on simply paying taxes. "It's the best tax shelter going," says an accountant. "My client just figures out what he wants to live on and we deduct the rest into his defined-benefit Keogh plan. He can also have an IRA. Now he can sock away big sums without having to incorporate."

To a certain extent, society has accepted the fact that business owners can avoid taxes on many of the personal expenses that wage earners find fully taxable, and then defer taxes on huge sums of their income by using fancy retirement plans. Whether we endorse these advantages to the self-employed or not, we are obliged to accept them. The fundamental change today is that wage earners are beginning to qualify for company-sponsored retirement plans in which their annual contributions can rise three or four times that of an IRA. And evidence is mounting that we will experience a profound explosion in both self-employed and salaried contributions to retirement plans in the years to come.

Building New Fortunes

If you want to become self-employed today you'll have to rely on your own instincts, choose a field that's just catching fire, and develop a new product or service that fills a need. It's not easy, but becoming an entrepreneur never has been. What's different today is that brains count for more than huge sums of capital. That's because today there are two extraordinarily favorable factors at work: a seemingly unending demand by consumers for specialized products and services and the tendency of big companies to become more efficient by shedding a host of products and services they previously made or provided.

The risks of self-employment clearly remain, but if you can overcome the fear of paying yourself a pay check, the opportunities have never been better.

7

Our Financial Security Blanket Wears Thin

The More We Have,
The Less We'll Get

Our nation built the entire structure of present economic life during the period from the turn of the century to the 1930s, when we had a homogeneous society composed mostly of nuclear families. According to prevailing conventional wisdom, only men would work, women would marry and raise children, and divorce would almost never occur outside of Hollywood. Retirement pensions (either industrial or governmental) were counted on to keep former workers happy and well fed in their golden years.

Now all those comforting myths have been shattered as emphasis shifts from the family to the individual. The post-war baby boom, the social upheavals of the 1960s, the readjustments of the 1970s, and the unprecedented diversity of the 1980s, have in a relatively short time changed our society into a bewildering variety of diverse groups with widely different needs and values. In short, we have become a decentralized society of individuals, yet the basic economics of working and retiring are still rooted back in the Depression.

Our nation's retirement system continues to be based on the Great

American Myth of a working dad and stay-at-home mom with two kids. Today, those traditional families account for only 7 percent of American households. Husband-and-wife households with only one spouse working outside the home account for only 14 percent, down from 43 percent in 1960. And the American lifestyle continues to become more diverse. At least a dozen separate types of households will eclipse the nuclear family of the working dad and stay-at-home mom.

The moneyshock is that in the future both men and women will have to retire later in life and will have to rely primarily on their own savings to do so. Social Security will become a program for the needy. Employer retirement plans will provide most workers with little more than token payments. To a large extent, retirement security will come less from employers and the government and more from individuals themselves. This shift has come about so fast that those of us who have only a decade or less before retirement age arrives will have little time to make the necessary transition from employer-paid and government-supplied benefits to forced savings.

Changing Demographics

If you're thinking of packing it in before your reach age 65, you're decidedly in the mainstream right now. Despite all the talk about doing away with the mandatory retirement age and allowing people to work until age 70, the trend today in America is in the opposite direction, toward early retirement rather than later. The government has been unable to get the message across that planning for retirement in the future will be based on either your continued employment or your own savings. Those of us with at least ten years until retirement cannot hope to duplicate the retirement plans of today's workers, where more than 70 percent of all working Americans drop out before age 65. They represent over twice the number of people who retired early just a decade ago, and the trend permeates all economic and social levels of our society. Today, the "normal" retirement age of 65 has given way to 62, when workers can still grab diminished Social Security benefits. And more and more people are retiring when they are 60, 55, and even younger.

This trend of early retirement also comes in the midst of a fundamental change in retirement policy as our nation moves from an industrial, highly unionized society to a service-oriented, non-union information society. For many current retirees who worked in an industrial society, formal retirement plans were tied to 30-year service pins, which in turn were tied to fixed pensions. In an information society, current workers are for the most part not covered by fixed pensions, and, for those who are, job changing has become such a way of life that pension benefits are seldom earned.

The problem today is that our nation's way of paying retirement benefits remains solidly rooted the early 1900s. But 50 years after the establishment of Social Security, President Reagan and Congress are learning how incredibly difficult it is to change a fixed way of retirement. If you alter or remove any of the well-established rules, the entire system can crumble. But whether or not change is mandated from the top, it will come anyway, just as it is coming to the banking world.

If you are single, the last thing that will give you any comfort is learning that you are a member of the fastest growing segment of our population. The total number of single adults 18 years old and over increased from 53 million in 1970 to 72 million in 1983. This is a remarkable one in four households, compared with one in ten in 1955. Among the never-married, divorced, and widowed, there are more kinds of single women than fit any simple profile. Being a single woman doesn't just mean being without a mate; in our male-oriented workplace, it can also mean being without a pension.

Ten million women are maintaining families today, compared with 5.6 million in 1970. Sixty percent of these women have children under 18 years of age. Of these women, 60 percent are working, nearly 80 percent of them full-time. The shocking figures of a changing American lifestyle: 59 percent of children born in 1984 are expected to grow up in single-parent homes.

An even larger segment is the group made up of two-income couples. Historically, married women were expected to become homemakers and remain financially dependent on their husbands. In 1890, when our retirement system was built, almost 22 million women worked outside the home, but married women accounted for only 4.5 percent of the total. Retirement benefits for these women could be avoided, pension designers reasoned, since most women would leave the labor force and become dependent on their husbands when their first child arrived. The moneyshock of it all: Social Security was never designed for working married women. Married women can, of course, earn Social Security benefits on their own wages, but those benefits are subtracted from what they receive as a spouse when their husbands retire.

The new family model, however, is the two-income couple. Women, in increasing numbers, single and married, are breaking out of the traditional "female" role. They are joining the labor force, going into the professions, and in many cases deciding to have a child later in life, in their thirties—if at all. Today, there are more women in college and graduate school than men, and it is through higher education that women are radically changing their traditional roles. Increasing numbers of women are studying law, medicine, and business—the traditional male bastions. During the last 15 years, the percentage of women lawyers, physicians, accountants, and auditors has steadily increased to the point that about 15 percent of all lawyers and physicians are women, and almost 40 percent of accountants and auditors are female.

The decline of gender-bound jobs is even more pronounced in vocations that were once sharply defined as being either "men's" or "women's." Today, women are butchers, brick masons, auto mechanics, truck drivers, and police officers. As a result, female stereotypes have begun to fade among fellow workers, according to Alma Baron, a University of Wisconsin management professor who conducted a survey of 8,000 male managers. The men who manage businesses responded with some interesting thoughts: 60 percent agreed that women were not reluctant to take risks; 85 percent didn't accept the statement that women lacked technical knowledge and couldn't understand technical matters; and nearly 90 percent no longer believed that sex itself barred a move up the corporate ladder.[1]

With the increase in working women, the comparable work issue has been taken to court. Women are insisting that they should receive comparable pay for comparable work. Why, they ask, should a woman working as a nurse, with a substantially higher education than a man working as a garbage collector, receive a smaller salary? The answer: Because women have always been nurses, men always garbage collectors, and men, along with their unions, have made the rules. And these rules, favoring men with families to support as opposed to single or married women dependent on their husbands, have gone unchallenged for decades. Our present pay inequity leads back to the basic nuclear family, with the working dad and stay-at-home mom. But today, the two-income family, in which the working wife shares the husband's financial responsibility for the family, has become more important. And the role of the married women will continue to change. By the start of the next decade, wives' salaries will, on average, make up about 40 percent of the family income, up from 25 percent today.

Now more than ever, a growing number of people are unable to fit into our nation's retirement policy. As the work force moves from supporting the all-American family to supporting the individual, we face a formidable challenge to our fixed-benefit retirement system. The magnitude of change in the nation's households over the past two decades has been so revolutionary that we can't conceive that our way of retirement has remained stuck in the last century. But it has! The lack of change in the way we provide retirement benefits is fundamental, yet it's so subtle that we tend not to see it—or, if we do, we fail to understand what effect it will have on our retirement security, so we ignore it. My prediction is that by the end of this century, employer-paid pensions will be a thing of the past, a 100-year-old phenomenon killed by soaring inflation, rising salaries, and a rapidly rising life expectancy.

Retirement Plans—The Basic Building Blocks

To understand how the pension pieces fit together and why our nation's pension system is in trouble, it's important to understand how pensions work. The larger patterns of changes in fixed-benefit pensions are not always clear. Helped by the news media, especially television, we see major corporations going out of business, laying off workers, closing down plants and offices. Yet we rarely pause to notice what effect this might have on the workers' pensions, or, for that matter, on our own.

There are two basic types of employer-sponsored retirement plans. One is a *fixed-benefit pension*, in which retirement benefits are usually tied to a percentage of the last five years' salary. Inflation-induced salary increases can boost the costs of a fixed-benefit pension to five or ten times the original cost estimates, which were based on salaries that remained constant. With a fixed-benefit pension the employer is guaranteeing to pay, at retirement, a monthly pension based on the employee's final salary, for the rest of his or her life.

The other types of employer-sponsored retirement plans are *contribution-type plans*. In a *defined-contribution plan*, the employer's only guarantee is to make annual contributions, usually based on a percentage of the annual salary. The benefits are whatever the money in the account will purchase at the time of retirement. In a *profit sharing plan*, the employer can make contributions only when the firm makes a profit, and then in an amount determined annually by the board of directors.

Employers with fixed-benefit pension plans, which guarantee to pay a lifetime benefit based on the worker's final salary, usually set the retirement age at 65. The selection of age 65 as the demarcation between middle and old age is arbitrary. It's believed to have originated in the social legislation of German Chancellor Otto von Bismarck.

Prince von Bismarck, one of the last absolute autocrats, fashioned Europe's first old age and disability plan in 1889 to be paid for by equal contributions from employees and employers. Over the next three decades, most other major industrial nations adopted a similar plan. But the United States, with a tradition of rugged individualism, held out, although this country had some private retirement plans, mostly provided by major corporations. Theodore Roosevelt proposed a system of social insurance when he ran for President in 1912. He lost his bid for the presidency and the idea of prepaying retirement benefits for American workers with government insurance did not resurface until the presidential elections of 1932. This time, Franklin Roosevelt, in a Depression-racked economy where the plight of the elderly had become desperate, campaigned for social insurance similar to that adopted by imperial Germany in the 1890s. To get this radical legislation through Congress, Social Security had to be a system funded entirely by payroll taxes paid equally by the employee and the employer. It was to be a contributory insurance plan. If you look at your pay check today, the deduction for Social Security taxes is referred to as "FICA," which stands for Federal Insurance Contributions Act.

For the retirement age, Bismarck picked the "safe" age of 70—well beyond the life expectancy of the 1890s. In the United States, encouraged by the spread of pensions overseas, workers began pushing for private employer-paid retirement at age 60. For obvious reasons, employers wanted to keep age 70. Since private pension plans were originally established primarily for economic reasons, to keep employees tied to the company, the employers' idea was to pay retirement benefits only as a last resort. As a practical matter, the adoption of age 65 as a compromise for the normal retirement age for America's pension plans assured employers, as it had Prince von Bismarck, that pension benefits would actually be more hope than substance. As late as 1900 our average life expectancy was only 47 and the number of American workers who survived beyond 65 totalled a mere 6 percent of the population.

The private pension plans established between 1875 and 1920 were a form of "pension arrangement." They were considered gratuities, not wages, and business owners were free to turn the payments on and off like a faucet. Workers, for whom the entire pension system had been established, had no rights in the plans—and none were ever intended. By the early 1900s, other forces were also beginning to change the face of American economic life. The economy had entered an era of "state capitalism" in which the power of the government was to be brought to bear on social problems too large for private enterprise.

In the 1930s, New Deal congressmen believed they were creating something new with the passage of Social Security, but in reality they were only expanding the federal government's already existing thrust into our nation's retirement security.

In policymaking, Congress shaped Social Security to a large extent from previous federal retirement legislation, mainly the Civil Service Retirement Act of 1920 and the Railroad Retirement Act of 1934. The civil service and railroad plans were, in turn, based on the private pensions of the late 1890s and early 1900s, which, in turn were based— you guessed it—on von Bismarck's idea of a 1889 pension plan. We are still working on von Bismarck's idea today.

Unlike other aspects of our lives that are changing, retirement plans are not a victim of high technology; they are a victim of inflation, and to a larger extent, the incredible skill the medical profession has developed in keeping most of us alive well into our graying years. The basic question for any fixed-benefit pension plan—private industry's or Social Security—is: Once retired, how long will the average retiree continue to receive a monthly check? In 1946, after World War II, when pension plans and Social Security first began paying off in large numbers, the life expectancy at age 65 was only 13.5 years. Today, according to the National Center of Health Statistics, life expectancy at age 65 is 17 years. That's a staggering 42 additional, inflation-bloated monthly benefit checks per retiree than our retirement system managers estimated they would have to pay just a few decades ago. Even more frightening to pension planners are those workers who retire at age 62 and receive, on average, 90 additional monthly benefit checks.

The attitude that "retirement plans always worked that way before and they will continue to do so in the future" has no place in the new American workplace. Fixed-benefit pensions have been overtaken by inflation and a soaring life expectancy. Their costs have skyrocketed, forcing more and more employers to look for other ways to fund retirement benefits. One of the first signs of change is the discovery by many major corporations in America that they have more retired employees drawing monthly pension checks than they have active workers taking home pay checks.

Changes in What Employers Will Offer

Employers, for the most part, are expected to make contributions to some kind of company retirement plan *and* to match employees' contributions to Social Security. That's the conception most of us have, based on a time when most of it was true. To be sure, some money is still being set aside by private employers with fixed-benefit pension plans; but, for a growing number of employers with contribution plans, the amount they contribute is only a small fraction of what's needed to do the job. Increasingly, workers are being asked to join voluntary contribution plans, such as 401(k) salary reduction plans, where they can use their own tax-deferred income to build up a nest egg for retirement expenses. Those of us who work, in short, are being asked to take responsibility for our own retirement security.

Since 1980, an increasing number of American companies—more than 500 major firms—have terminated their pension plans. Additionally, over 200 corporations now have notices of "intent to terminate" pending with the federal government's Pension Benefit Guaranty Corporation (PBGC), the agency that regulates and insures pensions. The House Committee on Aging reported that in 1984 alone almost 300 plans were scheduled for termination, roughly the same number of terminations as for the previous five years. So far, the largest termination occurred in June of 1985, when United Airlines dumped its pension plan. "Both our employees and our shareholders will benefit from the financial stability this action will provide us," John Cowan, United's executive vice-president said.[2]

In my opinion, the idea of doing away with costly fixed-benefit pensions will gain momentum in the next few years. Both the number of plans being terminated and the amount of money involved will escalate. For now, terminating pension plans has the support of the Reagan administration, but Congress and the unions are becoming uneasy over the prospect of millions of workers ending up with nothing but government benefits at retirement.

Why do employers terminate pension plans? Because they can avoid the horrendous costs of paying future pensions tied to escalating salaries. By paying off taxes and future pension obligations to active and retired workers (companies usually buy annuities for vested and retired workers), they can also use the surplus cash to repay debt, expand operations, or buy their own stock to make the company less attractive as a takeover target by corporate raiders.

What happens to the employees? They usually end up with some form of defined-contribution plan in which only the amount of contribution is set, not the benefits at retirement.

The downhill slide in available pensions is already apparent in the numbers coming out of Washington, D.C. Less than 55 percent of those who retired in 1984 qualified to receive a monthly pension check. The average monthly pension—and those who retired recently found lower benefits, adjusted for inflation, than those who retired in the late 1970s—was just $246. For single people 65 or older, the average company pension was only $156 a month. And of all presently retired workers, only one in six continues to receive a private employer-paid pension!

For women, the prospects are even dimmer. Although the law generally regards a married couple as an integral economic unit, our nation's pension system, including Social Security, continues to think in terms of "workers and dependents." In the eyes of Social Security the wife remains a "dependent," whether or not she holds a job outside the home, and retirement benefits will generally flow to her through her husband. The benefits she might receive under Social Security as a housewife or as a married working woman are usually about the same.

For example, a working male with a dependent spouse who has never worked outside the home can easily end up with more retirement benefits than a two-income couple with both spouses working outside the home and paying hefty Social Security taxes during their working lives. The Social Security rule that cheats most married women says that if a woman works and pays Social Security taxes to earn a benefit in her own right, that benefit will be subtracted from the benefit she receives as a "dependent" married woman. If her own earned benefit is less, she receives nothing for her working and tax-paying years. If her earned benefit is more, she receives only the difference. Of the 12 million women who retired married, only about one in four received the "difference" over their spousal benefits and this amount is only a small fraction of the benefits they earned during their working years.

One of the first signs of a basic change in our retirement system came with the passage of the Retirement Equity Act of 1984. It was a clear statement that American women are now deprived of pension benefits by loopholes that deny their contribution to our economy. The law now makes it easier for women to receive retirement benefits under employer-sponsored plans—either their husbands' or their own. As a symbol of equal rights, the Act now requires a spouse's written permission before a worker can waive payment of benefits for a surviving spouse. The Pension Rights Center believes that before the 1984 law about 10,000 widows each year lost their benefits when their husbands died before early retirement without signing over their benefits. An even larger number of widows lost pension benefits when husbands who had arranged for benefits to be paid only as long as they lived died during retirement. Another major victory for women was the change in the pension laws that allows them to stay within their employer's pension plan when they take time off to have children.

In spite of these improvements, for those of us in our middle years or younger—men and women—the future looks bleak. Changes in the laws help, but by themselves they don't create pension benefits or keep employers from terminating pensions. Ironically, we are about to come full circle to where we were in the 1890s: Most employees in the private work force will once again be unable to collect an employer-paid pension.

As I speak around the country, I am always surprised by people who continue to believe that a comfortable retirement income will somehow magically appear. After all, they say, they or their spouses are covered by some kind of retirement plan where they work. And with Social Security, they'll be on easy street once they're retired. What they don't understand is that companies that continue to provide employer-paid retirement plans are offering benefits that are more and more created with mirrors. Earning a pension is one thing; receiving it is another. The national trend of job-hopping is killing off future retirement income (a person is not on the job long enough to earn pension benefits) and it's accelerating much faster than even I supposed when I wrote *The Graying of America* in 1981.

Here is the way the pension game of mirrors is played. You must first understand the difference between "participating" in your employer's retirement plan and "qualifying" to receive any benefits from it. "Participating" means that the expanded rules now governing private retirement plans allow you to become a member of the plan and begin building credits toward a retirement benefit. "Qualifying" means you have actually earned a vested right, and your employer must pay you once you retire, or give you cash in the event you leave your job prior to retirement. Under current rules, a new employee can wait as long as three years just to become a "participant" in the company's retirement plan, and the employer can demand ten years of service in the plan before the worker "qualifies" or is fully vested. Normally you are not entitled to receive earned retirement benefits before you reach the company's stated retirement age. If you leave your job before you reach retirement age, most companies will buy out their future obligations with a tempting cash payout of the vested amount.

Of the over 48 million men working in 1983, only 60 percent, or some 28.8 million, were participants in pension plans. Of this number, only 17.8 million were vested and qualified to receive some form of benefit. In sharp contrast to these cold statistics, the number of younger and middle-aged men who will collect a pension has fallen to about one in five. For working women, the odds are a mere one in fifteen.

If this moneyshock does not trouble you, the way pensions are paid today should. With rising salaries, inflation, and soaring life expectancy in retirement, employers have put the brakes on pension benefits once you retire. Consider:

• *Inflation.* Private pensions are not indexed for inflation. The reasons? Indexing was never in the original rules used to establish pension plans, and companies don't like to write a blank check. Indexing pensions today could cost more than the current pension liability already on most companies' books. Only Social Security is indexed for inflation with cost-of-living adjustments each year.

• *Social Security integration.* More than half—maybe closer to 70 percent—of all company pension plans simply reduce their benefits by the amount of Social Security benefits you receive. In theory, this is to "offset" half of the Social Security payroll taxes the employer previously contributed. Let's say your company pension is a hefty $10,000 a year but it's "offset" by 50 percent for Social Security. If you're eligible for the maximum Social Security benefit of $8,633, your company pension could then be reduced from $10,000 to only $5,684. Again, the strategic resource in financial planning is information. If you expect to receive a pension of $10,000 as well as Social Security benefits, you will have overstated your income by almost 100%. Caught up in their own economic woes, companies have used "offset" pension plans to cut their costs in a hidden, yet totally legal, way.

• *Early retirement.* Because most private pensions base your retirement benefits on your average salary for, say, the last five years, early retirement can be very expensive for you. For example, if your pension plan reduces your benefits by 7 percent for each year you retire before age 65, your benefits at age 60 can shrink, both from the reduction in benefits and the lower average salary. If your salary rises by 7 percent a year, from $30,000 at age 60 to $42,080 at age 65, your retirement benefits could more than double.

The cold fact is that we are moving from a stable industrial society in which pensions were regarded as an unalienable right, to a highly mobile information society in which pensions will become an exception to the rule. Our nation's retirement policy has not yet embraced the future and faced these facts. Those who can accommodate in their financial planning for the ambiguity of this in-between period will jump ahead of those who hold onto the past.

From Social Security to Social Insecurity

Social Security has been the nation's biggest and probably most successful social program. Approximately 36 million Americans—one out of every six persons in the United States—now receives a monthly check that assures the old, the widowed, and the disabled that they will not fall into poverty. For the 120 million American workers who pay the taxes, Social Security offers the hope that they too will be taken care of in their old age.

But 50 years after its passage, Social Security, like our nation's private pension system, is faced with a fundamental question: How much can the nation afford? Social Security was never designed to meet all our income needs in retirement. With the budget crisis deepening in Washington, it's becoming clear to more and more Americans that the system is reaching a breaking point. Politicians in Washington, D.C., don't believe it, of course, but the reality of shrinking Social Security benefits remains. Our desire for financial security in retirement often overshadows reality. We tend to dismiss Social Security's problems as something to think about near retirement, yet we ignore the problem at great risk to ourselves individually and to our country as a whole.

To understand the fundamental structure of Social Security we must travel back to its inception. The Depression made plausible the new Keynesian theory that government could restore prosperity by discouraging excess savings for retirement and encouraging consumption. We have the result of this philosophy today—a society starved for savings and adroit at finding ways to indulge in excess spending. Even though we can now collect savings dollars and recycle them through the system instantaneously, our tax structure still penalizes savers and favors consumers who rush into debt.

The basic idea of Social Security—pensions for the elderly from taxes assessed on their earnings—fit the needs of the 1930s. In the 1980s, however, it's turning into a system in which benefits are paid to the present generation of retirees from taxes collected from the next generations—their children and their grandchildren. And even these taxes are not enough. Social Security is quite simply running out of ready cash to get through the 1980s. But this is not new.

When President Roosevelt announced the birth of Social Security in 1935, everyone who worked on the bill knew that, in time, the rising benefits would grow to be incredibly expensive. The Committee on Economic Security was given the task of developing an acceptable program for unemployment and old age insurance. As recounted in the *Morgenthau Diaries*, Harry Hopkins, head of the Federal Emergency Relief Administration, who had just seen the startling figures projecting Social Security expenditures in 1980 at over $1 billion, put in a phone call to another member of the committee, Treasury Secretary Henry Morgenthau, Jr. After all, in 1935 "$1 billion" was a staggering sum, and Hopkins found it hard to imagine that anything could some day cost that much. Hopkins asked Morgenthau if he expected difficulties in winning congressional approval for $25 million to $30 million for the pension bill in the current year, and the phone conversation went like this:[3]

Morgenthau: Not this year, but it's the thing that it runs into.

Hopkins: Well, there are going to be twice as many old people 30 years from now, Henry, than there are now.

Morgenthau: Well, I've gotten a very good analysis of this thing, and I'm going to lay it in her lap [Frances Perkins, Secretary of Labor] this afternoon. I'm simply going to point out the danger spots, and it's up to somebody else to say whether they want to do it. I'm not trying to say what they should do—I want to show them the bad curves.

Hopkins: I wish I was going to be there.

Morgenthau: I wish you were too.

Hopkins: That old age thing is a bad curve!

The "bad curve" in pension planning is the declining ratio between those who pay the taxes to support the system and those who are supported. In 1947, 22 active workers supported each person receiving Social Security benefits. In 1985, that figure has shrunk to only three active workers, and many experts believe it will fall to only two active workers for each beneficiary by the late 1990s. The bad curve has arrived with a vengeance. At the same time, maximum payroll taxes (for both employee and employer) have soared from $600 in 1974 to $6,000 in 1986. As the bad curve continues to unfold, taxes are expected to reach 20 percent to 25 percent of payroll by the end of the next decade. Harry Hopkins was right 50 years ago: "That old age thing is a bad curve."

What most Americans misunderstand about Social Security today is the right they think they have to the benefits from the system generated by the taxes they have paid. Each election, politicians looking for votes tell the elderly and the young they have a right to Social Security benefits high enough to maintain a comfortable standard of living in old age, including all the increases necessary to keep those benefits abreast of inflation. The facts are that the aged, the widowed, the disabled—and the young—have been promised more than the nation can give at a cost its workers can afford. And it's easy to see why.

Social Security was sold to the public as a prepaid retirement benefit
that would keep pace with inflation, financed by hefty payroll taxes.
That may make sense, but it's wrong. We pay taxes today, not to prepay
our retirement security, but to keep the system from drowning in red
ink.

There's no point in rehashing how we got into these difficulties,
the point is that our recent attempts to make the system sound have
failed. The problems we face in collecting and paying for Social
Security can be covered in two main points.

Never a Promise to Pay

From the start, Social Security has never made a promise to pay
benefits. The moneyshock of all of this: You are legally required to pay
taxes, but the government is not legally required to pay you benefits.
The larger image of many government programs is not always clear.
Helped by the news media, especially Congress, we have been led to
believe that somehow we have a vested right to future Social Security
benefits.

When you look at the original Social Security wall poster, tacked
up on bulletin boards when payroll taxes were first deducted from
workers' pay checks in 1937, your eyes are drawn to the simple, clearly
stated warning: "There is no guarantee that the funds thus collected
will ever be returned to you." And then the clincher: "What happens to
the money is up to each Congress." Congress changed the Social
Security law in 1939, 1946, 1950, 1952, 1956, 1958, 1960, 1965, 1967,
1969, 1972, 1977, and 1983. It will do so again.

An Unbalanced Scale

Visualize Social Security as a giant balance scale, with active
workers putting taxes on the left side of the scales, recipients taking
money off the right. In a pay-as-you-go system, as long as the same
amount of money is put on the left side as is taken off the right side, the
scales can stay in balance. During the Depression, when Social Security
was established, the elderly (age 65 and over) made up only 5.5 percent
of the total population. By 1980, their numbers had soared to 11.2
percent. By the year 2,000, government agencies believe, those age 65
and over could swell to over 15 percent of the total population. The
graying of America is rapidly tilting the scales out of balance. And even
this arithmetic doesn't take into account the effect on the system of our
remarkably extended lifespan. During the 1930s, the average 65 year
old could expect to live another 12 years. Today's 65 year old is

comparatively young at that age and can expect to live another 17 years. Centenarians are becoming almost commonplace.

Finally, Social Security benefits have risen much faster than inflation. The maximum annual benefit soared 200 percent during the 1970s, and between 1978 and 1982, it climbed another 40 percent. Dr. Rita Ricardo Campbell of the Hoover Institution in Palo Alto California says that since 1970, average Social Security benefits, adjusted for inflation, have climbed 37 percent; average weekly wages, again adjusted for inflation, have hardly increased at all. Today, a married man with a dependent spouse can retire on as much as $1,075 a month.

In 1965 Congress started payments, financed by Social Security taxes, to disabled workers and for Medicare to help cover hospital and medical bills for people 65 and older. Huge sums of money continue to slide off the right side of the scales under these programs. The $72-billion-a-year Medicare program faces insolvency by the mid-1990s, and Congress is more likely to use regular income taxes to bail out Medicare than to continue to raise Social Security taxes. General revenues are already being used to pay for a good part of the medical expenses covered by the program.

The good news is that we have tilted the Social Security balance scale so far to the right that the rate of poverty among the elderly has been cut in half, from about 30 percent in 1967 to 15 percent in 1980. "Social Security was a system designed to move us toward a world where the elderly were treated equally with the non-elderly," says M.I.T. professor Lester Thurow. "We have virtually reached that world."[4]

Social Security's fatal flaw is that everyone takes more off the scales than they put on. Right from the start, each lucky retiree has been guaranteed more money in the first year or two than was ever contributed over his or her entire working life. A man retiring in 1982 at age 65 can still expect retirement benefits worth almost three times the taxes he and his employer have put into the system, plus interest. If his wife doesn't work outside the home, he'll get back five times his investment. And that doesn't count what he can get from Medicare and other Social Security programs.

Federal income tax rates have been cut in recent years, inflation has weakened, and incomes have risen—yet many people still ask: Where does all the money go? It goes to Social Security, for one thing. Social Security taxes make up 60 percent of total federal taxes paid by low-income families, and 37 percent of federal taxes paid by moderate-income families. But that's only a taste of what's to come. With the balance scale now distinctly tilted to the right and more and more money being paid out in benefits, we'll need substantially higher payroll taxes to return the scales to an even balance. Congress has been busy pushing up the tax rate so that today we are locked into an effectively progressive Social Security tax structure. For example, under previous law the tax rate in 1988 would have been 6.45 percent of wages. Under the Carter administration it was boosted to 7.15 percent. Under the Reagan administration's 1983 law the 1988 rate will be again increased, to 7.51 percent of wages. The 1986 rate is 7.15 percent on a wage base of $41,700, or a maximum tax of almost $3,000 for the employee and the employer. By 1989, laws already on the books will boost the maximum payroll tax to over $4,000 for both employees and employers.

The bad news is that higher taxes will still mean lower benefits. The first wave of baby boomers reaching 65 just after the turn of the century can expect to get *less* than they and their employers paid in. In some cases, up-scale wage-earners who have paid the most in Social Security taxes may get back nothing!

The moneyshock is that the tax rates already on the books will not be nearly enough to provide the benefits Congress has already authorized. Dr. Rita Ricardo Campbell, author of numerous books and papers on Social Security and retirement, says the present benefits calculations for Social Security do not fully recognize the impact of a rapidly aging population and a declining birth rate. To pay the level of benefits already promised, she has concluded, would require a doubling in Social Security taxes by the time the baby boomers have retired.

Although half of America's workers already pay more in Social Security taxes than they do in federal income taxes, the bite in take-home pay from Social Security will loom even larger in the years to come. Those under 40, already struggling to stay afloat in choppy economic seas, say they can't afford to give up a hefty portion of their pay check to support retirees.

"An inter-generational conflict is brewing," warns Haeworth Robertson, a managing director of William Mercer-Meidinger, Inc. in New York and Social Security's chief actuary in the late 1970s. "It's not at all far-fetched to think that young people will soon stand up and say: 'I don't think the system is fair, and I'm not going to pay the taxes.' "[5]

Part of the problem is the double tax structure built into Social Security that takes an ever greater slice of the pay check. For example, an individual earning $30,000 in 1986 will pay $2,145 in taxes to Social Security. Let's assume the worker, a man, is married, files a joint return, and faces a marginal federal income tax rate of only 27 percent. He is paying federal income taxes of $579 (27 percent of $2,145) on income he never receives. Without adding state and local income taxes, the effective Social Security tax rate now becomes 9.10 percent, not the nominal 7.15 percent. This effective tax rate becomes even higher as you move up the salary ladder.

Unlike all other retirement plans in which taxes are deferred until retirement, such as IRAs, Keogh plans, and employer-sponsored salary reduction plans, Social Security socks the tax bite to us while we are working, paying our bills, and saving a little money for emergencies.

What to Expect

The good news is that there is a way out of our dilemma. With all the other financial restructurings, America will learn to live with a Social Security system like the one in effect in the 1930s. We are already in a transitional era, and the changes will occur very fast in the next decade. Much of what will transpire is already built into the system; the rest is waiting in the wings. Whether we endorse these fundamental changes in our nation's retirement system or not, we will be compelled to accept them. Why? Because if changes are not made, the system, already sinking into growing deficits, will simply disappear in a pool of red ink before the end of the next decade. This dismal long-term scenario can't be overcome by raising taxes alone. Benefits must be cut. Here is the moneyshock for Social Security coming in the next decade:

A Boost in Retirement Age

Today, two-thirds of all retirees collect Social Security before the "normal" age of 65. They have found out something the system already knows: Retiring at age 62 on reduced benefits gives them a big head start in total dollars received compared with someone retiring at age 65. Therefore, Congress will quicken the pace of moving the normal retirement age from 65 to 67 and will increase the penalties for early retirement, cutting back benefits at age 62 from 80 percent of those at 65 to 66.6 percent. For those individuals now under the age of 45, age 65 is considered early retirement. Social Security already offers a 3 percent boost in benefits for every year workers stay on the job past their 65th birthday. This will climb to at least 10 percent with income tax credits for working after the age of 65.

Increased Federal Income Taxes on Benefits

Today, rich retirees are the latest target for Social Security cuts. Before the end of this decade, almost all Social Security retirees will pay federal and state income taxes on half of the benefits they receive.

The taxation of benefits started in 1984 and Congress will continue to ratchet down the level of income in retirement subject to taxes.

There's an interesting sidelight to Social Security's tax-free benefits. In the early days of the program, in an attempt to get around a double tax deduction on the same money, the Treasury Department ruled that funds received in retirement were a "gratuity." But in 1983, looking for ways to give Social Security a cash transfusion while encouraging older workers to postpone retirement, Congress hit upon the idea of taxing benefits. The rationale for taxing to the grave is this: When your employer pays half your Social Security taxes he or she takes a tax deduction. The worker pays no tax on these employer contributions. When the retiree receives Social Security benefits, only half of the original contributions has been taxed. That's why the law now taxes 50 percent of your benefits.

The More You Have, the Less You'll Receive

Is Social Security going to become a program for the poor? Yes, I think it will. In 1983, Treasury Secretary Regan lofted a trial balloon on cutting benefits for upper-income retirees. Regan was quick to point out something that's been lost in time: When Social Security was begun half a century ago, it was designed merely to help people who otherwise would be destitute when they got older. Now, Regan said, it's been expanded to a point where it pays benefits regardless of wealth. The question today is, can we still justify that kind of program?

No one is talking about snipping so much as a penny off present benefits. That's political suicide. What is in the works is a change in the rules to make it more difficult for certain people to collect benefits. With a system rapidly running out of money, benefits in the future will have to be paid to those who have a real need. The logical extension of all this: Social Security is headed for a "means test," maybe before the end of this decade, certainly by 1995. Under a means test, you would begin to lose Social Security benefits as your total retirement income rose, and at some point you would not collect benefits at all.

More and more I am led to believe that you should make your financial plans on the basis that Social Security will fill a diminishing part of your retirement security package, not because the system is going broke, but because those who financially plan for their retirement will qualify for a smaller benefit each year into the future. Self-help has always been a part of American life. It's importance will increase as the government throws out more tempting tax-deferred savings plans like company-sponsored salary reduction plans and IRAs.

Even if we look forward only ten years or so, Social Security will under go a fundamental change. Accordingly, smart retirement planning requires that you accept these changes and take advantage of the growing number of tax-deferred savings plans that will spring up in the years to come.

Government-Induced Savings Plans

Now that we are moving in the direction of self-help, IRAs will expand at a rapid rate. They will become the "Social Security" for those who save. And why not? For most American workers, they can save at least *seven times* faster with an IRA than they can by first paying their taxes and investing what's left over. IRAs will change in some unexpected ways:

• *Home-buying.* IRAs will soon allow the individual to use the IRA as a joint investor in the purchase of a home. For the past several years, bills have been introduced into Congress to make IRAs more attractive to younger workers, and this is only the beginning of the future uses for IRAs.

• *Equal spouse contributions.* President Reagan has proposed that both spouses, even if only one spouse works outside the home, be allowed to contribute the full $2,000 for each individual.

• *Medical IRAs.* With Medicare on the critical list, programs being cut back, Medical IRAs will let people build up a nest egg for future health care costs. Each year a worker could contribute up to $500 tax free and the Medical IRAs would gradually offset Medicare bills as workers began to rely less on the Medicare system.

• *Soaring contribution levels.* Soon contribution levels to IRAs will match those of current-tax-deferred savings plans now available through your employer. This could double or even triple the contributions limits within the next few years.

Self-Help:
The Trend of the Future

For the past 50 years, the government and our employers were our buffers against slipping into poverty once we retired. Now we must abandon our dependence on others and learn to rely on and trust only ourselves. This is a fundamental change in the way we plan our retirement security. For most of our lifetime we have been told that the strength of our employer and our government was the only thing able to overcome the nagging fear that we would run out of money before we ran out of breath; so, more and more, we relied on these institutions to provide the safeguards for our future.

Now these institutions have failed us. Corporations have, by and large, taken away the guarantees of a fixed pension. Social Security will move further from our grasp at retirement. The moneyshock: We can no longer act as passive bystanders during the massive shift from institutional security to individual security. If we ask today, "Whom can we trust?" the answer is clear: "Ourselves."

Once again, those who are financially unprepared will receive Social Security and other benefits; those who have made financial plans will draw on their own resources. The good news is that we will be allowed to help ourselves with a growing number of IRA-type plans that can serve as a buffer against life's hard realities—retirement, illness, housing, and food.

The question is, will we be able to reclaim our traditional sense of self-reliance after half a century of relying on our employers and our government? I believe that we will. New opportunities, as yet unseen, will help to transform our lives and give us the courage to take action on our own.

8

Cashing In on Tax Trends

How to Keep More of What You Make

Geologists should understand better than the rest of us the federal income tax system. It erupted in 1913, yet the trend to change the way we pay federal taxes has evolved glacially, with an initial upheaval followed by stretches of quiet, broken occasionally by the ominous rumblings of tax reform. Right now it feels as though the geologic plates could be shifting again, but no one knows how far they'll move.

The latest tremors were set off by President Reagan's tax reform proposals to lower tax brackets and cut back on a growing number of tax deductions. While the current tax-reform convulsion is clearly the forerunner of a fundamental change in the nation's income tax system, it also has another, often overlooked, benefit: It will give people more freedom to control their own lives.

The Past: How We Got Here

Taxes—in the form of excise taxes, not income taxes—paid for our Revolution and the War of 1812. The first real federal income tax was imposed by the Revenue Act of 1861 to help pay for the Civil War. That tax lasted until 1872. Once the war was over, hard-pressed taxpayers went to court and federal income taxes were found to be unconstitutional. It took the Sixteenth Amendment to make federal income taxes legal in 1913.

At that time they were expected to represent only 1 percent or 2 percent of the taxpayer's income, and were to be levied only on the true fat cats in the country. The average wage-earner was never expected to pay such a tax. In 1916, IRS form 1040 had just seven paragraphs of instructions. For incomes of more than $20,000 the rate was 1 percent, or $200—a princely sum in those days, equivalent to about 25 percent, or $2,500 in 1985. For incomes of more than $40,000 it was 2 percent. The highest marginal bracket, on amounts over $2 million, was 13 percent.

In contrast, by the beginning of this decade middle-class wage-earners had become the counterparts of the fat cats of 1913. On a taxable income of more than $34,100, their bracket had soared to 50 percent, and the top rate had climbed to 70 percent for incomes of more than $108,300. Rising tax brackets spawned tax shelters, deductions, and tax credits, until today even the best tax attorneys and accountants find themselves lost in an endless tangle of regulations and tax laws.

In theory, revenue measures are born in the House of Representatives. They are then hammered into shape by committees of both houses of Congress with considerable help from lobbyists and the staff of both the House Ways and Means Committee and the Senate Finance Committee. The surviving tax bills are then knocked about and "marked up" until a joint committee produces the final version. If the bill becomes law it's usually signed by the President in time for the 6:00 news.

Not so well publicized is the fact that the whole process is a bit of a hoax. First there are multivolume loose-leaf tax reporting services addressing various aspects of the new law. Then an army of expert lawyers, accountants, and corporate tax managers ferret out the loopholes and pick apart what Congress has enacted. Finally, page after page of Treasury regulations (called "regs" by the tax people) begin to fine tune the law and start a process of damage control. These copious regulations, however, bring on an avalanche of court battles, where much of what Congress had in mind is circumvented.

Worse yet, tax codes have become a tool Congress uses to shape public policy. As one Congressman told me, "If you want more of something, tax it less; if you want less of something, tax it more. As a corollary, if you want more tax revenue you should find things you baffled, they are expected to dig deep into the shifting sands for the real meaning of the tax law. Consider the reflections of the famous jurist, Judge Learned Hand: ". . . the words of such an act as the income tax, for example, merely dance before my eyes in a meaningless procession; cross-reference to cross-reference, exception upon exception—couched in abstract terms that offer no handle to seize hold of—leave in my mind only a confused sense of some vitally important, but successfully concealed, purport, which it is my duty to extract, but which is within my power, if at all, only after the most inordinate expenditure of time. . . ."

This crazy patchwork of legislation and IRS rules has resulted in an obsolete, inefficient, and almost unworkable tax system that buries the IRS itself under a tidal wave of paper. Individual and corporate returns, computer tapes, and amended returns have now ballooned to 650 million—three documents and reports for every man, woman, and child in this country! The 1913 progressive tax system continues to send us into higher tax brackets where bigger chunks of our income are taken away by Washington. The natural consequence of this pernicious system is America's endless search for loopholes—and the willingness of some to commit outright tax fraud.

The Future:
Confronting the Challenge of the Underground Economy

Henry George (1839–1897) told us that "Taxation must not lead men into temptation by requiring trivial oaths, by making it profitable to swear falsely, to bribe, or to take bribes." A century later it apparently has. Today a growing number of citizens no longer face the bleak prospect of giving ever-larger chunks of their money to Uncle Sam; they have joined the underground economy—the "cash for services and no records kept" economy. The IRS could slash our soaring federal budget deficits by as much as $200 billion a year by simply going into our underground economy and collecting what is owed on legal income from moonlighting, tips, and unreported cash transactions. By grabbing this kind of money, Congress could cut the tax rate for millions of us who report our total incomes, and it could translate the meaningless phrase "tax reform" into something real.

No matter how sophisticated you are, the chances are that you have only a murky idea of the pervasiveness of the underground economy flourishing just beneath the surface where most law-abiding citizens live. The underground economy is dominated by the self-employed,

want less of and tax them more." This rule of thumb isn't effect
when applied to people, however. The tax system wanted fewer ri
people, so taxes were raised for them. But the rule did not work for ri
people because they had lawyers and tax accountants who we
smarter than the tax codes, so they avoided paying the taxes. Tl
system may not work for people, but it does work for things people ca
buy. I offer a few examples, but there are certainly many more possibil
ties than I can describe here.

If we have an energy crisis, tax incentives will encourage people t
build windmills on mountain tops to generate electricity. If we neec
more low-income housing, special tax credits and deductions should
do the job. If we want to encourage people to buy diesel cars and save
gasoline, we give them special tax credits. If we want people to insulate
their homes, we give them special energy tax credits. If we want
businesses to buy more equipment, we give them investment tax
credits. Congress has even filled the tax codes with special provisions
that benefit individuals, certain companies in an industry, and certain
employees (who may work in the same building, boat, or airplane with
other workers who don't benefit at all).

The laws, the regulations, and the rulings are often written in sand.
Each "up-to-date" tax report is replete with complex alterations in
existing law. Take the case of energy tax credits. The Joneses and the
Smiths each installed the same kind of solar hot-water system, with
roof-mounted solar-collector plates and a closed loop through which a
liquid heated on the roof is pumped into a heat exchanger in a storage
tank and back to the heat collector. Both Jones and Smith leaped at the
opportunity to save energy—and the U.S. Treasury paid 40 percent of
the cost of the new systems.

The Joneses, however, added an optional heating element for use
when solar energy is inadequate. If you're going to spend all that
money, they reasoned, why not have a system that would work during
overcast days? But the Internal Revenue Service, in one of its new
rulings based on the latest shifting sands, now says that only the Smiths
are entitled to the hefty energy tax credits because "the sole function of
the entire unit is the use of solar radiation to provide hot water for the
dwelling, so all components are eligible for the 40 percent tax credit
allowed on renewable-energy-source property."

In the Joneses' case, the shifting sands short-circuited their roof-
top energy source. The electrical-heating unit and the storage tank can
function independently of solar energy. These two elements serve a
dual purpose, and therefore, neither qualifies for the tax credit.

Or think of judges, who must work within the IRS tax code. Often from doctors, writers, and lawyers to barmaids, window washers, and small business owners—of whom the IRS estimates as many as 60 percent report less than their total earnings, and as many as 62 percent pay no Social Security taxes on these earnings. A former IRS commissioner explains that the failure to report income arises not so much "out of immorality as out of opportunity." Many small businesses, for example, offer their services at considerably lower cost than first quoted if payment is in cash without the need for a receipt.

A major component of the subterranean off-the-books economy is the exchange of merchandise or services without benefit of records or taxes. A beauty shop operator lives in a $100,000 home, yet reports income of only $20,000 a year from his essentially cash business. A doctor who charges $30 a visit sees more than 100 patients a week, yet reports less than $75,000 in income. A housewife moonlights as a bookkeeper for a local company, for cash. During evenings and weekends, a construction worker installs new bathrooms and refinishes basements for half the price charged by full-time competitors; he buys the material from cash-hungry suppliers and collects cash or barter for the work.

A lawyer I talked with acknowledges that he no longer feels guilty about the barter system. "I trade my legal work for car upkeep and repair. I've worked out the guy's divorce and he's given me tune-ups and a totally rebuilt car." Last year the Internal Revenue Service hired a professional polling organization to find out who the cheaters were. For starters, the IRS estimates that almost 30 percent of all taxpayers cheat, and that yuppies, as a group, cheat the most. Young urban professionals are consumers first, savers last. For them, saving on both income taxes and Social Security taxes is part of the fast track to high living. The under-35, white-collar, professional, and potentially up-scale taxpayers are the most brazen in cheating simply because, the IRS says, they have the greatest opportunity to do so. With high incomes, they often believe that they are only doing what others do and they are less fearful of tax cheating than any other age group. So called "scramblers," who are described by the IRS as young, largely blue-collar workers, are most likely to cheat on a smaller scale by not reporting second incomes and tips. The methodology of tax cheating follows a simple rule: Avoid taking money by means other than cash or provide the services or products in exchange for items of like value. In this group, the IRS poll found that tax cheating was most common among those earning less than $49,000 a year who live in the West. It was lowest in the Atlantic region.

The point is absolutely clear: While most of us report our incomes and pay what the IRS says we owe, the underground economy is multiplying, and experts believe that the deterioration in tax collecting is accelerating. Dealing off the books has become a middle-class phenomenon whereby some 25 million Americans cheat not only Uncle Sam but the Social Security system by not reporting billions in income. With about 95 million individual tax returns, the number of cheaters has soared to almost 30 percent. Five years ago, the figure for tax evasion was set at close to $200 billion. Now, it is around $500 billion. Some of that is inflation, but almost every other economic statistic is similarly inflated.

Among other things, the growth of the underground economy has brought us back to a tax-free barter system—plowing a field in return for a side of bacon. It suggests that many of the statistics for unemployment, income, production, and savings are way out of line with reality. It also suggests that much of what the government is telling us about our economy is a myth. For example, the economists reckon that inflation appears to be far higher than it really is because prices in the unobserved economy may be 20 to 40 percent lower than in the observed economy. And productivity, of course, is healthier in the underground economy because the reward is higher per hour of work when it goes untaxed.

We need to enforce the law. My own sense of it tells me that cutting income tax rates alone won't make people less inclined to cheat. We need to restore public confidence in the fairness of the system. To do that, we need a simple, easy-to-understand tax code without the multitude of loopholes that gives high-bracket earners—and their accountants—opportunities to slash their taxes at the expense of the rest of us. That's the key issue in the underground economy—the public perception of unfairness in the system. Be honest for a moment. Do you believe that all those people who live better than you pay their fair share of taxes? Or do you suspect they've exploited some tax shelter or manipulated the system in some dubious way?

Millions of Americans believe they pay more than their fair share of taxes. To back up their claims, they point to the Treasury Department's report that in 1983 some 55,000 taxpayers with incomes exceeding $250,000 paid a lower percentage of their income in federal taxes than the average middle-class family of four. At least 2,000 high-income "taxpayers" paid no tax at all. The Treasury report said that a family of four with an income of $45,000 paid an average of $6,300 in federal taxes in 1983. Yet some 30,000 taxpayers with incomes five times as much paid the IRS, on average, less than twice as much. For the super-rich, the numbers get even better. Side-stepping their way past the IRS, almost 3,200 taxpayers who earned more than $1 million in 1983 paid virtually no taxes at all. "If anyone had any doubt about the unfairness of our present tax code these figures should convince them," said Democratic Congressman J.J. Pickle of Texas.[1]

But individuals aren't the only ones who can evade the uneven tax code. Fifty major U.S. corporations paid no federal income tax during President Reagan's first term in office, despite earning nearly $60 billion in profits. Then, looking for some angles they may have missed, these same corporations got back about $2.5 billion in tax refunds. Forty companies, taking advantage of special tax incentives only a pork-barrelling Congress could bestow, got back $660 million, despite earning profits of more than $10 billion in 1984 The major corporations, with all their high-powered tax attorneys, offer a picture of unparalleled success in out-smarting the federal tax collector.

While cutting taxes to zero is legal under our current system of loopholes and tax credits, the fact that it's carried out in such a massive way leads millions of taxpayers to cheat the system in an illegal way. We need tax reform, but the IRS also needs to beef up enforcement. Less than 2 percent of individual returns are examined by the IRS and cutting corners here is both poor economics and bad government. The federal government takes in over $10 for every $1 spent on enforcing the tax laws. Unless the IRS cracks down on cheaters, the underground eonomy will continue to boom and the whole purpose of tax reform will lose its meaning.

We Must Reexamine Our Investment and Tax Structure

The way we pay or don't pay our taxes is forcing us to reexamine the whole tax structure. Tax cheating, legal avoidance, and endless loopholes have become so pervasive and so powerful that we must completely reform our methods of collecting taxes.

It's difficult to imagine that in 1963 the top income tax rate was 91 percent. By 1980 the top rate had declined to 70 percent. By 1984, it had dwindled to only 50 percent. And now, in 1986, the beginning of true tax reform has begun with a top rate of around 30 percent. (Most working Americans should find themselves in a 15 to 20 percent individual tax rate.) It started with President Reagan's tax reform plan to clean up the present loophole-ridden tax system and it ended with Congress enacting a major reform bill that dramatically affects the way we pay our taxes. The essence of the plan is to lower the income tax rates by limiting or eliminating a number of tax deductions, exemptions, exclusions, and credits. This makes it possible to significantly reduce tax rates for both individuals and corporations and it will cause the underground economy to rise to the surface. Another benefit to individual taxpayers is that big corporations will have to start paying taxes again. With everyone paying at least some taxes, small businesses and entrepreneurs will be on a more equal footing with the large, established firms.

I argue that tax reform is a change whose time has come. Some of the ideas I've covered in this chapter will be incorporated in laws passed during the 1985-86 session of Congress, or the following session, and the process of change will gain speed after the election in 1986. This is important to you because *your long-term tax planning should include less reliance on tax savings and more emphasis on receiving taxable income from your investments.* That's because the U.S. tax system will evolve toward lower tax brackets and fewer deductions. The crucial issue before Congress is not simply tax reform, although that's needed; it's the public's perception of fairness amid a growing number of loopholes and tax cheaters.

Tax Shelters Were Meant to Save Taxes, Not Make Money

A general partner forms a company, raises capital to make a public offering, and becomes responsible for the management and the debts of the new venture. There may be no intention to make the venture profitable until much later. Investors, called limited partners, are then asked to put up the money by buying limited partnerships. The lure of a business that sets out to lose money, and thereby create huge tax losses, is that actual dollar losses sustained by the limited partners are limited to the loss of their investment. However, any profit or paper loss from the business flows through to each individual limited partner in proportion to his or her investment.

For instance, a high-income individual can invest $10,000 in an oil and gas partnership, making up, say, 5 percent of the partnership's total investment. If the venture loses $500,000, the investor will be able to write off $25,000, or two-and-a-half times the original investment. The Treasury's report on 1983 incomes says that in 1982 more than half the partnerships in real estate and oil and gas were losing money, a sure sign that they were in the hands of tax-shelter promoters.

For high-bracket individuals facing the intense heat of 70 percent or more of their income going to the IRS anyway, tax shelters were as inviting as the express lane on the highway to Easy Street. The more they lost, the better the deal. By the late 1970s and early 1980s tax shelters had become as varied as some of the larcenous characters who dreamed them up. It became fashionable during dinner party conversations to brag about heavy tax write-offs in cattle feeding, oil and gas drilling, catfish, chinchilla and mink breeding, and almond growing. If early tax write-offs were the key, tax-shelter promoters would make the deal irresistible, offering to deduct from current taxes the entire first year's investment. The sharp promoters began to dangle the prospect of deducting even more. If you put up $5,000 and sign a note, you could deduct $10,000, even $15,000, in the first year. But all of this pales by comparison to the new tax shelters that fly in the face of the IRS.

Congress, by using tax incentives to spur investments, has itself created some of the most bizarre tax shelters ever to tempt the American taxpayer. How would you like to invest in a giant windmill that, on windy days, produces electric power? A limited partnership in wind turbines can let you reduce your income taxes, if you're in a 50 percent bracket, by $155,570 during the first five years of ownership. In California, where the windmill craze hit its peak in 1985, promoters were touting federal energy tax credits, federal investment tax credits, federal depreciation savings, state solar tax credits, and state depreciation savings. Windmills may be the ultimate tax shelter; their sole purpose is to allow you to pay your money to someone other than the federal government in order to avoid paying taxes.

Windmills don't appeal to you? You're in luck. When Spring comes it will be buffalo-calving season, and profit from one animal averages nearly $200 for its beef and another $200 for its hide. You can even fetch as much as $1,000 for mounted buffalo heads. What makes a 2,600-pound beast appealing as a trendy tax-shelter? It is 100 percent depreciable over five years.

"People set up shelters for coal deals, but there is no coal under the ground. We've had cattle shelters where there were no cows," says John Monaco, chief of the examination divisions of the regional IRS office in Chicago. The IRS, however, has been putting the coal in the ground and the cows in the corn since 1984, when a new tax law permitted tax gatherers to go after both the abusive tax-shelter promoters and the investors. Shelters with more than five investors, or those that attract more than $250,000 in investment money or promise a return of more than two-to-one in their first five years, must register with the IRS. As an investor, you'll receive a tax-shelter registration number and you must put this on your 1040 tax return. With the tax-shelter ID on individual tax forms, the IRS has a handy way to track down investors when a shelter runs into trouble with the tax collectors.

The IRS is not alone in its fight to squelch abusive tax shelters.

State securities administrators, working together, have begun a multi-state securities crackdown. To put the wheels in motion, the IRS will begin publishing names, addresses, and descriptions of abusive shelters to help investors and their tax advisers spot the offending shelter promoters.

Investing After-Tax Income Will Favor Cash Investments, Not Tax Deductions or Deferral

The fundamental change in the way we handle our income taxes—away from tax shelters and delaying taxes at any cost, and toward paying cash and earning solid income—will come about very fast. Today, with a top tax rate of 50 percent and President Reagan's tax proposals set to trim the top bracket back to 35 percent, investing in shaky tax shelters won't be the smart play of the future. In fact, saving taxes with a limited partnership tax shelter comes with a hefty penalty. Suppose you invest $20,000 in a typical shelter that runs 5 to 7 years. After a year, because of an emergency in the family, you desperately need the cash. With most shelters you're out of luck. Selling second-hand tax shelters is a chancy affair at best, and when you can, you'll be lucky to recover even a small part of your original investment. You'll get a better bonus by betting on cash income instead of tax deductions, and you probably won't lose your original investment, as you would in a tax shelter that can't make a buck and goes out of business.

At first blush it may appear that investors are continuing to buy oil and gas and real estate partnerships. And of course they are. The big change is that investments in real estate, for example, are not necessarily tax shelters. Investors are increasingly losing their appetite for tax shelters that use a lot of debt to get tax deductions. These now represent less than 25 percent of publicly offered real estate programs, compared with a solid 40 percent the previous year. On the other hand, *income-oriented limited partnerships* were up a thumping 75 percent in 1985. These are real estate partnerships that either invest in mortgage loans with no tax benefits or buy real estate for cash and provide limited shelter by passing along depreciation write-offs.

With tax reform, however, the future looks grim for tax shelters. The assault on tax shelters is part of the overall change in our income tax code. Lowering the top tax rate from 50 percent to around 30 percent diminishes the incentive for people to find ways to shelter their income. Those who try to defer taxes would find that the tax laws restrict many of the benefits of the shelters. The investment tax credit would be lost and real estate deals would be hurt by a cutback in depreciation deductions. But the biggest wallop would be felt by investors in paper losses—the heart of many hard-core tax shelters—now used to offset other income.

The rocket-powered growth, however, will be in new investments such as real estate investment trusts (REITs). Unlike a tax shelter in real estate with hefty tax write-offs, REITs pay fully taxable dividends. In other words, REITs are not tax shelters. They are more like a closed-end mutual fund invested in real estate. They trade like stocks, whereas limited partnerships offer almost no liquidity during their 5 to 7 year term. REITs pay no federal income tax themselves; the dividends flow to shareholders who pay the tax, and because REITs themselves get depreciation deductions to limit their own taxes, their typical range of yields to shareholders can run from 8 to 13 percent.

REITs (pronounced "reets") come in different shapes and sizes. An equity REIT specializes in real estate ownership. A mortgage REIT concentrates on lending. A hybrid REIT does both. A "finite" REIT will liquidate itself in a given number of years. Because tax changes will continue to undercut tax-sheltered syndications, the smart money, experts tell me, is going to REITs with a low debt in proportion to assets.

From Fixed to Variable Investments:
A Move as Important as the One from Loose Cash to Banks

Amid all the other financial restructurings of taxation and deregulation, the nation is rapidly moving to investments that combine guarantees with open-ended future profits. The fundamental change will be some form of government or private insurance to protect the investors' capital and fixed rate of return, like an insured CD, yet allow future income to soar with interest rates and inflation. Accordingly, successful investors will seek out these new *second-generation* investments that guarantee their principal yet leave them open to rising income potential.

The logical extension of this: *New investments will not limit your future return.* When you buy a bond today, you lock yourself into a fixed rate of return. If interest rates rise, you lose, because (1) your money now earns a rate below the market and (2) higher interest rates diminish the value of your bond. If you sell your investment you can take a hefty loss on your original principal.

No one can predict the shape or individual design of the new second-generation plans as they explode on the financial scene, but the basic factors of safety of principal, fixed income, and unlimited income potential will remain. For most conservative Americans, the new plans will put a considerable damper on fixed savings accounts. In my opinion, they are clearly the most important result so far of financial deregulation. To understand how the pieces fit together, let's look at three second-generation savings plans already available:

1. *EE U.S. Savings Bonds.* Here's a scenario for making better investments than banks, brokers, and S&Ls: Make up the rules yourself. The government did just that. The new EE bonds are second-generation savings plans because:

   a. Your investment is guaranteed by the government.
   b. You have a floor or minimum of interest return, which itself is also guaranteed.
   c. You have an automatic six-month interest adjustment to market rates.

2. *Total growth trusts.* This a new investment that gives investors 100 percent protection of their original investment, yet lets them invest in common stocks. With an investment life of about 7 years, half of the trust's funds are invested in zero coupon Treasury bonds which return the investor's entire original investment at the end of the trust's life. The safe return is based on zero coupon Treasury bonds.

With your original investment safe, the other half of the trust's funds are invested in common stocks that have a consistent record of above-average earnings and growth. People who would like to invest in the stock market but can't tolerate the losses associated with a volatile market will find that a total growth trust protects them from loss.

   a. Your investment will be returned to you through the Treasury bonds.
   b. You should earn a return each year from the common stocks.
   c. You'll share in the future growth of the common stock with an unlimited growth potential.

3. *Enhanced yield certificates of deposit.* Look again at how these new insured CDs, which are invested in real estate, fit the requirements for a second-generation savings plan:

   a. Your investment is guaranteed by either FSLIC or FDIC insurance up to $100,000.
   b. You have a floor or minimum of interest return, which itself is also guaranteed.

c. You'll share in all future interest-rate and inflation increases with an unlimited interest-income cap.

These real investments are also called *earnings-based certificates of deposits*. On my radio and television shows I call these new second-generation plans heads-you-win, tails-you-can't-lose. They are federally insured to $100,000 and they guarantee to pay a minimum rate of interest throughout the term of the certificate (usually 8 to 10 years), which itself is also federally insured. What makes them a second-generation investment is their ability to share in future profits of the real estate deals. Enhanced-yield insured CDs offer real estate developers a lower-than-market interest rate while the real estate developer, financial institution, and the investor share in the future profits of the deal. What's happening is not all that new, since banks and S&Ls have for years used depositors' money to make equity-sharing commercial real estate mortgages. In first-generation investments, the financial institution pays the saver a fixed rate of return for a fixed term (a savings account) and then loans the money to a real estate developer at a higher rate of return, with options to share in the profits when the real estate is sold. Quite simply, a second-generation savings plan cuts out the middleman and lets the real estate developer, the financial institution, and the individual saver share in the profits from completed shopping centers and apartment buildings.

The major change in the way we save and invest, as the top income tax brackets are lowered to 30 percent, will be a rush to those investments that first have value unrelated to their tax benefits. Losing money in a tax shelter that went bad when you were in a 70 percent bracket won't have the same appeal to future taxpayers in a 30 percent bracket. Guaranteed cash income with open-ended profits will replace tax reduction or deferral.

Saving Before-Tax *Income:*
Employer-Sponsored Savings Plans that Dodge the Tax Man

Amid all the confusion of where to save, there are growing signs of change. Instead of paying taxes and rushing into savings accounts or snappy investments with what's left over after Uncle Sam has taken his share, millions of Americans are finding they can sock away tax-deferred income five or ten times faster when they do so with their employer's help.

Congress is aghast at the size of the tax-avoidance industry it has created in its rush to take the heat off Social Security and allow workers to save for their own futures, yet Congress will play an expanding role in determining where we save our money by directing the sweet deals to where we work. The effort is a planned substitute for Social Security later on, of course, but it will shape our savings habits as nothing has in the history of our republic. Simply stated, the growing legion of middle-class savers who have discovered congressionally-inspired employer-sponsored tax shelters will undeniably be the smart savers of the future.

Employer-sponsored savings plans began in 1958 when Ike was in the White House and America had regained the lead in space by firing into orbit the first American earth satellite. On Capitol Hill, Congress was quietly putting the final touches on a bill identified only as the Technical Amendments Law of 1958. Unhampered by prior legislation, Congress fashioned the best tax-deferred savings plan ever presented to the American public, the tax-sheltered annuity (TSA). The only problem was that to take part in the TSA program you had to work for a non-profit organization. The original bill allowed only employees of privately supported non-profit organizations to qualify for this bonanza until the national teachers' union launched a massive lobbying campaign to allow their million-plus schoolteachers from publicly supported organizations to step inside the elevator before the door was slammed shut.

If you are among the select few who can grab this brass ring, the opportunities to save on taxes are breathtaking. When you instruct your employer to invest your money in a TSA, you are not required to report as current income the money thus deducted from your salary. TSAs are what a good savings plan should be and they remain today, almost 30 years later, the best IRA-type savings plan ever written by Congress. For starters, you can instruct your employer to contribute up to 16.6 percent of your pay—and you can also open an IRA! But the most important aspect of TSAs is their ability to let you go back and catch up for years when you may have made little or no contributions to your personal retirement savings plan. The "past-service allowance" can raise your contribution level to 20 percent of your gross pay plus $3,200, and you can have this credit prorated over future years to give you a level savings plan.

On the other hand, IRAs, which are available to most of the rest of us, are based on the premise that during our younger years, when we are often struggling to raise a family and buy a home, we have the same disposable income for savings as when our children are grown and a big chunk of our debts are paid. It's a faulty assumption and you and I know it.

Since TSAs were created long before IRAs, they have no early withdrawal penalty. Like IRAs, TSAs are not attachable in case of bankruptcy and they can be paid to a named beneficiary. Investment opportunities are almost as unlimited as those for IRAs. But TSAs extend beyond saving for your retirement. With the passage of the Tax Equity and Fiscal Responsibility Act of 1982, better known as TEFRA, TSAs allow the contributing employee to borrow up to one-half of his or her TSA account, to a maximum of $50,000, for the down payment on a principal residence. One twist in borrowing from a TSA is that you are, in effect, borrowing from yourself. Your interest payments and the repayment of the loan go back into your own account, and if you itemize on your tax return, you can take a deduction for the interest you pay to yourself!

TSAs, with catch-up features for older workers and assistance in buying a home for younger people, are what IRAs should be. Dozens of bills have been introduced into Congress to expand IRAs in these areas and I believe IRAs will soon permit access to your account before retirement.

Congress hatched the Keogh plan in 1962 as the government's answer to bargain-basement tax savings for nonincorporated business owners. Named after Congressman Eugene J. Keogh of New York, Keogh plans permit self-employed, nonincorporated business owners to set aside money on a tax deductible basis for retirement. In 1974, under the Employee Retirement Income Security Act (ERISA), Congress created the IRA, which did the same thing for individuals not covered by a retirement plan at work that the Keogh plan did for self-employed individuals. Under the 1974 law, the small business lobby hit pay dirt. Annual contributions permitted for Keogh plans were increased up to $7,500 and their contribution limits over IRAs have widened ever since.

The first IRAs were limited to 15 percent of pay or a maximum of $1,500, but problems began to surface almost at once. First, millions of workers covered at work by totally inadequate retirement plans were barred from opening an IRA. In some cases, they were covered under profit sharing plans, plans to which employer contributions were rarely made, but the law still didn't allow them to open their own IRAs. Also, self-employed business owners, unhappy with the $7,500 limit on Keogh plans, wanted the same generous limits for their Keogh plans that applied to corporate retirement plans.

Therefore, Congress expanded both plans in 1982, allowing *all* workers to open IRAs and boosting the limits of Keogh plans to $30,000 while the limitations on IRAs were raised from a mere $500 to $2,000.

($2,250 where only one spouse works outside the home.) It seems almost a simple-minded observation, but many American workers didn't like the fact that while they were making the same total income as a self-employed friend, they had less than one-tenth of their friend's maximum deductions under the law. Workers began to rain letters on members of the Senate Finance and House Ways and Means Committees. Every silver lining has a cloud, of course. If you work for someone else, the gap between you and a self-employed worker has since been narrowed—and in some cases eliminated—but only if you funnel your contributions through your employer.

The introduction of these saving plans—TSAs, Keogh plans, 401(K) plans, and IRAs—has profoundly altered the way American workers will save for their graying years.

We Must Balance Individual and Group Savings Plans

We are in the midst of a major shift from Social Security and individual retirement savings to employer-sponsored savings plans. In fact, second-generation tax-favored individual retirement plans have already begun. The transition time between the old and the new is collapsing as one idea follows another. Therefore, changes in the way we save for retirement will occur much faster as financial entrepreneurship booms. We are now entering that period.

Simplified employee pensions, or SEPs, are marching to the same drummer as TSAs. A product of the 1978 Tax Reform Act, SEPs allow your employer to make contributions directly into your IRA. Once the money is there, you have the same control over it as if you made the contributions yourself. The maximum annual contribution to a SEP-IRA is $30,000, but it may be no more than 25 percent of your salary. Most contributions work out to about 10 to 15 percent of pay—a substantial jump over the $2,000 IRA limit when you do it yourself.

Another second-generation plan has workers in growing numbers scrambling for something that may sound like the come-on of a con man. Employer-sponsored schemes bearing the uninviting title of 401(k) plans are named for the section of the Internal Revenue Service code that outlines the provisions. The idea is simple and perfectly legal. You voluntarily take a cut in pay—on paper—and your employer puts the salary reduction into a tax-sheltered 401(k) plan on your behalf. The bonus is that the amount you save isn't subject to federal income tax, which also trims most state and local income taxes. If you earn $40,000 and put $4,000 into a 401(k) plan, your taxable compensation falls to $36,000. As with an IRA, your earnings or profits on 401(k) monies are tax deferred, which means your savings can grow faster than in almost any other taxable investment you can make on your own. And, for now, you can have an IRA on the side!

The growth of 401(k) plans has been staggering. Sometimes called "salary reduction plans" or "cash or deferred arrangements" they were authorized by Congress in 1980. Because of a delay by the Internal Revenue Service in issuing rules for the new plans, they barely existed four years ago. In 1982, 1 percent of the 250 major companies in this country had them. In 1983, the number had risen to 43 percent, and by 1984 it had soared to 74 percent. From big names like General Electric, Ford, Quaker Oats, and RCA to the local employer with a dozen employees, everyone seems to be maneuvering into the fast-spreading plan that reduces both salary and taxes. The American Electronics Association is setting up an industry-wide 401(k) plan that any of its 2,800 member companies can join. All told, roughly 18 million workers—young as well as old—are now taking a cut in pay as a way to save both money and taxes for the future. A benefits consultant figures that two-thirds or more of eligible workers participate in 401(k) plans when offered the chance. "There's nothing else quite like this," he says. "The guy can cut his taxable wages, get the company to sweeten the pot, and boost his savings without costing him a dime, and he can often use the money to buy a house or send his kids to college."

More impressive is the fact that 401(k) plans dodge the tax man far better than an IRA. Maximum annual contribution, including employer contribution, is a hefty $30,000. For IRAs, it is $2,250 including spousal contributions. The big lure, however, is the features 401(k) plans have borrowed from the older corporate retirement plans, like the matching plan, in which employers typically kick in a contribution for every dollar the employee contributes.

Let's look at an employee who earns $40,000. With an IRA she might contribute $2,000, or 5 percent of her salary. With a 401(k) plan she might contribute 10 percent of her pay, or $4,000. The typical employer then boosts the savings by a matching contribution of 50 cents on the dollar, or an additional $2,000. Since the employee may also have an IRA, she can save $2,000 more. That's a total of $8,000, or 20 percent of her annual income—four times the limit of an IRA alone. Retirement nest eggs balloon when they are protected from the ravages of taxes. For example, if these contributions were made for ten years, beginning at age 40, the difference between saving taxes on $2,000 and on $6,000 of pay (with the employer putting in the other $2,000 in the 401(k) plan) is startling. Tax savings for the $2,000 IRA contributions totalling $20,000 would be about $460 a year, or $4,600. On the 401(k) contributions totalling $60,000, tax savings come to about $1,380 a year, or $13,800. That's a hefty $9,200 in outright tax savings in 10 years.

But the big bonus is earning income that is tax deferred. Assume that both the IRA and the 401(k) earned 10 percent annually for the ten-year period. The IRA account would total about $35,000 for a total tax-deductible cost of $20,000. The 401(k) would total about $140,250 for a total tax-deductible cost of $60,000.

What makes the 401(k) a second-generation savings plan and the IRA a first-generation one is the 401(k)'s ability to give workers access to their savings prior to retirement and then offer sizable tax benefits when they take the cash out in retirement. A big plus, especially for younger workers, is the employer's leeway in giving employees access to their 401(k) accounts during their working years. With an IRA, you can't take out your funds without a tax penalty until you reach age 59½ or become disabled. But if you leave your job with the employer who is sponsoring a 401(k) plan, your money can be withdrawn without a tax penalty or it can be rolled over into an IRA.

In addition 401(k) plans let you do something else that you can't do with IRAs: You can make withdrawals during your employment under what are called "hardship" provisions. While the IRS has yet to define hardship, it is commonly interpreted as a situation in which you are unable to financially provide for such major expenses as a home, college tuition, or big medical bills. In actual practice, the employer often determines what qualifies as a hardship. Some employers allow hardship withdrawals for legal expenses and home repairs, others for buying a car and commuting to work. Withdrawals from a 401(k) plan are current income in the year of withdrawal, but unlike an IRA, there is no additional 10 percent tax penalty for people under age 59½.

You may need to use the cash in your account but you'd rather not pay income taxes on the money you withdraw at this time. With a second-generation tax-deferred plan you don't have to. More and more firms now permit workers to borrow from 401(k) plans, with loans at the prime rate or less. If you borrow money from an IRA-like tax-deferred savings plan, you can use the money without paying any tax, because you are, in effect, borrowing from yourself.

401(k) plans not only let you avoid taxes when you put the money in, they almost dodge the tax man when you take the money out in retirement, using something called ten-year income averaging. If you take the money out in a lump sum, ten-year averaging could let you treat the payout as if it were received in 10 annual installments. Unlike an IRA, where your withdrawals are lumped on top of your current income, boosting your tax rate, ten-year averaging is separate from your other current income. Ten-year averaging can often cut your taxes to less than half of what you'd pay with an IRA.

The Death of the Pension System

We are in the process of making a massive shift from fixed pension benefits to an employer-employee financed retirement system. To many working Americans it might appear that tax reform has sabotaged their retirement security, but it is the only realistic course this nation could follow. As we've already learned, pensions have become too expensive for all but the wealthiest corporations and Social Security. We created the pension system over one hundred years ago when it was the practical way to continue some form of monthly wages for employees in retirement. Direct participation by workers in paying part of their retirement income simply was not feasible, so the employer set up the plan.

But then the issue of fairness became a consideration. Today, since mobile workers job-hop every few years—and don't work long enough with one employer to earn a pension—most working people wouldn't quality for a pension. It's a great idea to qualify for a pension benefit after only a few years on the job, but the added cost of hefty payments to most employees or cash buy-outs when employees leave the job early simply make pensions too expensive for most employers.

Today, to qualify for tax breaks, private pensions plans must follow federal rules meant to ensure fairness to mobile workers, women, and those who work past age 65. Laws now require the minimum time on the job needed to earn a pension be shortened from 10 years (it was 15 years during the last decade) to only 5 years. Companies would be forced to cover at least 80 percent of their employees if they offer a pension, not the minimum 56 percent previously required. And employers could deduct no more than 50 percent of the intended pension benefit for workers covered by Social Security in retirement.

This major reform to gain fairness now for retirement later would boost the cost of pensions because more people would collect them in retirement or when they leave their jobs during their working years.

We are in the midst of a major shift from employer-financed pensions to plans in which the responsibility for our retirement security is shared. Essentially, we are telling our employers, "Okay, if you can no longer pay the bills for a fair and reasonable retirement system, we want to help with our own contributions." *The fundamental change in retirement security is that in the future both the employer and employee will finance the benefits.* Both in our investing and in our retirement planning, we are becoming a nation of "self-help" independents—and not waiting for company or government hand-outs.

With tax laws squeezing pensions, most working people will be drawn to retirement plans (already on the books) to which they can contribute on a tax-deferred basis. These include TSAs (for school teachers and other employees who work for nonprofit organizations), 401(k) plans, Thrift plans, and SEP-IRAs (Employee-employer sponsored IRAs). IRAs will lose ground. When you can contribute up to $7,000 a year in a 401(k) plan with your employer matching your contributions, IRAs pale by comparison.

All the present impetus toward giving employees opportunities to fund a major share of their retirement benefits in employer-sponsored plans depends on how much cash an individual chooses to put into the plan and how successfully it is invested. Many people will not be able to manage those choices and will rely on Social Security and society when they retire. But many more will have undreamed-of opportunities to help themselves. They'll be able to boost their contributions as they near retirement age, make all their retirement savings tax-deferred, and with both their own and their employer's contributions, end up with a considerable monthly income when they retire.

This fundamental change in the way we save for retirement in the years to come will be known as "double-savings." As long as workers and employers join hands and work together both will be able to contribute almost as much as they want on a tax-deferred basis.

We Are Moving from a
Tax-Oriented Society to an Income-Oriented Society

Central to the whole issue of self-help in long-term saving and investing is the development of second- and third-generation plans. For investing, these plans will concentrate on earning taxable income in a 30 percent tax bracket with no limit on the future growth of the earnings. For retirement savings, the plans will focus on delaying taxes on money saved, rather than saving taxes on income already earned. They will give the young the incentive to save for a home and the middle-aged the opportunity to make up for lost time by boosting their savings as they near retirement.

If you look at the trends already underway beneath today's successful middle- and even upper-class investors, you can identify the probable sites of tomorrow's savings and investments. Today, with stocks and mutual funds dancing up and down on Wall Street charts, many Americans believe that anything fancier than old-fashioned fixed savings is too dicey in these turbulent times. But a growing number of smart investors are finding that they can get the same upside profit potential with a minimum of downside risks with the new second-generation savings plans. The plans offer the "magic three" of safety, guarantee of fixed income, and open-ended future income potential. As they did with tax shelters, investors will find they can have a piece of the action and a chance to earn big returns; yet they'll have a secure, highly liquid asset that can smooth out a bumpy financial road in a way tax shelters never did. With safety of principal and unlimited profit potential, smart Americans will no longer let banks and savings and loans borrow their after-tax savings in return for only a modest fixed rate of return. It's a radical change, of course, but individual investors put up most of the cash for real estate, land, and commercial development and the savings plans of the future will guarantee individual investors both a fixed return *and* a share of the profits to attract the cash.

As deregulation turns the financial business from being product driven to being more focused on customers, these second-generation savings plans will become more attractive than anything we can now envision. Some mistakes are probably inevitable, but in the long run enhanced savings plans will be extremely successful. On the other hand, the quickest way to the poorhouse will be to embrace an investment strategy based on fixed savings.

The simple rule of the future: It will be hard to prosper when you go for tax savings first and income second in your investments. Likewise, it will be hard to profit when you go for income first and tax savings second on your retirement savings.

In retirement savings, we are in the midst of a major change in the way we attract people's money. The Reagan administration wants to encourage savings for retirement, not pre-retirement. The trend, however, is clearly moving in the other direction, away from a forced choice in a closed system to second-generation savings plans like SEP-IRAs and 401(k)s. In a now-oriented society, many people recoil at the thought of tying up their money for 30 or 40 years. "When you lock up things tighter than a box," says a benefits manager, "you get the opposite of the intended effect. People won't save." I believe that the administration and Congress will in the end encourage pre-retirement savings as a way to boost the economy and give employers some control over a rapidly changing savings environment.

Simply stated, cutting the maximum individual tax rate to 30 percent, locking in fixed returns with unlimited upside potential, and developing employer-sponsored plans to save taxes and money both before and after retirement will have a profound effect on the way Americans handle their money. Whatever happens will happen fast, and you will come out the real winner.

While the shift away from first-generation fixed-interest passbook savings accounts and employer-paid pensions took 100 years, the present restructuring to second-generation enhanced earnings-based insured CDs and 401(k) plans took only four years. In the future, change will occur so rapidly in the new information and deregulated society that each investor and saver will assume a new responsibility, unknown to the previous generation. The strategic resource of the future will be information and knowledge, not hard cash.

9

From Expert Help to Self-Help

The Keys to Do-It-Yourself Financial Planning

Americans know more about investing than ever before, yet they often forget what their forefathers knew: Money is more easily lost than gained. Fraud stories are commonplace within the securities industry. Gypsters, with their hot tips, never give a sucker an even break.

Looking back on this decade, chaos in the financial markets will be the story of the 1980s. The chaos is reflected in the number of government securities firms, savings and loans, small brokers, and commercial banks that have failed; heavy trading in a number of complex new investments, such as stock index options, have made financial markets more frenzied and perilous.

The regulators are in place in the form of the Securities and Exchange Commission, the government agency created in 1934 to police the investment world. But with the SEC's leaky umbrella, individual investors are now at greater risk of losing their money through fraud than at any time in the past 40 years. The problem is that both by design and through financial deregulation, the agency has cut back on regulations and is unable to carry out its mandate.

And the disparity between the growing number of financial markets and the shrinking SEC work force is widening. For example, in the five years between 1979 and 1984 the securities markets have boomed. The daily share volume on the New York Stock Exchange rose by 184 percent, the number of stockbrokers by 50 percent. Meanwhile, customer complaints to the SEC soared by over 100 percent, and investor cases brought to securities dealers for arbitration jumped by 322 percent.

There was a time when most investors could understand what was going on in the financial markets. Today, however, legitimate investments are becoming more complicated because of a burgeoning number of new products, forcing people increasingly in turn to bankers, brokers, accountants, financial planners, even employers and department stores for advice and assistance in managing their personal assets.

Is It a Great Deal—or a Scam?

With financial deregulation tearing apart what was once an orderly market, there's an epidemic of financial swindlers and frauds. Even reputable financial institutions are using omissions and misleading statements with the intent of fleecing you as never before. The use of questionable gimmicks has proliferated to a point far beyond the ability of our federal and state enforcement agencies and regulators to eliminate them. Losses have spread to every part of the country, with investors in every profession and of all educational backgrounds taking the bait.

One of the biggest scams is also the oldest: the Ponzi scheme. In the past three years alone a staggering $2 billion has been lost in some 30 giant Ponzi schemes. These investment swindles are based on the real-life adventures of the Boston swindler Charles (Carlo) Ponzi. He came to New York City in 1903 at the age of 20, an Italian immigrant, penniless and unable to speak English. By 1920 he had moved to Boston, where he established a worthless company with the imposing name of "Securities Exchange Company."

Ponzi had discovered that international reply coupons (literally international postage stamps) could be purchased from post offices in America and redeemed abroad for a profit of as much as 250 percent, depending on the exchange rate. Originally, postal reply coupons had been established as a way for Americans to prepay postage for relatives or friends overseas, many living just above the poverty line and often hard pressed to come up with the postage themselves. The fact that reply coupons were seldom used by the public and could only be redeemed for postage stamps did not deter Ponzi; he was set to make millions from an idea that *appeared to make sense on paper.* By convincing the authorities and the public that he could make money buying and selling reply coupons, Ponzi set out to develop the country's first pyramid scheme.

He accepted "investments" redeemable in 90 days at 50 percent interest. Investors were to receive their profits from reply coupons; just how, Ponzi never made clear. At a time when Boston banks were paying 4 percent annual interest, Ponzi's scheme seemed to good to be true. Ponzi began methodically working the greed factor, using the little fish to catch the big ones; until by some estimates investors had poured as much as $15 million into the Security Exchange Company. The idea would work, Ponzi knew, only so long as the interest earned was paid out of the money received from subsequent investors.

Like a giant chain letter, the plan at first succeeded beyond his wildest dreams as more and more money poured in to cover the maturing 90-day notes. With riches far beyond anything he or his family had ever known, no expense was spared. Ponzi entertained lavishly, bought the best cars, hired his friends to lure more investors, and set out to enjoy the best that life could offer. But in the second year the scam ran into trouble. It had started with a come-on, offering something for nothing. Thousands bit while Ponzi flipped the money back and forth, but as the pyramid forced the payouts to soar, there finally came a time when no money was left in the till. What the fishes learned the hard way is that if you're going to make money in a Ponzi scheme, it's not enough to be the first one in; you have to be the first one out as well.

Ponzi lived 60 years ago, but his investment scams live on. Recently a new generation of greedy people jumped at what looked like a sweet deal: A 30 percent to 40 percent return in 90 days on "certificates of investment" offered by the Maryland-based Life Investors Group, a "financial planning" firm. Investors got bogus promissory notes for their money. When state investigators stepped in, they found a trail of nonexistent assets left after some $2.5 million had been gathered from 243 investors in the Washington, D.C., area. In Sacramento, California, another modern-day Ponzi took in $7 million from 250 investors by guaranteeing only 22 percent interest on phony real estate partnerships and money market funds. The promoter killed himself as deputy sheriffs prepared to arrest him on 49 felony counts of theft and fraud. The investors lost everything.

Today, newer Ponzi-like schemes are based on secured loans

obtained with inflated assets, often worth a fraction of their stated value. These investor rip-offs have become so commonplace that their inventors need a gimmick to make them interesting. In 1985, a group of Ponzis found one. The promoters discovered a ghost town just outside Dallas, Texas, where roughly 2,500 unfinished condominiums had been neglected and were in various states of decay. Chimneys had collapsed, uncovered walls let in the wind and dirt, and the condos looked like they should be torn down before they fell down. It was the ideal place for a real estate scam based, not on limited partnerships, but on individuals taking out home mortgages on the condominiums.

What made this pyramid scheme novel is that unlike the original Ponzi deal, the investors, who would provide the cash to renovate the condos, not only were promised a return of $200,000 in a two-year period with no cash up front, but they would also get $20,000 or more in cash at the time they took out the home mortgages, *without putting up a dime*. Once again the little fish—the construction workers, the secretaries—bit, and they brought in the big fishes—the lawyers, doctors, judges, and some of the city's big names.

About 400 investors formed the bottom of the pyramid. They were needed by the promoters because their net worth was the basis for the home mortgages, and guarantees on the land, and the construction loans. But to get the hefty up-front money—$20,000 for their signature on a loan form—many people exaggerated their net worth to qualify for the mortgage. Some were even lured into colluding in the fraud. An appraiser was bribed and the loan packages were financed at 110 percent of their stated value. Inside the financial scam, people got fees for finding the investors, fees for doing the paperwork, and fees for obtaining the mortgages.

When it became apparent that the promoters had pocketed the money instead of fixing up the condos for resale, this modern-day Ponzi scheme turned into one of the largest bank frauds in history: $500 million in bad loans. The FSLIC has already paid out $300 million on insured deposits used to make the real estate loans and $25 million more to try to sell the condos. Because the condos weren't finished and sold, the investors are personally liable for tens of thousands of dollars, and in some cases millions of dollars, in real estate loans they can never expect to repay. The promoters got the tens of millions of dollars and, like Ponzi, there is no sign of them or the money.

If you think the Dallas scam is unique, you are wrong. Secured loans of inflated value form the basis for scores of fraudulent schemes. The bank vaults in Zurich, Switzerland, would seem like a safe place to store a fortune in precious gems. The gems, supposedly worth $90 million, had been pledged as security for $45 million of bank loans. But when Swiss investigators unlocked the steel boxes in which the gems were stored, they found hundreds of rubies, emeralds, and sapphires worth 5 to 10 percent of their represented value. The appraiser told the shocked bankers and insurance men the gems were like those "sold by mail order in America—rip-offs." Sixteen banks in five countries, plus hundreds of individual German investors, may have lost as much as $135 million on this and other gem-related investment scams over the last five years.

Ponzi schemes and over-valued secured loans are merely a few of the investing and saving scams waiting to lure your money. Con artists are promoting phony tax shelters involving everything from drilling rigs that don't drill for oil to investments in records and films that have no audience. Stockbrokers churn your account to make their money on commissions and your capital shrinks; financial planners take a piece of the action for investing your hard-earned cash in two cows in Montana whose calves you are to sell, but they end up as hamburger instead.

In the explosion of investments brought about by deregulation, some of the new investment and savings plans seem, at first glance, weird, even if they are legitimate. The problem in this kind of market is that a crook can offer things that *look* like the same kind of unusual but legitimate deals, but they're not.

The next time you are intrigued by an investment or savings opportunity that sounds too good to be true, look for these telltale signs:

• *High-pressure tactics.* If you are asked to make a snap decision so you won't have time to investigate the promoters or their product, don't bite. An old saying on Wall Street comes to mind: There is always another stock and always another day.

• *Secured bank loans.* If the investment requires you or the promoter to rely on secured bank loans, you'd better think twice. Not only can the investment fail, but you could be held liable for not only your original investment but your share of the unpaid loans as well.

• *Telephone sales.* You may never know where the promoters are located, how to check them out, or if they'll be gone soon after you've invested your money. If they won't send you the information in the mail, it probably won't stand the light of day.

• *Inside information.* In the fast-moving world of money today, inside information is hard to come by. By the time you or your broker find out about it, it's old news. Unless you're a substantial client on a direct hook-up to the eyes and ears of Wall Street, don't bank on insider information. Besides, who would offer incredible riches to the average investor with a few thousand dollars to invest?

• *Fabulous returns.* Again, when it seems too good to be true, it probably is. If you can't get detailed information on how the investment is to generate the fabulous returns, or a list of investors who already receive these incredible returns, don't bite.

• *No-risk offers.* There are no risk-free deals any more. On government bonds, you can lose money. On insured CDs, you can lose money. On investment products from your broker or financial planner, you can lose a great deal of money.

The way to cut your losses is through self-help, not with so-called expert help. With deregulation, the burden of hanging on to your cash falls squarely on your shoulders. You will have to be less passive when dealing with your bank, broker, or insurance company. For example, even well-established financial institutions are misleading the public in the desperate battle for the consumer's dollar. Consumers Union, the publisher of *Consumer Reports* magazine, filed suit against the fourth-largest savings and loan in California, claiming it engaged in illegal and deceptive mortgage-loan advertising. Federal truth-in-lending laws are supposed to protect the consumer by requiring that advertisements specify how long a so-called teaser rate is good for. If you're going to lock up your savings for two years or take out a home mortgage for 15, you should know just how chancy the whole deal is before you plunk your money down or sign your name.

Consumers Union says the advertisements were illegal and deceptive by offering adjustable home mortgages at 9 percent but not warning the homebuyer that the rate could soar to 11 percent after as little as six months, and ultimately climb to as high as 14 percent. "It's not so much what the ads say, as what they don't say," a staff attorney for Consumers Union stressed. "Consumers tend to go for the lowest rate they see, but this is not a 9 percent loan." What's scary is that under a lot of adjustable rate home mortgages that have negative amortization, home buyers can make payments for three years and then face a loan balance that is substantially higher than when they took out the mortgage.

Some banks and S&Ls use misleading and deceptive advertising to try to swindle you out of your money when you withdraw your cash before the end of a CD's term. If you're not wary, you can actually get back less than what you deposited in an insured CD. The early withdrawal penalty is first subtracted from your earned interest. If your earned interest does not cover the penalty, the balance of the charges are subtracted from your principal.

In a blizzard of words and pictures about how safe and secure you'll be if you let them have your savings deposits, many large financial institutions cover the thorny issue of taking you to the cleaners with the simple statement: "Substantial penalty for early withdrawal." What they do not tell you in their advertisements, but what they say they tell you when you open an account in person or with their 800 phone number, is that if you withdraw your money in an emergency, before the maturity of your CD, you can lose several months of interest and, in the case of some major S&Ls, 2 percent of the money you've invested!

I asked an executive of one of these S&Ls why they did not make this clear in their advertisements. "It would have a negative impact on sales," he said. "Besides, with the mad scramble to bolster our deposits we're just doing what everyone else is doing."

S&Ls Are Sounding More and More Like Stockbrokers

On a radio program, I had as my guest a broker from one of the major S&Ls. The securities branch of the S&L was touting tax-free bonds, zero coupon bonds, and equity products. The conversation went something like this:

> "I see you're pushing double tax-free interest income at 9.5 percent at the same time your branches are offering fully taxable interest income at 8 percent," I said.
>
> "That's right. We want to offer our customers every opportunity to do business with us."
>
> "But when customers can get almost double the after-tax return on the products offered by the securities division, won't they yank out their money from your branches?" I asked.
>
> "They already are. We just want to hang onto the money and keep it from going to the brokers," he said.
>
> "I see. So that's why you've formed a brokerage investment company and why you're taking to market limited partnerships in real estate."
>
> "Yes. We intend to offer the services that brokers do where it will help our customers most."

One of the first signs of the new financial environment created by deregulation is that different financial institutions have begun to look alike. And companies are quickly moving toward becoming financial supermarkets. By the end of this decade, there will be little difference between what a bank, S&L, broker, insurance company, and mutual fund can offer the consumer. Yet when these varied institutions offer the same financial products, when they blur in our eyes as a bank or a broker, they will then all face the intense heat of competition and many will find that without their previous special niche, they will fail.

How to Find a Financial Planner

Anyone who wants to call himself a "financial planner" can be one, so hundreds of thousands of insurance agents, brokers, mutual fund salesmen, and tax-shelter promoters have entered this new game. Prudential-Bache Securities advertises not stocks, bonds, insured CDs, and insurance, but total financial planning. Merrill Lynch brokers are no longer account executives, they're financial consultants. Big accounting firms who used to just keep the books now have a director of personal financial planning in each office. Banks and insurance companies have scores of financial planners geared up to go after the middle-income client. And a swarm of independent financial planning firms fills the Yellow Pages.

If you want to get started planning for your own financial future they will give you a long questionnaire to fill out and send back with your check. In return you get a computer-generated financial plan. On the low end of the scale, Sears and several mutual funds will sell you a plan off the rack for around $25 to $50. Credit unions, which have entered the low-cost end of the jam-packed financial planning field, plan to roll out a $50 computer run that uses your financial data as the basis for a 30-page booklet with strategies for IRAs, savings, insurance, home financing, and college expenses. Brokerage firms and accountants prepare plans for $150 to $500. Financial plans that require personal interviews and an in-depth study of your financial affairs run between $1,500 and $10,000. Or you can do it yourself with the help of your personal computer and some of the good software programs that are on the market.

The basic premise—that you need a financial plan to develop your assets—is a sound one, but here again you need to guard against the gypsters specializing in fancy-looking financial plans that say nothing. James Karpen, director of enforcement for the Michigan Securities Bureau, says his office has seen computer-generated individual financial plans for middle- and lower-income people that cost as much as $1,500, and that they were basically worthless exercises—mostly just common sense.

The problem is not finding a financial planner; the problem is finding one that's qualified. No financial industry is so unregulated, so dimly perceived, yet can offer so much (and then often do so little), as the financial planning industry. From a few enterprising guys using a catchy term dreamed up by hungry insurance salespeople in the 1930s, there are now, by some estimates, over 250,000 financial planners in the country. They range from those with no relevant education or experience to MBAs and certified financial planners (CFPs).

Professionals within the industry and state officials are worried about the growing number of incompetent planners, many of whom have conflicts of interest, and some of whom are outright frauds. As a result, pressure is growing to create some form of regulation for this new industry of "financial consultants." The California legislature is considering a bill that would force all financial planners in that state to register as investment advisers. "If we force them to be considered investment advisers," says a consultant to the State Senate, "then we can seize records and slap civil sanctions on them." The hang-up is that bankers, followed by accountants, have muscled exceptions for themselves. The California Bankers Association argues that banks are already over-regulated, but in the financial planning field that's not true. There are no regulations at all to cover their growing presence in financial planning. Other states, like Arizona, Oregon, New York, Maine, Massachusetts, and Maryland have bills pending to register financial planners. The North American Securities Administrators Association (NASAA), made up of state regulators, examined financial planners' operations in 20 states and found almost $90 million worth of deceptive and abusive deals associated with people who called themselves financial planners. "What we're seeing now is the first stage of an epidemic of fraud and abuses arising from the underside of the financial planning industry," Wayne Howell, director of the Georgia Securities Division and NASAA president warns. "The current era is a made-to-order incubator for financial fraud."[1]

Registering financial planners won't transform the horde of insurance agents, stockbrokers, mutual fund salesmen, and independent financial planners into objective, qualified planners. You can't legislate intelligence or stanch the generous flow of bad advice, but the failure to register could become a felony, giving state officials another club to wield in their battle to weed out the charlatans and con artists.

Granted, there are thousands of well-qualified financial planners waiting to help you manage your money, but when an industry triples its size in a few years, thousands of unsupervised, unregulated, and unqualified frauds are also waiting to fleece you. "I can attest to the fact that there are substantial investment sums raised by financial planners that are passed into the hands of con men who are now facing criminal charges," says Robert J. Sullivan, a district attorney in San Diego, California. One investment come-on was a scheme to buy gold directly from a Nevada mine and sell it to California precious-metal dealers for a 120 percent annual return to investors. A call to any reputable precious-metal dealer could have disproved this claim, but investors never made the call. With promises of fabulous profits dancing before their eyes, they wanted to believe the financial planner, who in turn had hefty commissions dancing before his eyes. "The financial planners got exorbitant finders' fees," Sullivan said, "and financial planners rarely get prosecuted."[2]

Amid all this criticism, a basic fact remains: More than 10 million Americans could use professional help in planning their financial future. A good financial plan will help you track your cash flow down to the last dime, suggest ways to cut your taxes, boost your investment earnings, and set up special funds for the kids' education and your retirement. The increase in two-income families where each income can be treated separately, the confusion caused by financial deregulation, and the phenomenal growth in new ideas and products, require more information and planning. In the end, however, you'll have to make more agonizing decisions yourself than ever before.

Instead of constantly bemoaning the frauds some financial planners commit, let me help you find a qualified financial planner who might do you some good. Over the years, I have hosted money talk shows with financial planners, talked with them about their business operations, and received hundreds of letters from across the country about their activities. Here are some tips on finding a financial planner:

• *Make an initial office visit.* Most financial planners will give you a free or low-priced initial office visit to see if the chemistry between the two of you is right. Visit two or three planners so you can compare them. During the meeting, ask the planner if you will be dealing directly with him or her, or with an assistant. If the planner turns your work over to a junior associate, check that person out, too. Also find out what the planner would do in specific situations. You can judge very quickly by the answer if the planner operates within your comfort zone and will later steer you clear of investments that make you feel uneasy. In the end, the best financial planner is someone who thinks and acts like you do.

• *Check experience and qualifications.* A financial planner should have on file a statement about his or her background and experience. Does the planner have impressive educational qualifications, as indicated by sets of initials following his or her name on the letterhead?

The certified financial planner (CFP) designation comes after two years of college-like study, and is awarded by the College for Financial Planning in Denver, Colorado. The Institute of Certified Financial Planners (ICFP), whose members are CFPs, has educational standards and a code of ethics. The International Association of Financial Planners (IAFP) is a trade association whose members also abide by a code of ethics. And the chartered financial consultant (ChFC) is a designation given by the American College in Bryn Mawr, Pennsylvania, a life insurance-based group in which most ChFCs are also chartered life underwriters (CLUs). Finally, the National Association of Personal Financial Advisors (NAPFA) is a group of "fee-only" planners.

• *Learn how the planner makes money.* Most financial planners earn their income on commissions. Some charge a fee for their time and earn commissions on their sales. Some are fee-only planners who manage your financial assets without selling investments. At your first meeting, find out what fees, if any, you'll be expected to pay up front.

• *Find out how the planner works.* Will the planner provide references from three or more clients who have been counseled for at least two years? Ask to see examples of plans and reports drawn up for other investors. Some financial planners are "captive" agents of a large financial firm and they are usually required to place most of their business with their own company. Others are independent, self-employed planners who can recommend any financial product they feel might fit your specific situation.

Get Ready for More Products

Life was simpler in the 1960s. Everybody bought stocks and that was about it. Today, the proliferation of investments, from stock options to mutual funds, has put a strain on the industry's delivery system—the retail broker and financial planner working directly with clients—and that system hasn't changed much in decades. "We get at least one new product every day," a branch office manager for a large broker says. "They range from new commodity accounts to tax shelters and annuities. Brokers can choose from 300 or so of the 1,500 different mutual funds and dozens of tax-shelter programs and insurance products. It's really mind-boggling and my brokers all complain that there's so much to choose from it confuses them."

The seeds of broker overload were planted in the early 1980s, when rising inflation and interest rates motivated investors to do more comparison shopping. This led brokers to expand their product line

from stocks and bonds to insurance annuities, life insurance, specialized mutual funds, stock options, money market funds, and insured
certificates of deposit. Under deregulation, the brokerage industry
wanted to sell the latest and widest range of investments to keep their
customers away from the banks or insurance companies. As a result,
brokers and planners are under increasing pressure to sell a growing
number of new products and services, even though they may not fully
understand the risks and rewards of each new product. In the rush to
sell, many salespeople lean to the products with high commissions or
yield to aggressive product managers who apply the strongest pressure
to meet quotas. The pressure to sell is often greatest in the large
brokerage operations where the introduction of a new investment
product can launch a contest in which brokers can win bonus credits
and establish a ranking within the branch and the company.

The underlying problem, in a financial system ablaze with new
products, is that brokers and financial planners have to sell to eat.
Taking time to learn what they need to know about a score of products
or explaining the customer agreements you'll sign when you open an
account cuts deeply into the time they can spend talking to existing
clients and looking for new business.

When you open your stock brokerage account, your broker will ask
you to sign a few forms. These forms run between two and four pages
and you'll need a magnifying glass to read the small print. One part of
the form has an arbitration clause in which the customer agrees to
arbitrate any claims and thereby deprives him- or herself of the right to
sue the broker in court and the right to have a jury trial. Many
customers cross out the arbitration clause and this does not seem to
discourage the brokers from doing business with them. You must
receive a basic customer agreement when you open an account. If you
don't have your agreement, ask your broker to send you a copy.

When the financial environment changes as fast as it has for
financial products and services, the public also becomes confused. The
number of ways to save and invest begins to whiz by like race cars
roaring past you at track level at the Indianapolis Speedway. The roar
caused by the bewildering inundation of advertisements is not the
sound and fury signifying nothing, but it's close. We are told on radio,
television, and in the papers that this or that place to save or invest our
money offers a heaven-sent opportunity to cash in on the fast track to
riches. Our mind, meanwhile, is on our fears that we will somehow be
run over in the middle of the speedway by one of these new financial
products racing out of control.

"All of our research says today's client wants someone to talk to," an executive of a large brokerage operation said. "If a broker isn't willing to listen, he's going to be banished to the land of the fast sale and he'll probably work harder for less money." Brokers and planners are seeing one of the biggest changes in the industry since the invention of the telephone. Suddenly people want to come in and chat about their finances.

On my money talk shows, the 11 telephone lines are constantly flashing as people desperate to talk with someone about their personal financial problems wait their turn. For all their differences in outlook and needs in a seemingly derailed financial world, they are all searching for someone they can trust. In spite of the unprecedented number of financial products they have to choose from, most of the callers are simply looking for savings and investments that will help them hold onto what they already have. One call may be from a college student about to graduate, expecting to make $25,000 a year with $1,500 in savings. Then an older woman tells me that she and her husband depend on their investments to receive a "livable" income. "We don't have a broker or a consultant we can confide in, so any help you can give us will be sincerely appreciated."

Typical of the letters I get is one from a woman in Ohio who wrote, "I often feel like a complete idiot. Could you please recommend some reading material that would get us headed in the right direction? My husband and I make more than $50,000 a year, but we seem to just fritter the money away and I don't know where to start." A man in Texas wrote, "I'm just small peanuts but I can't afford to lose what I have. The more I see, the more appalled I become over how to deal with all the products on the market. Only those who started juggling figures at an early age or have an MBA can stay on top of this mess."

In the past we allowed ourselves to act as passive bystanders, handing over our money to banks and brokers. But today we are finding that the responsibility belongs only to ourselves, and that in many cases in a deregulated environment institutions have failed us. More and more we are becoming disillusioned, asking "What, or whom, can we trust?"

Self-help will be the password to success in the financial business of the future. And central to the self-help concept will be marketing, not sales. Marketing is finding out what the client needs, sales is selling what's on the shelf. The successful financial institutions will gear their business away from product-driven selling to customer-focused investing. Instead of selling products on the basis of high yields, fat tax advantages, and future growth, banks and brokers will listen to their customers and then tailor the sales to the individual's needs. In talking with brokers and financial planners who have yet to learn this lesson, I get the feeling that many of them already know what they will recommend to a client before he or she comes in the front door. And very often, it's what's on the shelf in the back room.

Unless brokers, mutual funds, planners, and insurance companies reconceptualize what business they are in, they will lose customers to the uncomplicated fixed-savings plans offered by banks and savings and loans. What you'll witness in the next few years are financial institutions moving into financial consulting. Financial products are worthless unless there is first a crucial understanding of how they work and how they fit into a person's overall financial plan. The successful firms will offer objective, easy-to-read books on financial products, retirement plans, and financial planning itself. Many financial planning firms already offer educational seminars where accountants, lawyers, and financial planners, in a classroom setting, help you understand how to put together a financial package to achieve your goals. Educating the investor and saver will become a booming business, and those firms that don't point out the advantages and disadvantages of their products will fail. With so much confusion, people want hard facts, not fine print that will leave them with surprises later on—the kind of surprises you can find in mutual funds and saving accounts today.

Redefining Mutual Funds

When you decide to invest in a mutual fund, you'll come face to face with a prospectus, a document that spills out clumsy jargon and looks so intimidating that you might at first glance think you're being sued for your run-in with a shopping cart at the supermarket instead of being solicited for an investment. The prospectus is the Securities and Exchange Commission's way of telling you what's inside the fund. It's objective is to communicate, in a brief way, the essential material you need to know, as well as to provide supplementary information to meet technical requirements. The prospectus describes: the purpose of the fund, its investment record, what it will cost you to buy and sell its shares, how the adviser is paid, who runs the organization, and whatever else the government considers "material." Generally, the latter is whatever language lawyers have thrown in over the years to protect themselves.

In the past, if the mutual fund had made money for its investors over the years, you didn't have any trouble finding the performance of the fund in its prospectus, along with its supposed ability to boost the net asset value of its shares. Today, however, much of the performance information is buried in financial tables. That's because when mutual funds strike out, they want another chance at bat. As one mutual fund manager said, "Who wants to see the box score of the last inning in boldface type going in?"

But it is in the disclosure of sales charges and annual fees that critics charge that most mutual fund prospectuses aren't coming clean. That's because the changing sales and fee structure has become a touchy issue for brokers and mutual funds. The director of the SEC's division of investment management, which is working on requiring more disclosures in prospectuses, warns, "What concerns me about the charges is that they get buried, so to speak. I don't think it's laid out as clearly as it should be in all prospectuses. It's there, but you basically have to hunt to find it." Of all the recent mutual fund changes, the biggest one for the investor has probably been the way many of the sales charges and annual fees tend to be hidden in what, at first glance, appear to be no-load funds.

Load vs. No-Load Funds

Henny Youngman is reported to have told of a compulsive gambler who bet on every basketball game his bookie could find. After a few weeks of betting on 50 or more basketball games—and losing every bet—he called his bookie and asked, "How many basketball games today?" The bookie shot back, "No basketball games today, but there are two hockey games." "What do I know about hockey?" cried the gambler. Investing is often compared to gambling—what do you know about sales commissions or load and no-load funds? The moneyshock is that no-load funds have become a new form of load funds and we may be losing more money when we don't pay a sales commission than when we do!

Most people fail to understand how important sales commissions can be in creating wealth. Typically, load mutual funds tack on an 8.5 percent sales charge. Say you invest $10,000 in a load mutual fund with an 8.5 percent commission taken off the top. Before your money begins to work for you, your capital has shrunk to $9,150. If you earn 8 percent and are in a low 33 percent tax bracket, you'll end up at the end of the year with about $9,640. At the end of the second year, your average annual rate of return for the first two years, based on this interest rate and tax bracket, *would be under 1 percent*. Over a longer period, the results can be devastating. After 15 years, at 10 percent interest,

$10,000 can grow to $42,000. Starting with $9,150, however, the total is only about $38,000.

What you're doing, in effect, is buying a set of handcuffs when you pay out all that commission money up front. The freedom to sell—and buy—is the key to successful investing. You can no longer adopt the old gambit of "buying, holding, and praying" that your investment will somehow go up when the news tells you otherwise. Yet, with hefty sales commissions fresh in their minds, many people are reluctant to sell. Their assets are diminished by high commissions and the falling value of their capital as they wait on the sidelines.

The basic problem with a load fund, therefore, is that the brokers and financial planners are eating from your plate. They collect a sales commission presumably in return for some kind of investment advice. You can easily obtain whatever information you want on mutual funds, their ratings, sales costs, and performance in financial magazines and newspapers articles. Two of the best sources are the special mutual fund issues of *Money Magazine* and *Forbes*.

This does not mean that you should avoid paying commissions entirely, but it does mean that a load fund or investment has to out-perform a no-load one. Some investments have more risk and the payoff can often more than make up for the up-front sales charges. I have recommended an 8.5 percent load fund (without sales charges on reinvestments) because of its track record of well over 20 percent annual return, because much of what it earns is taxed as capital gains, and because of its grandfathered ability to pay out principal first on a tax-free return of your own money.

None of this sort of disclosure comes as any surprise to your broker or financial planner, who knows what a growing number of American investors have already discovered: There is no evidence that in general load mutual funds perform any better than no-load funds. In *Forbes* magazine's recent mutual fund issue, half of its top 20 honor roll funds were no-load funds. Sales of no-load funds in 1984 reached some $20 billion, about 40 percent of all fund sales. In the first half of 1985, new records were again set, as no-load sales almost doubled to an annual rate of $40 billion.

More and more stock traders, as well, are discovering the impact of paying a hefty up-front commission. Discount stock brokers, offering to cut sales commissions by 70 percent, have quickly expanded nation-wide. They now do as much as one-third of the business on the stock and bond exchanges. Customer resistance to up-front sales charges for mutual funds has also forced the brokerage industry to mend fences by offering funds without sales charges.

Hybrid Funds

Full-load funds typically impose an 8.5 percent sales charge while no-loads do away with the one-time sales charge. Both types of mutual funds take a management fee, usually no more than .5 to .75 percent a year. Now, however, brokers and mutual fund managers have developed no-load funds that cut into shareholders' returns in ways that are not obvious to a prospective investor. They are tacking redemption charges on no-load equity funds, dipping in the funds' assets to cover marketing expenses, and charging investors special annual fees. Characterized as "hidden-load" funds, these investments are sold as no-load funds by brokers and financial planners under Securities and Exchange Commission rule 12b-1 that allows them.

Since 12b-1 funds have no front-end sales charges, the SEC does not require that they be called load funds. However, managers of rule 12b-1 funds can deduct up to 1.25 percent of the funds' assets each year for expenses. Since you can also expect any mutual fund to charge .5 to .75 percent of total assets for expenses of the mutual fund organization, many of these hidden-load funds nab investors for as much as 2 percent a year. Then you have to pay attention to the early withdrawal fees. Many equity products have redemption fees that begin at around 6 percent, then decline to zero after five years. Redemption charges, or "back-door loads," are a way funds can nab investors who sell their holdings before the fund managers can recoup the sales costs and the commissions paid to brokers. Mutual fund managers generally like the annual charges because they rise as the funds' net asset value rises. Over the long term, fund managers make a lot of money and their backsides are protected by the hefty redemption fees.

When you consider an equity fund, focus first on performance, not fees. The greater the risk, the higher the return (usually), and the less importance you need to give to fees. In comparing the old front-end load funds with the new hidden-load funds, you need to determine how long you plan to hold your investments for. For short-term investors, hidden-load funds can work out best. For long-term investors, the annual mutual fund charges end up being more costly. The rule works something like this: If you plan to hold the fund for 8 to 10 years or more, you'll do better by paying the traditional 8.5 percent (or less) load than taking a beating each year from the annual charges in a 12b-1. In a shorter period, you could come out slightly ahead of a full-load fund even if you paid the redemption fees. On fixed-income funds, front-end loads are usually cut to 3 or 4 percent. Money market funds are usually no-load.

Moving from Expert Help to Self-Help

Financial services have at last become market-driven. In the past, we were offered a limited array of simple products at standard prices, which were easy to regulate even though they didn't always meet consumers' needs. In the future, the role of product development will shift from the regulators to financial institutions themselves, creating a new era of financial services marketing. The menu of financial instruments, only now coming into view, will be developed with consumers' needs in mind, offering choices that were unimaginable at the start of the decade. And the pace will quicken over the next ten years.

To meet this challenge, you need to understand that self-help will be your first line of defense. If you seek professional help, just about the first thing you'll be asked is to complete a questionnaire describing your financial situation. Neither you nor a professional can develop an adequate financial strategy without taking into account the unique network of money relationships you'll face now and in the future. A business professor who teaches a popular course on personal finance says that even knowledgeable investors and financial planners tend to come up short. "It's amazing how many people take a long time to work up a net worth statement and how surprised they are by the results."

No matter how many books you read, how many financial planning sessions you attend, you need to first know where you stand and what your objectives should be to avoid the pitfalls of self-inflicted financial confusion. The endless supply of get-rich-quick tax shelters, easy profits in the stock market, real estate, and other investments can leave you wondering if you're missing the boat. The only way to know if you should jump on the boat or let it sail without you is to know where you stand and just what investments are appropriate for your short- and long-term goals.

Experts can help, but only you can tune up your record keeping, lay out your financial needs, and decide how much risk you can tolerate in building your financial security. Otherwise, in today's deregulated marketplace, you might as well hop a plane for Nevada and place your hard-earned money on number 18 at the roulette table.

10

MoneyShock

What's Ahead Is Already Here

To look up from the absorbing minutiae of daily existence and make a mental leap to the end of the century—even if it is only 14 years away— requires a perspective that most of us seldom find. It's often difficult to think beyond next week. But we are approaching one of those rare milestones in history where much of the past will give way to radical change. Changes in money, telephones, trains, and a host of other stable American industries are set to occur in the next 14 years. They may be simply coincidental with the turn of the century, but they will be so profound that they will force us to take account of ourselves, as individuals and as a society.

What I've attempted to do is look past next week or next year and set my sights on the financial marketplace that I believe is already coming into sharp focus. Naturally, the environment I foresee and the visions I describe are based on current trends. These impressions are subjective, written with the realization that they are only my idea of the shape of things to come. But I am convinced, nevertheless, that some- time in the next century, people will look back on the 1980s as the turning point for individual financial freedom and will see something that we can only now glimpse: a pattern, a new way of working, of saving and investing money, which will have become the foundation of society in the twenty-first century.

In fact, we are already in the midst of a major shift from a tightly controlled financial environment to a free, decontrolled money market. The shift from hiding our money at home to trusting a regulated banking system took several hundred years; the change in money management today is coming so rapidly that there is often no time to react before new products and ideas overwhelm us. Of all the changes that will occur in our society, none is more subtle, yet more explosive, I believe, than the shift from tight control of our financial institutions to a free, open financial marketplace. From the thousands of letters I've received from all across America, it's clear that people are confused and often unable to cope with a financial system that seems to have jumped the rails. But financial deregulation is no longer an idea whose time has come, it's a reality.

Financial deregulation is not alone. Deregulation is occurring everywhere. Changes that seemed impossible just a few years ago are now becoming commonplace. Much of this change can be traced to the deregulation of major industries in just the last five years. As a result, never before have consumers had so many choices in areas like travel, telephones, and of course, financial services. Let's look at three industries where massive change has already taken place:

Signs of Change

Trains

There's something wonderful about a caboose. Since the invention of trains, no kids' book was complete without the little red caboose at the back of the train. Before the adoption of air brakes, trainmen raced across the tops of cars from the caboose to apply hand brakes when the engineer's whistle sounded. But these charming anachronisms have been overtaken by high technology and deregulation; they are no longer needed as a lookout or conductor's office. Instead, they are headed for the junk yard or a spot in a municipal park, to serve as a reminder of a vanished past. In fact, railroads have travelled the same path that financial services are about to embark on: unlimited competition and wide-open marketplaces.

Before 1980, the continued existence of our tightly controlled rail system was threatened with collapse. A maze of regulatory measures prevented railroads from being competitive in terms of prices and services, and more than 20 percent of our rail system was operating in bankruptcy. In 1980, Congress enacted the Staggers Rail Act, which lifted some of the most crippling regulations. Since then railroads have expanded, competing with trucks and water traffic in a deregulated marketplace that has allowed computers and high-tech signaling devices to change the shape of trains forever. The most visible transformation may be the loss of the little red caboose, but that's only the tip of the iceberg in an industry that's awash with change.

Travel Agencies

Or consider the travel business. With the Civil Aeronautics Board's deregulation of the airlines came the proliferation of discount fares and fine print on those fares. New airlines sprang up all over America. But the rippling effect of airline deregulation has also allowed the giant travel agencies to gobble up the travel business. Big corporations are now doing business with big agencies, and consultants estimate that eventually a handful of mega-agencies could control over 50 percent of the travel agency market. Since anyone can now become a travel agent, small mom-and-pop agencies will gradually be replaced by the photo-drive-ups, banks, and discount stores, while middle-size travel agencies will find nationwide chains like American Express or Ask Mr. Foster luring away their big corporate accounts with computer services and hefty discounts.

Discount travel agencies that rebate part of their commission on most tickets to their customers will proliferate, just as discount stock brokers have quickly spread nationwide. "This is fast becoming an industry for big players," says a travel consultant. "Where there used to be hundreds of small and middle-size agencies, there will be a vast wasteland."

Telephones

The breakup of AT&T created seven regional telephone companies instead of one and then paved the way for the creation of some 300 long distance telephone companies throughout the United States. Coming all at once this can be highly confusing; instead of one you now must choose from dozens of long distance carriers if you want to continue to make long distance calls. And, of course, you have to sort through page after page of telephone bills from various carriers that now serve your home phone. But all of this change may pale by comparison with the new high-tech revolution that can make long distance telephone calls themselves obsolete.

A hundred years ago the telephone company offered a new service: long distance. It was expensive; miles of wire strung along telephone poles had to be paid for. With the advent of deregulation a century later, we learned that long distance service really didn't have to cost so much after all. The new discount long distance carriers told us we could cut our long distance bills by 30 to 40 percent if we'd just switch from the old telephone-pole mentality to the electronic age. But the era of long distance itself may be at an end as high technology propels us into the space age. Ever since it became possible to bounce a telecommunications signal off a satellite, every city in the country is, for all practical purposes, the same distance from every other city. What you're going to see is a groundswell of new companies with direct access to telecommunications satellites that will bring swift change to the long distance phone business.

Financial Globalization

Financial services on a global basis will follow the same trend exhibited by the railroads, travel business, and telephones here in America. Industries around the world will shed their little red cabooses and will let in anyone who wants to play, and much of what we have come to accept in saving and investing will become obsolete.

For example, in England the government-owned telephone company has been sold to the public as a forerunner of further deregulation. And in 1986 the deregulation of the London Stock Exchange will result in the formation of several American-style integrated securities firms in London. British merchant banks and stock exchanges, to fill the real or perceived gaps in their operations, are scrambling to turn themselves into financial money centers—both to accommodate deregulation and to ward off carpetbagging American banks and brokers.

Many Asian countries—Japan, Taiwan, and Thailand, for example—are slowly loosening the controls and moving toward free financial markets. The most vivid example, however, is Australia. Until recently, Australia's banking system was rigidly controlled. But market events much like those in America pushed the government into adopting major reforms in the global movement toward deregulation. The result is a financial system that, in theory at least, is as open as any in the world. But the benefits are not limited to the consumers alone. Foreign capital has flocked to Australia. By liberalizing rules for chartering foreign banks, Japan has opened its doors to the Australian banks.

The big benefit, when consumers and companies have a choice, is that the Australian economy will be spared the costs of evading, complying with, or propping up the inefficient regulations. Financial reforms have already transformed Australia from a backwater country to one of the world's major financial centers.

Opinions vary widely on exactly how much change will occur, how soon it will happen, and where it will take place. But massive changes in America and the rest of the free world's financial market-places are likely to gain momentum as regulatory controls continue to slip away. And the changes will almost certainly stretch well beyond the year 2000, which is only an arbitrary benchmark.

A Proliferation of Choices

In retailing, neighborhood stores are struggling just to stay afloat as giant corporations offer better selections and lower prices. More than 23 flavors of Nine Lives cat food, dozens of "low-cost" airlines, well over 160 shades of lipstick, and 5,000 videocassettes now fight for our attention. We can purchase the same financial product from banks, S&Ls, brokers, insurance companies, mutual funds, department stores. And these financial bazaars in turn offer us a plethora of ways to save and invest. From a society of limited choices, we may have reached a point where there are so many choices and so much information that many people simply can't decide.

The problems we face when an industry changes so fast is that many of us make our financial choices out of habit rather than by analyzing information. We are drowning in new products but starved for knowledge because the level of information is clearly impossible to handle on a day-to-day basis. Our minds, trying to expand to grasp the endless number of new financial products and services, are caught inside a classic shrink-to-fit denim.

Still, even if we can't focus on next week or next month, let's travel through time and take a peek at the financial industry at the turn of the century. The visions I see are not always consistent, nor sharply focused. Naturally, the future I depict is based on present trends that for the most part are already underway, and from what I've learned from talking with people inside the financial industry. I call it *financial futurethink*.

The Second Financial Revolution

As we move toward the end of this century we have to admit, if we are honest with ourselves, that the future isn't what it used to be. In the past we had fixed signposts and change occurred slowly, if at all. New ideas rarely led to new variations that formed the basis for whole new industries. At the turn of the last century, Charles H. Duell, director of the U.S. Patent Office, avowed that "everything that can be invented has been invented." Lord Kelvin, president of the Royal Society, agreed when he looked at the train. "Heavier-than-air flying machines are impossible," said he. It was also commonly understood that new ideas rarely came from existing products. Motion picture magnate Harry M. Warner asked, "Who the hell wants to hear actors talk?"

But the 1980s ushered in two radically new changes that will reshape the way we save and invest our money as nothing has since the invention of the banking system. The first, financial deregulation, will break down all the old accepted ways of where and how we save and invest. The second, high technology, with its supercomputers, will create hundreds of new financial products and transmit them to millions of individuals in a revitalization of personal services.

Deregulation will continue to spread across the nation; it has taken on a life of its own. When tight controls of financial institutions begin to loosen, it happens in ever-widening circles, like rocks thrown into a pond. Congress, the government, and private industry will be unable to put the genie back in the bottle because, once unleashed, basic changes create more changes and reversing the trend becomes impossible.

Within the next year or two, after the government's argument about non-banks has run its course, interstate banking will be inevitable. There are about 15,000 banks in this country—at least ten times as many as in any other Western country. Most of the banks are small, with two-thirds of them controlling only about 10 percent of the banking assets while 100 of the biggest control more than half. The reason there are so many banks (and savings and loans) today is that states, with the federal government's approval, have protected their own banks by keeping out-of-state banks from jumping state lines. During this period of protectionist banking, the financial industry as a whole achieved an equilibrium of sorts, where any change would affect the special niche of banks, brokers, mutual funds, and insurance companies and was, therefore, resisted. This protected right to operate in segments of the financial market, analogous to the territory of kings, was achieved in much the same way: by the submission of the citizenry.

Then in the 1980s, deregulation suddenly shattered this assumption. It first swept over the telephone, trucking, and airline industries, and by 1983 it was banging on the banks' doors. Financial deregulation's message was that market dynamics, once unleashed, will quickly leave static laws behind. Opinions vary widely on exactly how fast deregulation will completely break up our banking and financial services industry, but I believe nationwide banking with mega-financial firms offering a wide range of financial products will be a reality well before the end of this decade.

Already, the Federal Home Loan Bank Board wants to give interstate branching powers to savings and loans that spend their own money to buy insolvent savings institutions. The rewards—the franchise rights—would be in proportion to the savings that the FSLIC would realize by not acquiring the hundreds of insolvent thrifts now on its books. The U.S. Treasury has its own plan to rescue the ailing thrift industry. It would give big non-banking organizations, such as Sears, Roebuck & Co., the right to buy scores of insolvent savings and loans and then convert them into commercial banks. The Treasury plan represents a view within the current administration that the thrift industry should be merged into the much stronger commercial banking industry or acquired by the giant corporations who are already moving into the financial marketplace.

Major financial firms recognize the inevitability of this and much of what will occur in interstate financial networks in the next few years will be the purchase of hundreds of S&Ls and banks. This all assumes that everything goes according to the plan now envisioned by most experts. If it doesn't, if one segment of the industry jumps out to lead the charge toward one-stop shopping, things could then happen even faster, as each mega-financial firm tries to establish its own turf in the expanding marketplace.

High technology, often viewed as cold and impersonal, will actually be the key to personalized services for financial institutions. Computers will be instrumental in bringing many new products and players into the money game. Computers are nothing more than a tool to manage complexity, but once that tool is in place, rising computer capabilities invite more complexity and a greater number of products and services. High technology has also enabled financial firms to react quickly to shifts in consumer demand. Millions are being spent on computer programs that will create new financial products, some of them as yet undreamed of, and it is clear that the company that gets there first will have an enormous advantage.

Even as we stand on the threshold of a computer revolution, high technology remains for the most part dependent on data transmission. To bring on the first high-tech revolution we relied on the combined technologies of the telephone, the microwave, and the satellite for data communications. For the future, however, to carry the soaring data requirements of the growing information society, the emerging communications network is expanding into thin air with FM radio stations leasing unused spectrum space to carry data that otherwise would be compressed into phone lines and limited satellite space.

Here's how thin-air data transmission will work: Customers will send the data to the radio network, which in turn will send it out to its affiliated FM stations. The local stations will then rebroadcast the signal over an unused slice of their radio frequency simultaneously to thousands of subscribers, each of whom will have special decoders and printers. Radio waves will not only let financial firms and individuals receive vast quantities of data on a nationwide basis at low cost, but they will also seriously affect the number of people using the current means of data transmission—the telephone and the U.S. mail.

The futurethink of high technology is a vision of high-powered computers that can provide special financial products on a personalized basis to millions of people over radio frequencies at a fraction of today's cost. In short, we are about to embark on a future where, for the first time, we have a financial system based on unlimited choice of products and services with the high-tech skills to deliver them into our homes and local one-stop financial shopping stores. The resource is not only renewable but self-generating as financial products and high technology expand into the twenty-first century.

Changes in Financial Institutions

Financial futurethink is based on two powerful forces: deregulation and high technology. While their arrival may be simply coincidental, it's not unthinkable that both forces, working together, will provide that one rare occasion that results in profound change for not only this decade, but for the next century as well.

As we look to the future, we are reminded of other profound changes that also had unintended consequences. The invention of the chimney in medieval times permitted people, for the first time, to have privacy. They could live in separate rooms instead of huddled around a central fire. The effect on society was far greater than the simple invention of a chimney.

The elevator made modern skyscrapers possible, changing forever the city skyline and forcing millions of Americans onto the highways. With large populations living outside a city's center, retail managers had to change their way of thinking—and the result today is the suburban shopping center.

Financial deregulation will have the same long-term unintended consequences. In a technology-driven, information-intensive society, deregulation will create a brand new market for ideas and money. And the changes have only begun.

Banks and Savings and Loans

The bank of the future will be lined with computers—souped-up descendants of the automatic teller machines and interactive video computers that give customers information without the help of a teller. Those banks that escape the shopping malls, K mart department stores, and one-stop shopping centers will be tiny—about one-tenth the size of a conventional branch. Branch tellers will give way to more sophisticated financial counselors, equipped with desk-top computers, who can plan a customer's complete financial portfolio and can offer insurance, mutual funds, bonds, and savings accounts as well as brokerage, travel, and tax help.

Banks and S&Ls will cease to be separate financial entities and will merge into one industry. They already offer virtually the same products and services. Clearly, the nation will no longer need banks as banks and savings and loans as savings and loans. As these institutions offer the same retail products and services, the distinction between them blurs and together they become just another way to save and invest. But without their previous special niche, their special federal protection and assistance, most of them will become casualties of the fast-changing second financial revolution. At least 12,000 of the 15,000 currently operating banks will either be merged into larger mega-banks, or go out of business by the end of this century. Small to medium-sized savings and loans will shrink out of sight even faster, since most of the S&Ls today face the same problem that full-service gas stations did in the last decade: They can be replaced by self-service one-stop shopping centers.

If banks and S&Ls expect to compete, a new approach must be used. They can no longer rely on their high-priced services as a magnet to pull in the savings, such as checking accounts, safe deposit boxes, federal insurance, and personal loans—many other financial firms offer these. And the trend to one-stop financial shopping will make their expensive one-product branches unprofitable.

Banks and S&Ls are left with the hard cold fact: Anyone can loan money and offer checking accounts and credit cards, but not everyone can attract consumer deposits in a profitable way. For example, to boost the usage of automatic teller machines, more banks and S&Ls will follow the lead of the University of Connecticut's Student Federal

Credit Union, which turned its ATM into a lottery game. The credit union programmed its ATM to give away one $50 bill for every three hundred $20 bills it distributes. The ATM, at random, slips the free $50 bill into the withdrawal slot of the lucky customer. By making the ATM a game of chance, transactions at the ATM are up a massive 650 percent. Futurethink for banks and S&Ls sees them addressing problems in a way that will allow the mega-banks that survive to become a major force in our financial system.

First, the mega-banks and thrifts will expand into one-stop shopping centers. They will combine savings, loans, mutual funds, insurance, discount stock brokers, travel agencies, and retirement planning in one office. The mega-banks will be a wonderland of financial adventure with tie-ins and special discounts on a wide range of products. They will operate on a nationwide basis because the bigs will gobble up the smalls as the mega-banks and S&Ls jump state lines all across America.

Interstate banking is fast becoming a reality and Congress shows no signs of lessening the pace as it tries to accommodate it, respond to it, and shape it. Starting October 1, 1986, Arizona will follow Alaska and Maine by allowing its commercial banks to merge with or be acquired by any out-of-state bank, subject to approval by state and federal authorities. Already, in a scene that's sure to be repeated all across the country, some Arizona banks have begun the mating dance with the New York and California giants. A bank executive says of the rush to interstate banking evident in the sunbelt states. "Everything's for sale if there's enough money there."

Takeovers have already been arranged and are simply on hold until the date when they will be finalized. It is expected that United Bank of Arizona, the state's fourth-largest bank, will be bought by British-owned Union Bancorp of Los Angeles; Arizona Bank, the state's third-largest, should go to Security Pacific Bank of Los Angeles. Citicorp, Chase Manhattan Bank, and Manufacturers Hanover Bank, all of New York, already operate non-bank financial services in the state and are expected to pick up their share of the booty.

California and New York have reached an agreement that would open California to interstate banking if California lawmakers approved the proposed plan. In January 1987 the agreement would allow cross-border bank acquisitions in a nine-state Western region. In January 1990 (if not before), the arrangement would be extended nationwide.

But non-banks, or consumer banks, may make full-service interstate banking irrelevant. That's because the Supreme Court has swept aside a major obstacle to the spread of non-banks by ruling that the

Federal Reserve Board lacks the authority to regulate the newly emerging limited-service non-banks. The Court held that the federal Bank Holding Act was intended by Congress to exempt non-bank from board regulation, even though today they provide many of the same services as full-service commercial banks.

In the rush to deregulation, the decision was a victory for companies like Merrill Lynch, Sears Roebuck, General Electric, and J. C. Penney that already offer banking services in competition with full-service banks. Preliminary applications for more than 300 non-banks have been approved by the comptroller of the currency. All of this, of course, will increase the pressure on Congress to rewrite and modernize federal banking laws that date from the Great Depression. Congress can't reverse the trend to interstate financial money centers, but it could give every financial money player an equal opportunity to better serve the consumer with increased competition.

Next, banks and S&Ls will franchise their financial products and services the way McDonald's and Wendy's franchise food. They'll rush into retail locations like K mart discount stores, Safeway food stores, shopping centers, and airport terminals. Franchising will allow megabanks to once again open branch offices, but at a fraction of the cost of brick-and-mortar buildings.

In attracting deposits, a major change will occur by the end of this decade. No longer will one-state banks and S&Ls wait for depositors to walk through the front door of their offices; they will let other people sell their insured CDs in thousands of offices nationwide. Already, brokers offer bank and S&L insured CDs to their customers at better rates and terms than those sold over the counter in the banks' and S&Ls' own lobbies. Banks and S&Ls began selling their insured deposits through middlemen because they needed deposits faster than their "say-nothing" advertising and branches could pull in the cash. What they found was that with thousands of offices nationwide, brokers could not only generate the funds faster, but at a lower cost.

By the end of this century, banks and S&Ls will offer their financial savings plans through their one-stop shopping centers and through their own full-service brokerage firms. The products will be creative and attractive and, most important of all, many will give consumers the opportunity to share in the profits without incurring the corresponding losses. Earnings-based CDs will become a vital factor in attracting the money this nation needs to provide the mortgages for real estate construction. Other savings plans will be designed to attract consumers with special needs. An example of the future already exists in the six-year zero coupon insured certificates of deposits offered by the Philadelphia Savings Fund Society. PSFS is the largest savings bank and the fifth largest thrift institution in the United States.

The zero coupon FDIC insured CDs, with a 10 percent yield to maturity computed on a semiannual basis, will double your money in a little over six years. In other words, you invest $500 and collect $1,000 at maturity. Consumers can use these zeros for their IRAs or to build a college fund for their kids' education. The glimpse of the future is that the Philadelphia bank no longer has to wait for money to come in the front door of its branches. By going directly to the brokers, it can sell its savings plans instantly in thousands of offices nationwide.

Other financial products will put the mega-banks and S&Ls on a collision course with brokers and mutual funds. A good example is the Pacific Horizon Fund, the brainchild of Security Pacific National Bank, one of the larger banks in the country. To sell its funds in offices across the country, the big bank put Dreyfus Mutual Funds to work. Dreyfus offers the bank's family of funds without a sales charge, hidden fees, or penalty on redemption, and your money, starting with only $1,000 has complete liquidity at the ten-current asset value.

Pacific Horizon Funds include a government money market portfolio, money market portfolio, high-yield bond portfolio, and aggressive growth portfolio. Not bad for a bank that a few years ago offered passbook savings and checking accounts. The financial futurethink of the bank is this: We manage huge sums of money every day; why not manage our customers' money as well? In the bank's brand of aggressively managed funds, you are told that your money will be managed by the bank's successful investment team, that yields can rise 3 or 4 percent above those on insured CDs and money market accounts, and that you'd be a fool not to take advantage of such a sweet deal. It makes you wonder why, when there's a fund like that with no sale charges and with complete liquidity, you should put your money in a low-interest certificate of deposit with a fixed interest rate.

By the end of this century, mega-banks and S&Ls will find a new niche by inventing new mutual funds, insurance products, insured CDs, and money management accounts. And they'll offer these products through major branches, through money shops in retail stores and shopping centers, and through brokers and mutual funds. The mega-banks and S&Ls will make acquisitions and expand nationwide, following the path already set by the mutual funds and brokers.

Brokers

The financial futurethink for securities firms also includes one-stop financial centers. Why? For the same reason Wall Street firms do most everything: There's money to be made. They already offer the same services you can find at a bank and S&L, including checking accounts, home loans, insured CDs, money market funds, and credit cards. And they will offer these products and services through their own banks (which are in the form of low-cost sales offices, not the huge money palaces of the past).

Brokers could replace banks and S&Ls as the primary retail money gatherers. They will sell their own financial products and those of other brokers, and don't be surprised if your broker asks you to invest in bank or S&L stock and insured CDs. Merrill Lynch, for example, will unleash its 10,000 domestic salespeople to sell its services to small businesses and their owners—the same market that keeps much of the nation's smaller banks alive. Discount brokers will continue to grow, not only by selling stocks and bonds with a hefty commission discount, but also by selling insured CDs. For example, Charles Schwab tracks a wide range of bank and S&L CDs around the country and find the highest yield for your savings dollar.

On the consumer side, brokers will move into financial planning in a one-stop center with insurance, mutual funds, banking services, stocks, bonds, and savings accounts. In a real sense, the future is already here in a Sears department store. Called Sears Financial Network, Dean Witter Reynolds—the big broker—now sits side by side with an insurance company, a real estate firm, and a savings and loan. the futurethink for brokers is this: Walk-in traffic in a Sears store helps brokers land new accounts at *four times* the pace of conventional broker offices. Department stores aren't the only way to pull the public away from a formal brokerage setting; high-traffic discount stores, travel agencies, and airports are effective—even Grand Central Terminal in New York will do as well.

Brokers will increasingly reach out to the middle class as well as to the traditional up-scale investors by offering a wide range of savings, banking, credit, ATMs, loans, and investment plans. By doing so far away from the formal structure of Wall Street, they will soak up a big chunk of the savings that would otherwise have gone to the one-product banks and S&Ls.

Brokers will also become the nation's real estate agents. Real estate is a major part of one-stop shopping, giving brokers the inside track on mortgages, insurance, and the lucrative home equity and personal loan market. Merrill Lynch is already the nation's second largest residential real estate firm. Its network includes 43 major markets in the United States, with more than 12,000 agents and 400 residential sales offices.

In the home mortgage market, capital markets are on the verge of replacing thrifts as the primary source of mortgage funds. Repackaged real-estate-backed securities are bringing in money from worldwide capital markets. In the new wave of deregulation, thrifts are the least equipped to originate home mortgages, because we're now entering the era of the securitization of mortgages.

Actually, we are also in the midst of converting home equity into cash at a record pace. The home equity loan is a glossy name that the brokers have given to that old American lending practice, the second mortgage. People who would turn up their nose at the thought of a second mortgage, with its connotation of desperation borrowing, seem eager to risk their collateral for a home equity loan. And the brokers are only too glad to give them the cash. In 1985 alone, home owners scooped up $75 billion in home equity loans, thus doubling in a single 12-month period the total amount of these home loans. Wall Street brokers, drawn by the magnet of some $4.3 trillion of unmortgaged equity that still remains to be tapped as collateral for new home equity loans, will push these high-profit loans as if they were simply a variation on credit card loans.

By combining all these financial services, brokers will become banks and S&Ls, but they will be more. From a nationwide base of low-cost offices, their salesmen will also provide a low-cost and quick way to sell investments and insurance and raise deposits. Banks and S&Ls, walking a banking tightrope, will find that making loans with money that brokers have raised will eventually leave them at a disadvantage in the fight for the consumer's dollar and business. The financial futurethink is that banks and S&Ls may not be able to reclaim their once-primary role as the nation's money gatherers, but may become dependent on brokers for their source of deposit funds.

In our future, as in our present, there will be winners and losers. For most of the banks and S&Ls, the future is grim. When America discovers that brokers have bought banks, that they can take bank deposits, make loans, sell investments, real estate, mutual funds, and insurance, a new set of financial players will emerge in the deregulated marketplace.

Mutual Funds

The financial futurethink for mutual funds is that they will become both middlemen (allowing brokers, banks, S&Ls, and financial planners to sell their funds) and securities brokers and bankers themselves. For some, it will be like walking both sides of the street, but I believe they will pull it off.

Mutual funds already have ground-floor offices that resemble those of banks and brokers, and these will expand nationwide as the funds begin to offer many of the same financial products and services that brokers and banks do. Some 62 years after mutual funds were invented in Boston, customers stand three deep at the Fidelity Investor Center in downtown Boston (don't you just love the names we've attached to managing money?), where they can trade securities or switch mutual funds. Nearby, an automatic teller machine is spitting out money. And above all this bustling activity, flashing signs tout mutual funds, retirement accounts, and money market funds. Fidelity Mutual Funds is already the second-biggest discount broker, after BankAmerica's Charles Schwab, and it's taking on Merrill Lynch's highly successful Cash Management Account. What is less well known is that it's a big player in managing payroll deductions under employer-sponsored retirement plans and in offering mutual funds, money market funds, and cash management.

Since many mutual funds already own banks, insurance companies, and discount brokers, the name "mutual fund" is now only a holdover from the days when their business was limited to managing such funds. Dreyfus Mutual Funds, for example, started its Dreyfus Consumer Bank in 1982 in East Orange, New Jersey, and it has written millions in mortgage loans and sold its gold MasterCard to customers across the country.

Yet the restructuring of the mutual fund industry has not only allowed a growing number of financial giants to invade the market, but it also has mutual fund operators gritting their teeth over the rush of non-mutual fund companies invading their turf. Take Sears, Roebuck & Co. They have taken all uninsured money-market fund and turned it into a money market trust that's invested in safe U.S. government securities. It's like an insured money market account that requires a minimum investment of only $1,000 and additional investments in amounts of $100 or more.

Security Pacific National Bank, through its subsidiary, Security Pacific Corp., became one of the first banks to enter the mutual fund field in 1984. First National Bank of Chicago has a family of mutual funds called First Lakeshore Funds and Chase Manhattan Bank offers Park Avenue Funds, a triple tax-free fund (federal, state and city taxes) for New York City residents.

My picture of the future for mutual funds is not in sharp focus. With some 1,200 mutual funds struggling for investors' attention and a new one born almost every day, the market is already awash with funds. Some mutual funds may retreat into their former role as middlemen who manage the funds while others sell their shares directly to the public; others will take on the brokers head to head in a battle to carve up the consumer market. Most of the evidence to date indicates that the mega-mutual funds of the future plan to let the investor play the stock market through their discount brokerage operations, or invest in mutual funds rather than investing directly in stocks. They'll offer checking accounts, credit cards, savings plans, money market funds, and fancy asset management accounts. If that is the case, brokers and mutual funds will merge into brokers/mutual funds by the turn of the century. In the fast-moving world of deregulation that lies ahead, these two similar financial institutions will not be able to remain apart. They will merge because each can duplicate the other's products and services, and in the public's mind they will be perceived as one-stop shopping centers.

Insurance Companies

Of all financial players in the 1980s, insurance companies are in the most trouble. To the public they are nothing more than a horde of salespeople hawking just one product: insurance. To break out of the mold will require a shift away from basic century-old insurance values. Some companies have put their salespeople to work selling auto and home-owners' insurance, mutual funds, and securities, in addition to life insurance, as a last-gasp effort to keep their people employed. But the trend is clearly moving in the other direction. Most life insurance today is sold by stockbrokers, financial planners, banks and S&Ls, and through direct mail. That's because life insurance is no longer thought of as both death protection and a handy savings account for retirement. High interest rates killed the savings feature; IRAs and 401(k)s the retirement aspect.

To stir things up and break out of their image, several insurance companies have begun selling their product on a private label basis. That is, they supply the product (life insurance) and financial firms, such as financial money centers in supermarkets, department stores, and banks, sell it as their own life insurance product. Other life insurance companies have already bought brokerages, real estate firms, and banks. Those that remain one-product firms in a growing era of one-stop shopping will disappear into oblivion.

Success in the life insurance business has always been based on high-commission salespeople selling the product in the customer's home or office. But paying the high overhead for big buildings and delivering the highest commission paid our for any financial product on the street has forced many insurance companies to collapse into the arms of brokers, mutual funds, banks, financial planners, and the K marts of the financial world, who can sell the product in greater volume and at a much lower cost. And, as always happens in the financial world, the one who makes the sale will eventually become king. Mutual funds, brokers, and banks will simply buy up many of today's insurance companies.

The financial futurethink for life insurance companies asks whether they will devour brokers, mutual funds, and banks, or be devoured by them. Metropolitan Life Insurance Company, trying to shake off its insurance name, acquired Century 21 Real Estate, the nation's largest real estate sales organization. Century 21 has about 6,500 offices with 75,000 sales personnel operating in all 50 states, Canada, and Japan. With Century 21, Metropolitan Life will move into mortgage origination, home insurance, real estate syndication, and add all this to its MetFirst Financial Company. Metropolitan is clearly on the path toward one-stop financial shopping.

John Hancock Mutual Life, whose agents already sell a complete financial package, has acquired the oldest brokerage firm in the West, Sutro & Co. Prudential Insurance Company has taken the same route; they bought the big broker, Bache. Prudential-Bache Securities now combines insurance with stocks and bonds and a whole range of financial services. Prudential is also grabbing a big share of the banks' and S&Ls' home mortgage business with their new subsidiary, Prudential Home Mortgage Company.

The Prudential system relies on toll-free telephone numbers and computers to cut the time and cost involved in the blizzard of paperwork that many banks and S&Ls use to approve home mortgages. "We are talking about cutting out 50 to 100 basis points (.5 to 1 percent) of unnecessary cost by having an efficient information system," says an executive of the National Association of Realtors. "Financial firms may not be able to compete unless they have the information to tie into computers that know where the pots of money are." Mega-companies like Prudential, Sears, and General Electric will increasingly dominate the mortgage business because they have both the capital and the technology necessary to deal efficiently with individualized mortgages. Local banks and S&Ls will find that their competitors are not across town but across the state and country, and in many respects the weakest link in the future of money—the insurance companies—may turn out to be the one segment of the financial industry that steals the bread-and-butter home mortgage business from them.

Insurance companies will have to keep checking over their shoulder for non-insurance companies that may be gaining on them. Weyerhaeuser Company, a name synonymous with big timber operations, is a good example. Weyerhaeuser entered the insurance business with a tax-deferred annuity policy and soon these policies were being sold by many of the nation's savings and loans as a way to attract tax-deferred funds. Insurance was one thing, but the big timber company was after the magic of one-stop shopping, and its growth is a vivid example of how insurance companies, like brokers, mutual funds, and banks, will grow in the years to come.

Weyerhaeuser Mortgage Company, a subsidiary of Weyerhaeuser Real Estate, is the fifth-largest mortgage company in the United States. With that kind of clout, Weyerhaeuser got control of the 15-branch Republic Federal Savings and Loan Association, headquartered in the Los Angeles area, and entered the S&L business. Now a company that started out in the financial world selling insurance is set to expand into one-stop shopping across America. "By taking on a weak S&L, Weyerhaeuser is playing a good-guy role," a securities analyst said. "Sugar daddies with deep pockets make for strong S&Ls. The Federal Home Loan Bank Board will look kindly on it if it makes a move to acquire other, healthier associations either in California or in other states."

Someday, perhaps near the end of this century, people will look back with a touch of nostalgia at one-product insurance companies with their person-to-person sales representatives. They were a great social invention of the twentieth century, but they will soon be history. Insurance services will be a part of each financial firm's list of products and we will find some fairly innovative transition techniques for the different insurance products that will be used to lure our savings and investments.

Non-Banks

The terms non-bank and consumer bank have been coined to refer to non-banking companies that have entered the financial market on the cheap. With their financial clout, they have entered the market, through the cracks created by deregulation, by simply buying a thrift, bank, mutual fund, or insurance company or by including a financial firm in their existing shops by renting out space. Many of these giant corporations have been in the financial market for some time, but they have been limited to making loans and selling insurance to customers who purchased their products. Now they are setting their sights on the general consumer market.

As we move toward the end of this century, we are shifting from a financial consumer's market long dominated by banks, S&Ls, and brokers to a nationwide market dominated by the giant non-bank companies. Our attention has been diverted to the changing role of banks and brokers, who are already in the money game, and we have not caught up with reality. That's because the change caused by giant non-bank companies is so subtle and so fundamental that we tend not to see it.

Financial futurethink tells me that the big winners in the battle to restructure our financial marketplace will be some of the best-known names in American industry, names like General Motors, General Electric, and Ford Motor Company. They will do battle with the retail giants like Sears, J. C. Penney, K mart, and 7-Eleven. These mega-companies, with names long familiar to the public, have already entered the marketplace, and where they have, their financial clout and marketing savvy have pushed aside many well-established financial firms. Their entry—as far-reaching as it has been—is but the tip of the financial iceberg. As financial deregulation cracks open the entire industry, large companies will gobble up more and more of the national consumer market.

New Hunters and Gatherers

We are living in a period of transition, caught between Depression-era statutes that set strict limits on financial services and an era of deregulation in which market dynamics are leaving static laws behind. And the future is coming into focus very fast.

Five years ago, if someone told you that Sears, the big merchandise house of garden tractors, hardware, and pantyhose would own and operate a major brokerage firm, a nationwide real estate firm, and a savings bank you might have found it hard to believe. But not anymore. Not when a company that makes pens can own a bank, a savings and loan, and a life insurance company. Not when supermarkets and furniture stores can, next to their meat counter and loveseats, open a bank and sell life insurance and mutual funds to their shoppers.

We have always had changes in the financial services industry, of course, but they have been subtle changes in products, not changes in the services financial firms provided. Today we are in the midst of a financial revolution, and for the most part, it's just begun. Those who master the ambiguity of this in-between period and who can anticipate the new deregulated era will be winners. They will find the new tax-savings plans, the high-yield income funds, and the second-generation investment products. Those who hang onto the past will be the losers.

They will remain glued to the fixed-rate bank CDs and low-interest money market accounts.

In the years to come, shopping nationally for the best rate of interest—a practice foreign to most of us—will become a priority to those people who want the most for their hard-earned cash. With toll-free numbers, wire transfer of money, and more awareness on the part of the consumer, shopping nationally for good interest rates will gradually take over the way we save our serious money.

The trend to shop for higher insured CD rates is vividly illustrated by the fact that, for the first time in 22 years, a new federally chartered savings institution has opened in Massachusetts—the New England Federal Savings Bank. It will operate without branches from a second-floor office in the Boston suburb of Wellesley. By doing away with many of the expensive overhead costs associated with "Main Street" banking, the bank plans to pay higher interest rates on insured deposits.

The founders of the bank believe that, in recent years, a sophisticated market has developed: Consumers are now accustomed to dealing with financial organizations almost exclusively via mail, toll-free numbers, and ATMs. They feel that the lure of higher interest rates on insured CDs will be more powerful than the massive hometown buildings of yesterday. What savers have learned, as savings spread nationwide, is that federal deposit insurance, not the bank, protects their savings accounts. And, of course, that federal insurance works just as well in any state of the Union.

To show you what I mean in dollars and cents, a major bank or S&L in your hometown might offer 8 percent on a one-year insured CD. Another financial institution elsewhere in your state or across the country might pay 10 percent on that same insured CD. That's a boost in your earned interest of $20 for every $1,000 you save. And that's equivalent to 25 percent more in interest. For the consumer who wants the best deal for his or her money, the opportunity is no farther away than the nearest telephone.

In the hotly competitive battle to lock up money in a savings account, a fierce rivalry will unfold among financial institutions around the country. Today's spread from the lowest to the highest return on insured CDs and money market accounts of as much as 2 percent or more will narrow, but great opportunities will remain for the smart "nationwide" saver.

Financial futurethink pushes us to the limit of our fertile imagination. We no longer live in an age when most of America's banking laws were written. Lines will be redrawn between different kinds of financial providers, and as different types of companies merge with one another, lines will disappear completely. If that were not enough, there are even more changes on the way. It can be argued that in addition to the convergence of insurance, banking, and brokers, the financial services business and the information services business are fast becoming indistinguishable. Those who believe that financial institutions in a high-tech age will remain separate entities must also believe that compartments separating financial firms are watertight, and in spite of deregulation can be kept that way. But the marketplace shows us every day that those compartments are even now leaking. Once they are given leeway to expand, products, technology, and competition never stand still. My own vision of the future tells me that much of the financial industry today is sailing on a doomed *Titanic* with the watertight doors thrown wide open.

Thousands of financial firms are going to merge into bigger money players and will offer all kinds of wonderful reasons for doing so. None of them will be true. They will merge for survival or they will die separately. The concentrated financial system that will result isn't yet visible. We'll begin to see it in the next few years as we drive down a major thoroughfare, watch television, or read our newspapers. What we'll see is a small number of mega-financial firms spread out across the country offering us one-stop financial shopping. We will no longer use the words bank and broker to describe those firms; they'll be financial supermarkets. For most people, it will make money management more convenient. Competition and the introduction of new products will boost our returns and give us the freedom to choose among a wide range of options.

Whatever the final design may be, it must allow for still more change. Otherwise, we will not have learned from our past mistake of believing that any financial system can be static. I believe that changes will occur on a more frequent basis and that we are only now coming into a new era of financial opportunities for the consumer. Those opportunities will allow each of us to build a solid financial future in a truly free financial marketplace. I hope you find your dream of financial independence. I know you'll have the opportunities to do so.

Glossary
of Economic
and Investment Terms

Here are some definitions of many of the terms used in the book, plus other terms you might come across when you save and invest your money, plan your retirement income, or seek tax-deferred or tax-free ways to accumulate money.

My definition isn't authoritative; its purpose is to make the idea more intelligible to someone who is not familiar with economic and investment terms. In most cases, I've defined a words as they're generally understood in the financial world or as I've used them in the text.

Adjustable Rate Mortgage (ARM)   Mortgage payments can adjust to market interest rates. ARMs have a lower initial interest rate over fixed rate mortgages because lenders can adjust interest rates as their cost of funds rise and fall.

AMBAC   American Municipal Board Insurance Association.

Annual effective yield   The total interest earned at the end of a year. This can be the stated interest rate if the account is based on simple interest, or the total interest earned if the rate is compounded during the year.

Annuity   A contract with an insurance company that promises to pay fixed amounts periodically (monthly, yearly, or whatever) over a given period of time or for life. You can buy an annuity with a single payment or with periodic payments made over several years.

Annuity, fixed   An investment, usually from an insurance company, that guarantees fixed payments, either for life or for a specified period.

Annuity, joint and survivor   A contract, usually in a pension plan, issued by an insurance company, that promises to pay a regular sum to the annuitant for his or her life and then to continue the payments for the life of the surviving spouse.

Annuity, tax-deferred   A contract with an insurance company in which the investments to build the annuity accumulate on a tax-deferred basis until the money is taken out. The income is then taxable as received. Congress recently changed the laws so that withdrawals are taken out of the interest portion first, and are therefore taxable income, and you can pay a 5 percent penalty if you withdraw the money before age 59½ or within the first ten years of the date of the annuity. *See also* Tax Equity and Fiscal Responsibility Act of 1982 (TEFRA).

Arbitrage   Buying and selling at the same time in different markets. Sometimes securities or currencies sell for different prices in different markets and arbitrage traders try to take advantage of the difference—called the "spread"—to make a profit.

ARM   *See* Adjustable Rate Mortgage.

Ask price   The price at which a broker/dealer offers to sell unlisted stock or other investment products.

Automatic Teller Machine (ATM)   An electronic machine, usually at a bank or savings & loan, that allows the use of an ATM card for banking services. You can make deposits and withdrawals from your account. Most ATMs operate 24 hours a day, seven days a week.

Average annual yield   On savings accounts of over one year, the average annual yield is your return each year. This will vary based on the interest compounding method used.

Back-door load   A sales commission, usually on a mutual fund, that applies at the time of redemption. The sales charge can be reduced every year you hold the investment and it can reach zero after several years.

Back-end sales charge   A sales charge or sales commission that is paid when the investment is sold. Without an up-front sales charge, you pay a hefty sales commission on the total amount of your withdrawal—including not only your investments but all the interest or profits earned prior to withdrawal.

Bank holding company act   A company that owns or controls two or more banks or other bank holding companies.

Bear market   Term used to describe a period, usually on the stock exchanges, when the price trend is down.

Bid price   The price that a broker/dealer will pay to buy an unlisted stock or other investment products.

Big board   Another name for the New York Stock Exchange.

Blue chip   Term used to describe companies that are nationally known, enjoy wide acceptance of products or services, and demonstrate good ability to pay stockholders a regular dividend.

Break-in service   A pension plan that requires the employee to work continuously for a certain number of years to collect a pension at retirement. A break-in service can occur when the employee is fired, is laid off, or quits and returns to the company.

Broker An agent, often a stockbroker, who buys and sells securities, commodities, or other property on commission.

Bull market Term used to describe a period, usually on the stock exchanges, when good news pushes the price trend up.

Cafeteria-style fringe benefits plans Corporate benefits package that includes such options as putting pre-tax wages into a "reimbursement account." The money never shows up on a W-2 form and the employee can withdraw the money tax-free to pay for fringe-benefits-linked expenses such as legal advice, orthodontic work for dependent children, care of elderly parents, home/auto insurance, even a live-in housekeeper.

Call option A right to purchase a specified investment at a fixed price on a specified date, or, in most cases, prior to the specified date.

Call privilege The right of a bond issuer (the company, city, or state that issued the bond) to repay the bond prior to its maturity date. When interest rates fall the bond issuer may want to call the old bond and issue a new one at a lower interest rate.

Capital The money paid into a company by its stockholders. It can also refer to the net assets of a person or a firm.

Capital gains tax A federal tax on profits made on the sale of investments. If you hold investments for one year or less, and therefore make short-term gains, your capital gains are taxed as ordinary income, based on your personal tax rate. If you hold the investment for more than one year, and therefore make long-term gains, the maximum income tax rate is only 20 percent—and many times it's a great deal less.

Cash management account An account, usually offered by brokers, that allows you to invest part of your money and hold the surplus in a money market account.

Cash value life insurance Whole life insurance that, in addition to paying benefits in the event of death, acts as a savings plan to keep the premiums level during your lifetime. The owner can borrow against the cash values in the policy during his or her lifetime by paying the insurance company the annual interest rate established in the policy. If a loan is outstanding at the time of death, the face amount of the policy will be reduced by the amount of the cash value loan before payment is made to the beneficiary.

Certificate of Deposit (CD) A fixed rate deposit (or short-term savings) for a fixed period. CDs are represented by a certificate, from a bank, savings & loan, or stockbroker. Most CDs are federally insured.

CFP Certified financial planner.

ChFC Chartered financial consultant.

Closed-end investment company An investment company, often a mutual fund, that issues a fixed number of shares.

Collateral An asset that is pledged for a loan, to be forfeited if repayment is not made.

Commission The broker's fee for buying or selling securities or for acting as an agent for property.

Common stock fund   A mutual fund that invests all or most of its assets in common stocks.

Compound interest   Interest that is allowed to accumulate and that earns additional interest on the retained interest income.

Compound tax-deferred interest   The magic ingredient of all retirement plans. Interest that is allowed to accumulate on a tax-free basis; the full amount of the interest is put to work to earn more interest income.

Contrarian   A person who adheres to the theory that no matter what the public believes will happen in the market, it will move the other way. Most stock market gurus who provide inside information on the market are contrarians.

Contributory retirement plan   An IRA, TSA, 401(k) plan, thrift plan, or other employer sponsored plan in which the employee makes regular voluntary contributions from his or her pay check.

Coupon rate   The annual rate of interest, as a percentage of the face value, paid by a bond.

Custodian   An agent that keeps investments. All IRAs and Keogh plans require a custodian to maintain assets and make reports of changes in the account.

Dealer   An individual or firm in the securities business acting as a principal rather than as an agent. Dealers buy for their own accounts and sell to customers from their own inventory. Unlisted over-the-counter stocks are often bought and sold by dealers.

Defined-benefit plan   The correct name for a fixed benefit pension plan. A pension specifies the size of the benefit (usually in relation to the employee's most recent salary) and specifies when the benefit can be paid. The cost of the plan is paid entirely by the employer.

Defined-contribution plan   The correct name for a money-purchase pension plan. The cost is paid by the employer; however, the benefits employees receive will be only what the money in their accounts will buy when they retire. The employer is only required to make a contribution, not to provide a certain guaranteed benefit at retirement.

Deflation   The opposite of inflation. Deflation usually causes a fall in the general price levels.

Demand deposit   Bank deposits that can be withdrawn without penalty at any time; for example, deposits made into a passbook savings account.

Dependent status   That part of the pension law that refers to benefits for dependent members of the family. Usually, retirement benefits—private or Social Security—are not available to dependents until the worker who earned the benefits has retired. This also applies to divorced women, who may be entitled to Social Security benefits based on their ex-husband's contribution, but who must wait until he retires to collect.

Deposit account   A bank account with withdrawal restrictions. Also called a "time" deposit because you agree to lock up your money for a set period of time.

Depository Institutions Deregulation and Monetary Control Act of 1980
Federal legislation that provided for deregulation of the banking system.

The act, among other provisions, phased out regulations on interest rates for banks and S&Ls and permitted stockbrokers to offer checking accounts. Deregulation was completed, effective April, 1986.

Discount bond   A bond that is selling, or was issued, at a dollar price below the par value. When interest rates rise after a bond is issued, the bond can trade at a discount because its current yield is below the going rate of interest.

Discount broker   A broker who only buys and sells stocks and bonds. Without offering advice, making a market, or helping customers to buy and sell, discount brokers have cut commissions by as much as 75 percent. Most of the new discount brokers are springing up in banks and savings & loans.

Discount rate   The interest rate charged by the Federal Reserve Bank on loans to commercial banks.

Discretionary account   An account in which you empower a bank, broker, or financial adviser to make investment decisions on your behalf.

Dividend   A payment by the corporation to its shareholders. The amount can vary with the corporation's profits and the amount of cash on hand.

Dollar-cost-averaging   A method of buying the same security at regular intervals with a fixed dollar amount. The idea is to buy when the price is low and when it's high and to make purchases in good times and bad—and to thereby average out the price of the stock.

Dow Jones averages   The stock averages you see in the newspaper. There are three Dow Jones averages: one for transportation stocks, one for utilities, and one for industrial stock averages. The most widely quoted is the industrial stock average.

Earned income   For tax purposes, income from wages, salary, or self-employment. Earned income is the only source you have to make contributions into IRAs and Keogh plans.

Earnings-based CD   An insured certificate of deposit invested in real estate that is guaranteed by the FDIC or the FSLIC. Income is interest only, without the possibility of appreciation.

Economic Recovery Tax Act of 1981   This law gave us across-the-board income tax cuts, reduced long-term capital gains taxes, made headway against eliminating the marriage tax penalty by offering a "working spouse deduction," and made a substantial reduction in estate and gift taxes. This is also the law that gave us the new expanded IRA and Keogh plans. Not only is every worker eligible to open an IRA, but maximum contributions were boosted to $2,000 for individual IRAs and to $2,250 for spousal IRAs.

Electronic Funds Transfer (EFT)   Using computers to instantly transfer money from one financial institution to another. EFT can be done between financial institutions almost anywhere in the world.

Employee Retirement Income Security Act of 1974 (ERISA)   A law that cleaned up private pension abuse, provided pension plan insurance through the Pension Benefit Guaranty Corporation (PBGC), and gave us IRAs for employees who were not covered by a retirement plan where they worked.

Equity investment   An investment in stock in which you are at risk if the value of the company goes down. Often equity investments in smaller firms do not pay a specific return to the investor.

ERISA   *See* Employee Retirement Income Security Act of 1974.

Ex-Dividend   Without dividend. The buyer of an ex-dividend stock does not receive the recently declared dividend. When stocks go ex-dividend, the stock tables include the symbol "X" following the name.

Federal Deposit Insurance Corporation (FDIC)   A federal agency established in 1933 that guarantees up to $100,000 for each amount on deposit in member banks.

Federal Home Loan Bank Board   The federal agency that oversees savings & loan associations.

Federal Reserve Act of 1913   This act established the Federal Reserve System to regulate the U.S. monetary and banking system. The Federal Reserve System (the Fed) is made up of 12 regional Federal Reserve banks, their 24 branches, and all national and state banks that are part of the system.

Federal Reserve System   The country's central bank, made up of 12 Federal Reserve Banks and supervised by a Board of Governors that operates outside the control of Congress and the President. Familiarly known as the Fed. The current chairman is Paul Volker.

Federal Savings & Loan Insurance Corporation (FSLIC)   A federal agency established in 1934 that guarantees up to $100,000 for each account on deposit in member savings & loans.

Financial supermarket   Company that offers a wide range of financial services under one roof.

Fixed-rate mortgage   A conventional mortgage in which the interest rate does not fluctuate with market conditions.

Float   In banking, the time between the deposit of a check in a bank's account and payment of the funds to the customer's account.

401(k) plans   Employer-sponsored salary reduction plans in which contributions are tax-deferred. In many 401(k) plans the employer also makes a contribution based on the employee's payment to the plan.

Front-end load   Sales charges applied to an investment at the time of initial purchase. Charges are usually deducted from invested funds.

FSLIC   *See* Federal Savings & Loan Insurance Corporation.

General obligation bonds   Municipal bonds sold to finance public improvements, such as building and maintaining streets, water systems, schools, and police and fire stations; repaid by taxes.

Ginnie Mae   Mortgage-backed securities of the Government National Mortgage Association (GNMA). The government's way of providing money to the mortgage-lending institutions in order to bring investment funds into the real estate market. Ginnie Maes can be purchased in mutual funds, investment trusts, and (in amounts over $25,000) in bonds.

Glass-Steagall Act of 1933   Act authorizing federal deposit insurance and prohibiting commercial banks from owning brokerage firms.

Government National Mortgage Association (GNMA)   *See* Ginnie Mae.

Great American myth   The idea on which our nation's retirement system is built; namely, that today's American families consist of a wage-earning dad, a stay-at-home mom, and two kids. Today, such families account for only 7 percent of all American households.

Growth fund   A mutual fund whose rate of growth over a period of time is greater than that of the market in general.

Hidden-loan funds   Mutual funds that appear to be no-load, yet have a back-end load on redemption. These funds often charge higher-than-average annual management expenses.

Income fund   A mutual fund with a primary objective of current income.

Individual Retirement Account (IRA)   Anyone with earned income can open an IRA with tax-deductible deposits of up to $2,000 per year ($4,000 for a couple in which both work) or $2,250 for a couple with one working spouse.

Inflation   Not an increase in prices, although prices do increase. A decrease in the value of your money—every dollar buys less.

Institute of Certified Financial Planners (ICFP)   A non-profit, professional organization in which membership is reserved for financial planners who have earned the Certified Financial Planner (CFP) designation from the College. The address is 9725 E Hampden Ave, Suite 33, Denver, CO 80231.

Interest rate   The rate at which money is paid for the use of money. Annual interest rates are expressed as a percentage of the amount invested. For a bond, it is called the coupon rate.

International Association for Financial Planning (IAFP)   A non-profit professional organization with over 12,000 members in the United States. The IAFP has a code of professional ethics for its members. The address is 5775 Peachtree Dunwoody Rd, Suite 120C, Atlanta, GA 30342.

IRA   *See* Individual Retirement Account.

Issuer   The seller of a bond: state, municipality, or corporation.

Jumbo Certificate of Deposit   An insured CD with a minimum denomination of $100,000. Banks and S&Ls maintain a separate market for jumbo CDs and offer higher interest rates than on regualr CDs.

Keogh plan   Like an IRA, but available only to self-employed individuals. (Also called an HR-10) If you are self-employed, you can contribute as much as $30,000 in a Keogh plan *and* make the maximum contribution into your IRA.

Less-than-round lot   A stock transaction that incurs special charges (less than 100 shares) and possible delays in executing your order to buy or sell. *See also* Odd lot.

Leverage   Any arrangement in which you can control a large sum of money with a small down payment.

Liabilities   All debts and claims against a company. When liabilities exceed assets the company is insolvent.

Limited partnership   A partnership in which investors have a limited liability for the partnership's obligations.

Liquidity   You are said to have liquidity with your savings and investments if you can turn the assets into cash quickly.

Listed stock　　The stock of a company traded on a securities exchange.

Load fund　　A mutual fund that charges a sales commission at the time of purchase.

Management fee　　The fee paid to the investment manager of a mutual fund. The fee, usually about .5 percent up to .75 percent of the average net assets annually, is paid by the mutual fund's shareholders. Not the same as the sales charge, which can be paid at the time of purchase or at the time of sale.

Margin　　The down payment you make to buy stocks. The balance of the purchase price, usually borrowed, is a loan at prevailing interest rates.

Marketability　　Ability to sell an investment at the market rate at any time. When you invest, be sure to check the marketability of your investment so that if your needs change or your investment goes sour you can sell quickly and easily at the market rate.

Market order　　The order given to a broker to buy or sell securities at the best available price.

Maturity　　The date on which a contractual obligation is due, such as the repayment of a bond.

McFadden Act　　A 1927 amendment to the National Banking Act, the McFadden Act is best known for barring banks from opening offices outside their home states and denying nationally chartered banks the right to open branches within a state unless the state-chartered banks have equal rights.

Medical Expense Reimbursement Plan (MERP)　　A corporate plan whereby employees can have the corporation pay their out-of-pocket medical bills.

Money market account　　A savings account at a bank or S&L that pays current interest on savings deposits.

Money market checking　　A checking account that pays current interest on money in the account.

Money market fund　　A mutual fund that invests in only money market instruments and pays the current interest earned on those investments.

Municipal bond　　A bond issued by a state, county, city government, or public agency. Income from municipal bonds is free of federal income tax.

Municipal bond insurance　　Private insurance companies provide policies guaranteeing municipal bonds for the payment of interest and protection in the event of default. The insurance can be purchased either by the issuing government entity or the investor. The two major insurers are American Municipal Bond Assurance Corporation (AMBAC) and Municipal Bond Insurance Association (MBIA).

Mutual fund　　A fund that invests in stocks, bonds, or other securities. The fund assumes the obligation to redeem its shares at the net asset value of the fund upon request.

National Association of Securities Dealers (NASD)　　An association of brokers and dealers in the over-the-counter securities market. NASD is the watchdog of the industry, with power to expel members and enforce rules of fair practice for the public good.

National Association of Security Dealers Automated Quotations System (NASDAQ)　　The name given the automated information network that gives brokers and dealers price quotations on securities traded-over-the-counter.

National Credit Union Association (NCUA)   This is the government agency that regulates credit unions. NCUA also insures each credit union account up to $100,000 on the same basis that the FDIC protects savings accounts in S&Ls.

NDIGC   Nebraska's Depository Institution Guaranty Corporation.

No-load fund   A mutual fund that imposes no sales charges (load) at the time of purchase. Funds are bought directly from the fund companies, rather than through a broker or financial planner.

NOW account   A negotiable order of withdrawal, or a NOW account, is, in effect, an interest-bearing checking account.

NYSE   New York Stock Exchange, the nation's leading stock exchange.

Odd lot   An amount of stock less than the established 100-share unit of trading. On an odd-lot market order, the price is based on the first round-lot transaction that occurs on the stock exchange floor following receipt of the odd-lot order. There is an extra charge for odd-lot trading over round-lot trading.

Option   The right to buy or sell specific securities or properties at a specified price within a specified time.

Ordinary income   For tax purposes, income from all sources except capital gains.

Over-the-Counter (OTC) market   A market that trades in unlisted securities, conducted by broker/dealers through negotiation rather than through the use of an auction system as in the stock exchanges. The quotes are offered as "bid" and "asked."

Par value   The face or dollar amount of a security.

Pension Benefit Guaranty Corporation (PBGC)   A federal corporation established in 1974 to guarantee basic pension benefits in covered plans of 25 or more employees when the company pension plan is terminated.

Personal Indentification Number (PIN)   A number given to a depositor, which must be used along with an ATM card, to operate an Automatic Teller Machine.

Pink sheets   A daily publication for the National Quotation Bureau that lists the bid and ask prices of unlisted, over-the-counter stocks.

Preferred stock   A class of stock with a claim on the company's earnings before dividends can be paid to common stockholders. Preferred stock usually has a priority over common stock if the company liquidates.

Premium   The amount by which a security is selling above its par value. Can also refer to the premium an issuer of bonds or a buyer of stock will pay to get their hands on the security.

Pre-retirement income   The last salary you earn before you retire. Pension plans use this figure to determine benefits. You can judge the value of any retirement plan by how much of your pre-retirement salary it replaces.

Price-earnings ratio   The price of a share of stock divided by the earnings per share for a 12-month period. For example, a stock selling for $50 a share and earning $2.50 a share has a price-earnings ratio of 20 to 1.

Prime   The part of common stock on which the owners retain the voting rights and receive the dividends. Score holders get any price appreciation.

Prime rate   The interest rate banks charge their best customers. Changes in the prime rate are an important indicator of the direction that interest rates in general are headed.

Profit-sharing plan   A retirement plan in which the company makes contributions depending on its profits. The employer has no obligation to make a contribution and, in most cases, it can't unless the company makes a profit in that year. The employee's benefit depends on the amount of money on account upon retirement.

Prospectus   A booklet, required under the Securities Act of 1933, that introduces new securities to the public. It describes the company, explains what will be done with the money, and provides important information to potential investors.

Purchasing power   The value of a unit of money or other asset measured by the goods and services it can purchase. Purchasing power increases when the same amount of money will buy more goods and services, and it falls when it takes more money to purchase the same amount of goods and services.

Put   An option to sell a specified number of shares at a definite price within a specified period of time. The opposite of a call option.

Ratings   Usually refers to a bond's quality. The two nationally recognized ratings are from Moody's Investor Service and Standard & Poor's (S&P). The top three grades you should be looking for are AAA—prime grade, AA—excellent grade, and A—high grade.

Real Estate Investment Trust (REIT)   A company, usually traded publicly, that manages real estate in order to earn profits for shareholders. REITs comprise equity REITs which invest in real estate and mortgage REITs which lend money to building developers.

Recession   A period during which unemployment is usually on the rise, business slows, and our standard of living declines.

Red herring   A preliminary prospectus used to obtain an indication of interest from the public of a new issue. Named because of the red ink on the cover.

Registered representative   A full-time stockbroker who is licensed with an exchange to do business with the public. Also known as an account executive or customer's broker.

Regulation "Q"   The Federal Reserve Board ceiling on the rates that banks and other savings institutions can pay on savings accounts. Regulation "Q" was phased out in 1986 when interest rates were deregulated.

Replacement ratio   The difference between your last working salary and your income in retirement. For example, suppose your last working salary was $25,000. If your retirement income is $6,250, your replacement ratio is 25 percent. Social Security now averages somewhere between 21 percent and 33 percent, depending on your last working salary. Usually the higher your pre-retirement salary, the lower your replacement ratio in retirement.

Resistance level   The price level at which a stock has previously experienced a great deal of buying and selling. If the stock is trading at a price somewhat below this level, the old level is said to represent "resistance."

Retirement Equity Act of 1984   As used in this book, the law that grants spouses an automatic right to share in the distribution of funds from either spouse's pension.

Revenue bond   A municipal security backed by and expected to repay the bond holder with earnings or revenues of a project, such as tolls from a bridge.

Risk   The possibility of loss when you save or invest your money. Usually, the greater the risk the higher the rewards.

Rollover IRA   An IRA established to receive money "rolled over" from an employer's retirement plan. You can roll over any amount and continue to delay taxes, but you must roll over the money within 60 days of receipt to avoid paying income taxes in the year you receive the money.

Round lot   The regular-size stock transaction (100 or more shares) that does not incur special charges.

Sales charge   The cost or sales commission you pay to buy or sell stocks, mutual funds, annuities, or other investments. The sales cost is taken off the top of your investment so that your actual investment is less than the money you invest.

Score   Half of a common stock on which the owners receive only the price appreciation. Prime holders retain the voting rights and receive any dividends.

SEC   *See* Securities and Exchange Commission.

Second generation savings plans   Savings plans that allow the investor three advantages: A federal guarantee of principal, a guaranteed rate of return for the life of the investment, and an opportunity to share in the profits or the rise in interest rates while the investment is held.

Secured loan   Loan for which collateral is pledged to guarantee its repayment.

Securities and Exchange Commission (SEC)   Established by Congress in the 1930s to help protect investors. It is the watchdog over much of the securities business.

Self-directed IRA   An IRA that can be actively managed by the account holder. Usually you'll pay a set-up fee and an annual management fee for these IRAs.

Self-employed income   Income earned when you work for yourself or with a partner in business. You pay self-employment rates for your Social Security contribution, which are much higher than the rates paid by people with the same income who are employed by someone else. Self-employed individuals can open a Keogh plan and an IRA.

SEP/IRA   *See* Simplified Employee Pension.

Short sale   When you sell a stock you don't own in the belief that the price will go down and you can buy it back at a profit. When you buy a stock and invest in the stockmarket you are said to have gone "long." You are now buying before you sell, the opposite of a short position.

Simplified Employee Pension (SEP/IRA)   Allow employer contributions to IRAs based on a percentage of the employee's salary. With an SEP/IRA you may also open your own regular IRA.

Speculation   Any investment that attempts to make a profit from a change in price. Usually associated with a high-risk investment in which large profits are expected in a short time.

Spread   The difference between what the seller wants and what the buyer is willing to pay. Usually refers to unlisted stocks and bonds in the OTC market. The spread is the difference between the bid price and the ask price.

Stock dividend   A dividend paid in securities rather than cash.

Stop-loss order   Instructions given to a broker or bank to sell your investment if the price drops to a pre-set level. The stop-loss order then becomes a market order and your investment is sold as soon as a buyer can be found.

Street name   If you buy securities from your broker they will normally be held in the name of the broker rather than in your name. They are said to be held in Street name. If you want to hold your own securities, be sure to tell your broker.

Summary plan description   A booklet your employer is required by law to give you when you join your company retirement plan or whenever you ask for one. The booklet, which is to be written in "easy-to-understand" English, tells you how your retirement plan works, how you can benefit during your employment, and how to determine what your benefits will be if you leave the company or retire.

Supply of money   Amount of money in the banking system. The Fed is using the money supply as a way of determining future interest rates.

Switching   Moving assets from one mutual fund to another within the same family of funds.

Tax credit   A dollar-for-dollar reduction in your tax bill. If you have a $100 tax credit you can take $100 off the amount of money you would otherwise send the IRS at tax time.

Tax deferral   The delaying of a tax liability. For example, with an IRA you don't avoid taxes, you delay them until you retire.

Tax Equity and Fiscal Responsibility Act of 1982 (TEFRA)   This law reduced our deductions for medical expenses, casualty losses and increased Keogh plan contributions up to $30,000 a year. The law included a withholding tax on retirement plan benefits under pensions and IRAs, but the withholding on dividends and interest was voted down by Congress before it could take effect.

Tax-free income   Usually income or interest received from a municipal bond. To be free of both federal and state income taxes you must invest in municipal bonds issued by the state in which you live.

Tax shelter   An investment (usually a limited partnership) that provides tax deductions and/or tax deferral. Usually sold to people in the high-tax brackets who can afford to lose their money if the investment goes sour.

Tax-sheltered annuity   Called a TSA, this retirement savings plan works much like an IRA but it's available only to employees of non-profit organizations, such as school teachers.

TEFRA   *See* Tax Equity and Fiscal Responsibility Act of 1982.

Ten-year rule   A rule of Social Security whereby a divorced spouse must have been married for at least ten years prior to the divorce to collect benefits on the work record of the ex-spouse. Benefits are paid then only if the spouse has not remarried.

Thrift plans   An employer-sponsored savings plan in which the employee makes voluntary contributions into the plan and the employer matches the money according to a prearranged formula. For example: For every dollar you contribute into the plan your employer could put in 50 cents. The interest income or profits inside the thrift plan are tax-deferred until the money is taken out.

Time deposit   A bank or thrift deposit in which money remains on deposit for a fixed number of months or years. If you withdraw the money prior to the agreed-upon date, you can face a substantial early withdrawal penalty.

Treasury securities   The way our government borrows money to keep its financial house of cards from collapsing into a sea of red ink. Treasury bills (T-bills) are sold at public auction on a discounted basis (sold for less than the face value of the security and then redeemed at face value). Three-month and six-month T-bills are usually auctioned weekly on Mondays. The minimum investment is $10,000 with multiples of $5,000 above that. Treasury Notes mature in ten years or less; Treasury bonds mature ten years or more after issue.

Trustee   The person who controls the trust, often with powers to buy and sell investments for the trust.

TSA   *See* Tax-Sheltered Annuity.

Underwriter   A securities firm that purchases an issue of new stocks or bonds from the issuer and then offers them for sale to the public. Banks, now barred by law from selling stocks and bonds, expect to underwrite municipal bonds as a first step back to becoming a full underwriter of stocks and bonds.

Unearned income   For tax purposes, interest, dividends, capital gains, rental income, and other forms of non-business income. You can not make contributions to an IRA or Keogh plan with unearned income.

Unlisted   A security not listed on any stock or bond exchange.

Variable annuity   An annuity that's invested in a portfolio of stocks or other investments that can rise or fall with the market. Unlike a fixed annuity, there are no guarantees as to the value of principal because the portfolio performance will vary.

Vesting   Your right to receive your employer's contributions and the earned interest in the retirement plan when you change jobs prior to retirement. The vesting schedule is based on years of service. The law now requires that you be 100 percent vested after 15 years' service. Until that time you earn "fractional vesting." You can find out how much vesting you have earned and how much money you can take with you if you change jobs from your Summary Plan Description booklet.

Warrant   The right to purchase securities at a stipulated price within a specified time limit. Warrants are often offered with securities as an inducement to buy.

Withdrawal penalty   If you agree to lock up your money in a time deposit for a fixed number of months or years you can be charged a withdrawal penalty if you take out the money before the end of your time deposit.

Whole life insurance   *See* Cash value life insurance.

Yield   The interest or dividend you expect to earn as a percentage of the current market value of your investment. After-tax yield is the return realized after income taxes, if any, have been substracted.

Zero coupon bond   A bond that does not pay annual interest and is issued at a discount price. The return on the bond is strictly the compounding effect of the stated interest rate over the life of the bond. Like U.S. Savings Bonds, where for $18.75 you can buy a $25 bond, a zero coupon bond can take $4,500 and in 17 years hand you back $30,000.

Sources

Chapter 1

1. *The Nation*, June 28, 1933, p. 709.
2. *Business Week*, April 23, 1979, p. 85.
3. *Business Week*, April 23, 1979, p. 84.

Chapter 2

1. *Time*, December 3, 1984, p. 50.
2. *Associated Press*, Washington, D.C., May 29, 1985.
3. *Newsweek*, January 7, 1985, p. 40.
4. *Ibid.*, p. 41.
5. *Forbes*, April 22, 1985.

Chapter 3

1. *Wall Street Journal*, July 25, 1985.
2. *Forbes*, December 5, 1983, p. 151.
3. *U.S. News & World Report*, May 28, 1984, p. 74.
4. *Fortune*, October 15, 1984, p. 185.
5. *Forbes*, February 25, 1985, p. 53.

Chapter 4

1. *Los Angeles Times*, October 9, 1984.

Chapter 5

1. Address by Edward R. Telling (Chairman and CEO, Sears, Roebuck and Co.), Economic Club of Detroit, March 11, 1985.
2. Said during appearance on "Moneytalk" radio program on station KGO in San Francisco.
3. *Wall Street Journal,* July 31, 1985.
4. *Ibid.*
5. *Wall Street Journal,* April 26, 1983.

Chapter 6

1. *Business Week,* September 16, 1985.

Chapter 7

1. *Wall Street Journal,* June 6, 1981, p. 1.
2. *U.S. News & World Report,* July 29, 1985, p. 65.
3. Henry Morgenthau, Jr., *Morgenthau Diaries,* vol. 3, pp.58–60, Franklin D. Roosevelt Library, Hyde Park, N.Y.
4. *Time,* May 24, 1982, p. 19.
5. *U.S. News & World Report,* August 12, 1985, p. 4.

Chapter 8

1. *Time,* August 12, 1985, p. 14

Chapter 9

1. *U.S. News & World Report,* August 26, 1985, p. 55.
2. *Business Week,* July 22, 1984, p. 114.

Index